NEW HAVEN PUBLIC LIBRARY

3 5000 09384 4032

OFFICIALLY WITHDRAWN
NEW HAVEN FREE PUBLIC LIBRAR

D1058632

Also by Susan Sheehan

Life for Me Ain't Been No Crystal Stair

A Missing Plane

Kate Quinton's Days

Is There No Place on Earth for Me?

A Prison and a Prisoner

A Welfare Mother

Ten Vietnamese

Also by Howard Means

Money & Power: The History of Business

The Visionary's Handbook
(with Watts Wacker and Jim Taylor)

C.S.A.

The 500-Year Delta
(with Watts Wacker and Jim Taylor)

Colin Powell

NEW HAVEN FREE PUBLIC LIBRARY

THE BANANA SCULPTOR, THE PURPLE LADY, AND THE ALL-NIGHT SWIMMER

Hobbies, Collecting, and Other Passionate Pursuits

Susan Sheehan and Howard Means

FREE PUBLIC LIBRARY
133 ELM ST
NEW HAVEN, CT 06510

Simon & Schuster
New York   London   Toronto   Sydney   Singapore

NEW HIGH PUBLIC LIBRARY

SIMON & SCHUSTER
Rockefeller Center
1230 Avenue of the Americas
New York, NY 10020

Copyright © 2002 by Susan Sheehan and Howard Means
All rights reserved,
including the right of reproduction
in whole or in part in any form.

SIMON & SCHUSTER and colophon are registered trademarks
of Simon & Schuster, Inc.

For information about special discounts for bulk purchases,
please contact Simon & Schuster Special Sales:
1-800-456-6798 or business@simonandschuster.com

Book design by Deirdre Amthor

Manufactured in the United States of America

10   9   8   7   6   5   4   3   2   1

Library of Congress Cataloging-in-Publication Data is available.

ISBN 0-7432-0122-1

To Mary Sheehan, and to Pat and Shari, Gene and Marcia
And to Mary Ellen Willcox

Contents

Preface

This book began with a conviction and a premise. Our conviction was that there was a story waiting to be told about the way we Americans spend our leisure time. Our premise was that if we pursued our conviction, we would open up a world of enormous variety and surprising depth. We believe we were right, fortunately, on both counts.

Statistics on how Americans use their time are all over the place and often seemingly contradictory. We are working longer hours, some studies say. We're playing longer hours, others contend. The truth, to the extent it can be isolated, would appear to be that we are doing both, in part by stealing time from sleep and family rituals such as the evening meal and in part by using technology to blur the line between work and play. A cell phone can turn a golf cart into a serviceable office just as effectively as a laptop can transform a commute on the Long Island Railroad into an eBay opportunity.

If the ratio between work and play remains the same, though, a qualitative gap has opened between the two. Once, we defined ourselves by the jobs we did: we were an organization man or a union man, a homemaker or a working woman. Studs Terkel's wonderful 1972 oral history, *Working,* got to the heart of those jobs and the attitudes behind them as no other book has done. Today, jobs and even careers are transitory. More and more, we divide ourselves into tribes according to our leisure allegiances, and those allegiances can cross all sorts of once unbridgeable divides of race, gender, and class.

Bumper stickers tell the story as clearly as anything: I LOVE MY [fill in the blank]. I'D RATHER BE [fill in the blank]. The average supermarket parking lot is chock-full of these decal testimonials to an astounding array of avocations, amateur sports, and hobbies. The magazine racks offer proof as well: there is hardly an activity imaginable that doesn't have its own monthly publication, or even two or three.

Most powerful of all—the great glue of the webs of association that have grown up around these amateur pursuits—is the Internet. If you can't find a home page with dozens of links for a hobby or sport or collection you're interested in taking up, chances are the hobby or sport or collection doesn't exist. Internet-related businesses get all the attention in the press, but the interface between the World Wide Web and leisure time is where the real action occurs.

More than anything else, what's celebrated in these pages are the people who let us into their lives and pulled back the curtain for us on their own passionate pursuits. We had no idea at the outset that we were going to find a man who makes pyramid sculptures out of bananas or a woman whose marble collection is so extensive that she paves her driveway with the excess and invites neighborhood children to take their fill. We had never heard of Jim Dreyer, whose swims across the Great Lakes are the sort of epic adventures out of which myths get built. James Pettus, a one-handed veteran and government driver who lives for his bonsai trees, was completely below our radar screen, as was Robin Tarbell-Thomas, an amateur baker and cook who could cover her walls with the ribbons she has won at Iowa state fairs.

We didn't look, we should note, for the merely average. Many people have taken up in-line skating, but very few people have taken it up to the extent that San Francisco lawyer Steve Everett has. Many people have collections of military memorabilia, but no one has a collection of Indochinese military decorations to surpass that of John Sylvester Jr. Talking birds and their owners are all over the place, but very few talking-bird owners are as dedicated and as knowledgeable as Peggy Dickson. Train buffs are legion, but only the very rare buff ever comes into possession of his own steam locomotive or sets out to convert his yard into a miniature railroad as Steve Spreckelmeier has done.

So much of reporting is a matter of getting people to talk about subjects they would rather not talk about and say things they would rather not say. We didn't have that problem in interviewing people for this book. One of the difficulties of having so much commitment and so much expertise in what are often narrow fields is that attentive audiences can be hard to come by. We made ourselves that audience, and for the most part, the words poured forth.

No one sets out to build the definitive collection of precanceled stamps or to eat at every American McDonald's or to travel to every country in the world for frivolous reasons. The commitment of time and emotion is too great. Of necessity, a passionate pursuit is a window into a life's history—into the deep roots and complicated forces that propel us to devote so much of our time to something that might seem trivial or narrow to others. We wanted to get to that deeper level, and we thank our subjects for indulging us.

"For me, the pleasure is in the chase, and for a while in the acquisition," the cosmetics executive Leonard Lauder told us about his postcard collection. "Possession is far less exciting. I don't ever really want to have a complete collection. I prefer infinity to completion."

So it is with this book. Our gallery is far from closed. The pleasure for us has been in the chase. Possession in our case is impossible—we borrowed these passions, we couldn't own them—but like Leonard Lauder, we prefer infinity to completion.

PART 1

Artful Expressions

One

Doug Fishbone:
Lots of Bananas

As a youngster in Queens, New York, Doug Fishbone assumed he would grow up to be a doctor "because that was in the rhythm of the household and my father was a surgeon." One night, back when *M*A*S*H* was a hit television show, he was awakened by a bad dream: "I was performing surgery and I killed the patient." After he graduated from Amherst, where he was a music major, his substitute-career thought was to be "a wheeler-dealer business type." He spent some time in Israel selling a stretch fabric made of acetate and spandex, called Slinky. "I'm an easy-going guy, not a real grab-'em-by-the-lapel salesman, so I operated at a net loss," Fishbone, age thirty-two, says.

Fishbone returned to New York, got a job "in the financial field," and took some art classes. First he worked with clay, then with bronze. "I loved art and I hated my job, so I quit the financial gig and decided to devote myself to becoming an artist." As part of his preparation, he took a job at a bronze foundry in Long Island City. "Most of the guys I worked with were Ecuadorians. I used to go to salsa clubs with them to drink and dance. After ten months of learning how to weld and chase metal, I figured I wasn't going to learn much more. It was time to move on."

He was taken with the idea of going to Ecuador, heard about an art residency program in Cuenca, a city considered one of the nicest in the country, submitted a pack of photographs of his clay and bronze sculptures, and was invited to come. He arrived in March 1998. "You can live like a prince in

Cuenca for fifty dollars a month. I was able to work almost full-time on my art instead of wearing a tie and scrounging to make a buck."

Fishbone went to a blacksmith's studio through the art program and worked on a piece of conceptual sculpture, completing a *bosque,* or forest, consisting of fifteen narrow forged-iron poles with tops in a curved horn shape—a design taken from traditional blacksmith window grilles. One day in the spring of 1999, he was walking along a road near El Arenal, an open-air market. He saw vendors sitting next to vast quantities of bananas, which they sold by the bucketful to passersby who bought them to feed their pigs. "I like to be inspired by what I see, and what I saw were bananas," Fishbone says. "Lots and lots of bananas."

At a party, Fishbone had met a man who worked for the Banco Central. "I convinced the bank's director of cultural programs to let me put a mountain of bananas outside the bank. Then I had to find a supplier of bananas who could come up with a large quantity of bananas at short notice. I asked around and found a fellow named Miguel Mejia, with whom I made a deal for two hundred fifty cases of bananas—that's about twenty-five thousand bananas—for about one dollar per case. Many purchasers ship or store bananas and buy them unripened, but I had to have bananas that would be a rich golden yellow on the day of the installation in August 1999. The wrong color would have derailed the whole conceptual angle of the piece. I needed gold-colored bananas as the basis for the financial metaphor, which is crucial to the interpretation of the work. The bananas represent the wealth of the country and its environmental resources. Because they are not durable, even the banking system is based on a commodity at risk of rotting."

Everything went smoothly. His distributor showed up with a truckload of bananas, and Fishbone spent the day piling them up by hand, on top of a metal armature he borrowed from the blacksmith from whom he was taking informal classes. "Miguel came by later in the day with some of his daughters to help me, which was unexpected and very nice of him. A while after the show, I took his entire family out to dinner, and we ate a huge banquet of *cuy,* which is roasted guinea pig.

"The plaza of the Banco Central is a beautiful outdoor space framed by a number of dark buildings, and the image of the bananas worked perfectly there. Everything was set up on a Friday and left under a tarp overnight for the Saturday morning exhibition. It was covered like a Christo because I didn't want the bananas exposed to the sun. I could rest easy, since the bananas were watched over by several guards with submachine guns who normally guard the Banco Central at night, it being a federal institution.

"On Saturday the show was attended by several hundred people. The bank hired a rock group and gave out free ice cream and beer to lure younger and older people to the show, in case the promise of free bananas was not appealing enough. I think the director of the bank was fairly worried about the political tone of the piece, since in Ecuador it is a very touchy issue, and runs the risk of being misinterpreted when a work like this is staged by a gringo artist. The director of the bank had initially told me, only half jokingly, that he might lose his job if people assumed I was arrogantly pointing my finger and saying 'Look at this banana republic.' So the event was turned into a rather fantastic spectacle centered around my bananas, as opposed to the more austere conceptual work I had originally envisioned.

"It went very well. Within an hour and a half of my invitation to the audience to eat the bananas, not a single piece of fruit remained. The whole sculpture had been devoured or hauled off. People came from everywhere, carrying boxes and sacks, loaded up, went off, and returned for more. I saw a number of women in traditional dress come from the market to acquire bananas to resell in the market. I like the metaphor of eating the piece. The frenzy of it all was really remarkable, and lent a kind of absurd theatricality that took me by surprise, and added to the conceptual impact. And the piece was constantly changing shape as people carried bananas away with abandon. Not just poor people but rich people. The local Rolex dealer walked off with a bag of bananas in one hand, a Louis Vuitton bag in the other. As the pickings got slimmer people figured they would take whatever was useful. I had used some cardboard crates to give the piece more heft and people lifted those, too. This was mildly irritating, since I had to pay Miguel for them. Even the high-quality plastic tarp I bought and laid on the ground to keep the bank plaza from getting too dirty vanished. Thankfully, I didn't have to clean up a single thing, so after the show I thanked a few people at the bank, made sure my friend retrieved his steel armature, and walked home."

Fishbone returned to New York in September 1999. He taught art to kids after classes in a public school in Brooklyn and worked as a temp for an investment banking firm. He had made connections in Guayaquil, Ecuador, before leaving Cuenca. In April 2000 he flew to Guayaquil to do another banana sculpture. He went by bus to Cuenca to speak with Miguel Mejia and with the blacksmith. "It might have been cheaper to use a distributor in Guayaquil, since the cities are four or five hours apart by bus, but I felt lucky to have a banana distributor I knew and trusted. All I had to do was tell Miguel the quantity I needed—forty thousand bananas this time. And the color: golden yellow on May fourth. And the location: this time the banana sculpture was inside the gallery of a woman with a great reputation for staging alternative projects by young artists.

"At six A.M. on May third Miguel arrived with the four hundred cases of bananas—Cavendish bananas, which I was told are the most popular in Central and South America because of their size. It was a rough day, as Guayaquil is swelteringly hot. I hired a few guys to help unload the truck and to carry the cases up two flights of stairs to the gallery space, but I must have lost a few pounds from all the lugging and piling. A hell of a job.

"As in Cuenca, the piece was installed by hand, piling up the bananas on top of the steel structure. Miguel helped me all day, an enormous advantage. The setup was fairly straightforward and we finished about six P.M. the night before the show. Ultimately the form of the piece owed more to chance than I had hoped, since one of the sides of the pile of bananas collapsed, starting a mini-avalanche just as I was ready to go home for the night.

"As a result of the heat, the bananas below, which were under the most strain, started to soften and in some cases liquify. I was worried that one dicey part in front was going to avalanche downwards, since there was a frightening overhang of bananas that seemed itching to fall out of the pile.

"This brings up an interesting point. Though I try in some ways to sculpt the pile of bananas, ultimately I have no control because it will collapse here or there, altering the shape I am trying to construct. That's one problem when you're working with an impermanent material. Thankfully it held its form pretty well, and the show went on without crisis.

"It was well attended. Because the show was in an indoor setting, the crowd was just a little smaller than the one in Cuenca and was largely comprised of art students from universities in Guayaquil. I had rented and set up lights and they brought out the color of the bananas with a very expressive richness. An unforeseen element that added greatly to the show was the intense smell of bananas. The aroma, which wafted all the way out to the street, and the absurd beauty of an enormous pile of fruit in the middle of the gallery made for an unusual art-going experience.

"My conception of the piece is that in addition to its intellectual content, it must be first and foremost an interesting piece to experience visually. With the additional impact of the smell, and of course the free food, I am hopeful people felt they got good value out of the show. Even if they hated it, they got free food, which is more than you can say for most exhibitions.

"The show lasted about three hours. Toward the end we began inviting kids off the street to come in and take the bananas. In a country as poor as Ecuador it would be obscene to use so much food and then waste it, and I was worried that since we were using a gallery and not an easily visible public space, we would not be able to give away all the bananas. However, a lot of people came in off the street and left loaded with food.

"It was a bit uncomfortable to see beggars in the gallery mingling with gallery goers drinking rum supplied by a beautiful young woman in a red dress sent by the rum company which sponsors the gallery's openings, but it added to the impact of the piece as an indictment of global forces that conspire to impoverish vast numbers of people—these very people, to a large degree. I went back to my hotel more exhausted than I had ever been. Oddly enough, throughout the whole setup and staging of the piece, I ate only two bananas. I had a rum or two.

"The next day we arranged for the cleanup. There was still a good deal of food left over. We continued to invite people in and arranged the leftovers in crates and bags to be left on the street. Guayaquil is a very poor city. I was pleased that I was able to give away all the fruit—ripe fruit, of excellent quality—and that for at least a day or two there were fewer hungry kids in the neighborhood. Ecuador is going through an enormous economic crisis and there is no money for cultural projects. So I footed the entire bill, including all my personal expenses, hence the need for my daytime clerk job in New York. After a week's vacation, I flew home and went back to work."

In November 2000 Fishbone took time off and flew to Costa Rica to do another banana installation, and in May 2001 he did the "banana piece" in Poland. Both times, all his expenses were paid and he was glad: "For me to spend two thousand dollars is a lot of working in an office."

His banana installations have received some publicity and he hopes that if he does the banana piece in a few other places around the world he will have built up a reputation as a conceptual artist who can deliver a basically abstract and hard-to-put-together project. "It's forced me to become very resourceful," he says. "I'm like a commando. You can drop me anywhere in the world and I'll get the job done. I just need cheap or free bananas."

Fishbone has conjured up other projects he would like to try, closer to home. He would like to spend a week from 9:00 A.M. to 5:00 P.M. in a Plexiglas tank in the middle of Grand Central Terminal, reading. "I'd be at leisure while all around the train depot people would be scurrying around. I'd like to try to make the point that people in New York City live in a manic way." He also likes the idea of filling up a Manhattan art gallery with a large quantity of soil imported from Cuba. "You can't do anything simpler than dumping dirt on a floor," he says. "People would be standing around drinking wine on this 'foreign soil' that for so many Americans has become supercharged."

Fishbone is currently attending Goldsmiths College at the University of London, where he expects to receive an M.A. in Fine Art in September 2002. With an art degree he will be able to teach art "unless I hit the big time before that and become the next Jeff Koons or Christo. This may not be the most likely of things to happen, but one has to dream."

Two

James Pettus:
Essential Natures

"I started doing bonsai in the early nineteen-nineties," James Pettus is saying. "My sister was in a bonsai club, and she knew how I'm a nature guy from the heart. I was always one to be out in the woods, hiking and stuff. So she said, 'Why don't you join one of the clubs, too?' I'd seen bonsai when I was stationed in Okinawa, and I said, 'Isn't that hard?' But I went to a meeting, and I was hooked. And the more I got into it, the more fascinated I was."

James Pettus was born in Washington, D.C., in 1942, and raised in the northwest part of the city. After attending Bell Vocational High School, he joined the army and served just shy of thirteen years in Okinawa and elsewhere. Pettus would earn his graduate equivalency degree and rise to the rank of sergeant before losing his left hand in an automobile accident during an army recruiting swing through Virginia. He returned to D.C. and, since the mid-seventies, has worked as a driver in the motor pool of the United States Department of the Treasury. Most days, James Pettus is delivering documents to and fro around the nation's capital.

As it turns out, there couldn't be a much better place to live and work in all of America if bonsai is going to get into your blood. The federally administered United States National Arboretum—a lightly visited, 444-acre swath of green in northeast D.C., not more than fifteen minutes from James Pettus's home—is the repository of the National Bonsai and Penjing

Museum, and Warren Hill, the museum's curator, has been a mentor to bonsai enthusiasts from all around the Washington area.

"The more I talked with Warren Hill, the more contagious it became," Pettus says. "My wife thinks I'm addicted, and I think I might be. I can't pass a nursery or greenhouse unless I stop. Most of the time, I don't stop to buy something, but there are so many varieties and different styles. I'll see something I don't have, and I just have to buy it."

"Bonsai" is a Japanese word—it translates literally as "tray-planted"— but the practice of bonsai appears to have originated in China and spread to Japan as part of a general infusion of Zen culture from the late twelfth through the early fourteenth century. Over the subsequent centuries, bonsai developed into such an elaborate art form, filled with windswept-looking, seemingly ancient dwarfed trees, that it can seem a formidable undertaking, even for the highly talented. But in fact, bonsai has never strayed far from its etymological roots: the term still implies nothing more than a tree—any tree—planted in a tray or pot. And that in turn means that bonsai is pretty much anything you want to make of it.

"Bonsai doesn't stipulate any species," Pettus says. "Me, I want to try them all. I don't kill too many now, but my first two years, oh, I did 'em in because it's like a living art. When you first start, you see somebody's collection or something at the National Collection, and you think, I want one just like that, but there's no such thing as instant bonsai. You can train a tree for years before you even put it in a bonsai pot, and it's only when it becomes accustomed to the pot, that shallow pot, that it becomes a bonsai."

"Accustomed" is the key word in that last sentence. Creating a tree that looks good in a bonsai pot is one thing; creating one that can sustain life, and be sustained, in an environment that a tree was never intended to live in is something else entirely.

"The tree is like a sculpture," Pettus explains. "The statue, they say, is already in the marble. It's the same with the tree: I just release it. You see the design and shape of the tree, and you refine it by root pruning and wiring. You start whacking and cutting, and you put it in a bonsai pot and say, 'Oh, that's beautiful!' Then two months later, you say, 'Oh, it's too strenuous on the tree.' They tell beginners not to spend too much because you are going to kill trees. Now, I don't mind spending three hundred or four hundred dollars for a tree, and I've seen people spend more than that. A hundred dollars isn't nothing for me to spend on one if I see something in it that I want."

Since they lack natural sources of nutrients, bonsai are dependent upon their keepers for survival. Constant trimming is necessary, not just to maintain an aesthetic principle but to keep the proper balance between root, branch, and foliage.

"You have to furnish everything. It's worse than your kids," says Pettus, who has three grown daughters and two grandchildren. "I'm out there in the morning before I go to work. I'm out there in the evening after I get home. My wife says, 'What are you doing?' But there's always something to be done, especially if you have a big collection."

Pettus estimates he has 150 trees under some form of cultivation. Of those, maybe 50 are in the shallow pots that define the art—"bonsai that I consider show worthy." But even a tree that is only waiting to have its true size and form discovered and released has to be tended.

"It's hard to take care of them. I'm always busy. I tell my wife, 'You know where I am—I'm out in the yard.' Even if you don't do nothing but keep a tree from becoming root-bound, you've got to repot it every two years."

Bonsai also demand shelter in the winter, not from the temperature but against windchill, and the more trees you have, the more complicated providing shelter becomes.

"They can survive the freezing," Pettus says, "but the windchill will dry out the branches because of the small root size, and then they'll die. A lot of people dig a hole and bury them in the ground. A lot of people put them in the garage. When you've got quite a few, you've got to go beyond that."

Early on in his bonsai career, Pettus constructed a cold frame from plastic sheeting and pressure-treated lumber to preserve his bonsai and other trees, but like his current collection of plants, the cold frame is only a way station on the path to the fulfillment of his ambitions. A general renovation of the main Treasury building, next to the White House on Pennsylvania Avenue, produced a windfall of thirty to forty large wooden windows dating from early in the century, and he expects to make those windows the centerpiece of his new and greatly improved cold frame.

"They were stacking them up, getting ready to haul them away," Pettus remembers. "I said, 'Well, I could use those.'"

Rather than convince James Pettus that he is in control of the bonsai, all this hard work at keeping his plants alive and healthy seems to have taught him an almost opposite lesson. In his labors, he has found rest. Through his striving, he says, he has escaped striving. The more godlike his dominion would seem to be over his trees, the more he has discovered the cessation of his own ego. The Zen of bonsai has become the Zen of James Pettus.

"Oh, you're so content tending the plants," he says. "You're at peace. You become closer to nature. Once you see what it takes to keep a tree alive, you realize the old saying 'He's got His eye on the sparrow; I know He's watching me.' You think, Gee, I am just a little speck in the overall picture.

"Your ego doesn't come into play because you know that if He's keeping the tree alive, then He's keeping you alive. It's not you that's keeping you alive. You think, Look, I wasn't raising my kids. I was a caretaker, just like I'm a caretaker of the trees. And if you read how the monks and Buddhists originated this form and sense the fulfillment they got from it, you don't get big-headed. You realize that you're a little speck in a great big ocean, a grain of sand on the beach. It becomes almost therapeutic. I can go out there and stay all day and be just as content and won't be worried about nothing."

Bonsai also seems to have united James Pettus's two heritages—African American and Cherokee—and made him whole.

"I spent summers in Ahoskie, down in North Carolina, when I was a boy because that's where my mother is from," he says. "The stuff I learned about down there was always in the woods. I'm part Native American— that's why I can go out in the woods all day and feel content there.

"When I'm trimming a tree, I feel that I'm doing something special with it. I'm communing with it, becoming a part of it. You can't hear the tree, but you can sense the life in it. It becomes a part of you, and you become a part of it. You can sense when it's lacking something, but you can't put a finger on what it is. You have to get that feeling first.

"It does wonders for me. I used to do bad things. I was always running the streets and doing different things with my friends. Now, my friends don't even call me. My wife doesn't worry about me no more either, and she used to worry quite a bit."

Bonsai enthusiasts can spend thousands of dollars on accessories, from finely tempered steel pruning shears to every sort of pot and gadget, but the tools of James Pettus's art are everyday ones. He prunes his trees with discarded surgical scissors that his wife, a registered nurse, brings home for him, and he does his fine work with suture scissors. For shaping branches— bending them to fit a design—Pettus uses bricks, fishing weights, and monofilament fishing line. When he pulls bark off a tree trunk to create a driftwood look, he secures the edges of the remaining bark with trusty Elmer's glue. The bonsai themselves are sometimes foraged, too.

One day, Pettus was driving by the headquarters of the Washington Metropolitan Area Transit Authority—overlords of the region's Metro subway system—on his way to delivering a sheaf of documents to the Federal Communications Commission when he saw workmen yanking trident Japanese maple seedlings out of a patch of ivy.

"I saw them pulling them up, so I stopped. 'Can I help you?' they said. 'Can I have the ones you pull up?' I asked. You collect trees wherever you can."

Pettus took home nineteen of the baby Japanese maples and planted them together. The survivors have created a stunning design—a complete miniature forest in a shallow pot, the sort of place he can still walk through in his mind.

Pettus's hook left hand and his long salt-and-pepper queue give him a distinctive appearance, but the disadvantage of having only one hand to do complicated shaping also has stimulated his creativity, he says. Many bonsai enthusiasts will wrap a branch in stiff wire to achieve a desired angle or shape, a technique not easily available to a one-handed artist. The creativity, in turn, has led him to deeper insights about the nature of bonsai.

"If I want to wire something up, I've got to use my feet. I can hold the branch where I want to with my feet, but I don't have the same sense of feel that I'd have with two hands. That's why I don't like to wire. I'd rather use weights and string. Then you read that the Chinese would rather prune than wire because of the wire cutting into the bark. They want to stay as close to natural as possible. Wiring isn't natural, but pruning and making it go a certain way, well, that is. With wiring, you're going against the nature of the tree. You try not to make a tree do things that aren't in it. You want to refine what is already there."

Refining what is already there also requires seeing months, even years ahead to what will be there, and that may be the hardest challenge of all for a bonsai artist.

"You can see the design in your mind's eye, but you can't see the finished product. You've got to have the patience to wait two or three years. It can work on you. I use paper towels—I'll conceal a branch from sight and see how it looks if that branch wasn't there. I'll take the paper off and say, Oh, I can't do that. But then I'll cover it up again and have another look. I've done that three or four times in a day. You know it isn't going to happen today. It isn't going to happen in three or four years. You've got to visualize way far ahead."

When it does all come together, though—when you can step back and look at a bonsai and see the refinements in it, the years it took to redefine the branches and turn root stock into trunk, the meticulous pruning that has created a dense foliage—when you can see how all that effort has come together, the moment, James Pettus says, is magical.

"You sense that it's content, it's comfortable. Everything is like it should be, and you can tell that the tree is happy.

"I think the main thing this has taught me is patience. We live in a world that goes zoom, zoom, zoom. We can have breakfast here today and dinner in Europe. The world is shrinking, and we're constantly on the move. We want it now, want it now. Bonsai takes you away from that. It gives me a relaxing period. I'm not concentrating on nothing but my trees. The therapeutic value is immeasurable. You can't put a price on that."

Three

Robin Tarbell-Thomas:
To the Fair

Some pastimes are handed down from one generation to the next. Robin Tarbell-Thomas, who at the age of forty-one has already won more than three thousand ribbons for baking and cooking at the Iowa State Fair, is the granddaughter of the late Mildred Phillips, winner of more than five thousand ribbons at the state fair, county fairs, and festivals. She is the daughter of Olive Jean Tarbell, who has won more than two thousand ribbons at the Iowa State Fair, county fairs, and festivals and is still competing. Thomas's great-grandmother, Eva Horstman, won a blue ribbon for a cake she baked in her wood-burning stove and sent with a neighbor to a nearby festival: the neighbor owned a car, the Horstmans had only a horse and buggy. Tarbell-Thomas is the first member of the family to have won all her ribbons at the Iowa State Fair, one of the best-known state fairs in the country.

Robin Tarbell-Thomas lives in Centerville, Iowa, as her grandparents did and her parents do to this day. At the age of five, she asked Santa Claus for a Suzy Homemaker oven, and Santa brought it. The stove's four tiny top burners didn't work—"the knobs turned on and off but they were just for show"—but the oven was heated by one 100-watt light bulb. She could bake four tiny cookies in it. She wanted the stove so she could "bake and take" to the Iowa State Fair, but in the nineteen-sixties there were no categories for children under the age of ten. She used her turquoise mini-stove to bake for her parents and her two older brothers, "and they said the cookies or the four bites of cake the Suzy Homemaker accommodated were delicious, even though they probably weren't."

She first entered recipes in the Iowa State Fair in 1975, when she was fourteen. She has entered the fair every year since, with two exceptions. She graduated from high school in 1979, took a secretarial course at a community college from the fall of 1979 to the spring of 1980, and worked the midnight to 8:00 A.M. shift at Union Carbide during the summers of 1979 and 1980. "I couldn't get to the fair those two summers," she says. "I was on the graveyard shift and helping my dad on the farm in the hayfield, and I also helped my grandpa Phillips mow the Haines cemetery near Centerville during the summer." In December 1980, she started working in the Appanoose County Courthouse, where the hours are 8:30 A.M. to 4:30 P.M.; the family farm was sold in 1980, and she hasn't missed taking entries to the fair for over twenty summers. In the 1982 competition she won 57 ribbons, 17 of them blue.

Most years since then, she has increased the number of entries she has submitted and has won more ribbons. Two of her best years were 1995, when she received a total of 258 ribbons, 121 of them blue, and 1997, when she won 231 ribbons, 131 of them blue—the largest number of blue ribbons ever won at a single fair.

Tarbell-Thomas shares Vince Lombardi's philosophy: "Winning isn't everything, but wanting to win is." She loves the spirit of competition, looks forward to seeing the other competitors ("We send each other Christmas cards, we talk a couple of times a year, we're like family"), and loves to bake and cook. "Cookies are my favorite thing to make, probably because I started with cookies, and candy is my second favorite."

The Iowa State Fair is held every August in Des Moines, a two-hour drive from Centerville. Tarbell-Thomas begins to prepare for the pickling and canning classes months ahead of time. "By January I've already canned a few fruits, like apple chutney and pears, and a few vegetables, like End of the Garden Relish," she says, and she usually has an idea or two for new recipes for cookies and candy.

The Iowa State Fair's "Premium Book" arrives in the mail during the first week in June. It lists all the different divisions and classes being offered that year. "You go through it and you get so excited," Tarbell-Thomas says. "You want to take this and you want to take that. Many classes don't change, but sometimes old classes are eliminated and new ones are added and it's fun to see what the new ones are." All she has to do by July 1 is pay an entry fee—thirty dollars for 151 entries or more. She has another month to decide on the specific 151, 251, or however many entries she will take.

Robin Tarbell-Thomas receives three weeks of annual vacation plus comp time. She and her husband, Jim, the owner of T'NT Auto Sales ("He buys wrecked cars, fixes them up, and sells them") and their daughter Molly, now nine, go on a one-week vacation in June, when Molly gets out of school. "One year we went to Niagara Falls, one year to South Dakota." July is Tarbell-Thomas's busiest month. "I don't bake and freeze cookies until July," she says. "I think if I baked them in May or June they would lose their taste and texture.

"The best recipes are my grandmother's and even some from my great-grandmother. When I find a good recipe, I usually stick with it." Blue ribbon–winning recipes are published, so, in theory, anyone who reads the recipes could duplicate them. "If someone who doesn't bake tries a blue ribbon recipe, it would take some practice to get the same results," Thomas says. "But if someone bakes a lot, they should be able to get the same results I do." That doesn't seem to happen, because Thomas has won blue ribbons in many cookie classes year after year after year. Her winning ways may help explain the fact that several years ago, the fair instituted a new rule prohibiting blue-ribbon winners in a particular class from competing in that class the following year. "If I win the blue ribbon for a cookie in 2001, my mother might compete in that class in 2002," she says. "We've competed against each other a few times but we don't really like to do that. When I first started entering the fair, I had to compete against my Grandma Phillips because they didn't have that many categories to enter. There are more every year."

Tarbell-Thomas attributes her success at baking for ribbons to experience. She doesn't make beginner's errors, like not knowing that cookies must be displayed only on white paper plates (the use of colored plates is prohibited and disqualifies entries). "I don't use cheap plates because certain cookies leave buttery oil spots," she says. "I buy the more expensive plates that don't show spots. I want everything to be elegant." She also bakes and freezes six of every type of cookie. She chooses the four best to enter at the last minute. Entries must be wrapped in self-adhering, see-through plastic or Ziploc bags, or they will be disqualified. "You want air in the bags, so they are puffed up and don't touch the entry."

She believes she has learned, over the years, what the judges are looking for. "You have to use fresh ingredients, especially fresh spices," she says. "They can tell if they're not fresh. Appearance is really important. I try to do a little bit extra, like drizzling the cookies with melted almond bark or Wilton's baking chips or adding candied cherries, bits of fruit, nuts, or candy on top of the cookies." Tarbell-Thomas allows that sometimes varying a recipe pays off. She thinks she won a blue ribbon for her grandmother's Rocky Road Candy because she added macadamia nuts to it. She is convinced she won with her pumpkin bar recipe by adding dates and orange marmalade to it. And she once bought rose water in a drugstore and used it in a recipe for pink sugar cookies she found in a booklet her mother had received over forty-five years earlier as a wedding present, and that cookie was a winner. "But it doesn't matter how many extras you add if the entries don't taste good to the judges," she observes. The cookie division is generally judged by six to ten judges. They never see the names of the entrants until after they have chosen the prize-winning cookies.

Taking to the fair is a family collaboration. Robin's father is her official taster. "I like to have Dad sample all the cookies I'm going to enter," she says. Ivyl Tarbell also cuts up the cardboard that must be placed underneath the rolls and breads Tarbell-Thomas enters. Robin's mother, "O.J.," babysits for Molly. "I work full-time," Robin says, "including July." Mom also washes dishes and cookie sheets and mixing bowls ("It would take too long to keep running the dishwasher"), shops at farmer's markets for fresh fruits and vegetables, and helps fill out the three-by-five-inch and four-by-six-inch index cards that must be submitted, often in duplicate, with entries. Molly unwraps "boughten caramels for cookies and bars whose ingredients include caramels."

Jim Thomas makes sure to have a van, a station wagon, or a big car in good working order to transport the family and the entries to the fair. He also made eight large trays with handles to hold Robin's entries ("Each tray can hold ten six-inch plates, so Jim's carrying case accommodates eighty entries"), and he does some of the almost daily driving.

In July Robin works until 4:30 P.M. as a legal secretary for the county attorney and bakes cookies late into the night in her one oven. She bakes all day on weekends. She makes candy a few days before the fair ("Candy can't be frozen") and doughnuts and muffins at the last minute. "I don't think I could take a lemon meringue pie to the fair," she says. "It would be hard for it to survive a two-hour trip in A-1 condition. If you live ten or fifteen minutes away, you can just run over with it. A two-crust pie can travel. I entered a cherry pie once, but didn't win. Just for entering I received a Diane Roupe cookbook, and that's why I entered. I'm not a pie maker. I rarely enter casseroles because people who live in Des Moines are at such an advantage with those. They taste best right out of the oven. But I don't want to enter all eight hundred food categories anyway, so that's fine."

Tarbell-Thomas takes about two weeks of vacation time in August.

"Since I've been grown, I've never slept in Des Moines during the fair," she says. "I have to go back home either to get more entries out of the freezer or to bake more things. One night during the fair I don't go to sleep at all. That's usually the night before cookies are judged. That's my biggest day." Tarbell-Thomas is rail thin. She says that as a child she liked to sample cookie dough before her mother put it in the oven, but she looks as if she hasn't sampled dough or eaten a cookie for years. "My dad worries about me and tells me to drink a chocolate malt every night so I don't lose too much weight while the fair is on."

In 1999 Tarbell-Thomas entered all sixty-three classes of cookies at the fair, and won blue, red, or white (first-, second-, or third-place) ribbons in thirty-eight categories: peanut butter cookies, peanut butter balls, butterscotch gold-nugget bars, chocolate-chip cookies, white-chocolate-chip cookies, chocolate drop cookies, chocolate crackles, chocolate-caramel delights, glazed fruitcake bars, lime meltaways, orange marmalade pumpkin bars, Austrian peach cookies, Italian sprinkle cookies, Dutch spice cookies, Chinese almond cookies, lebkuchen, Amish sugar cookies, California cookies, coconut macaroons, oatmeal cookies, jam sticks, spiced applesauce cookies, sour cream–date dreams, frosted orange cookies, sugarless fruit bars, fat-free ginger cookies, nut-butter dream cookies, sugar cookies, almond-raspberry cookies, raspberry swirls, butterscotch bars, raspberry-filled white chocolate bars, Neiman Marcus bars, triangle pyramids, sunburst lemon bars, Ranger cookies, and Grandma's cookies. That year, her lime meltaways won third overall prize in a competition held by the magazine *Midwest Living,* for which the prize was fifteen pounds of C&H sugar. In 1986, 1990, 1991, and 1994, she won Best Cookie of the Iowa State Fair, sponsored by the Archway Cookie Company. "My recipe went to the national contest and one year I placed third and one time twelfth. My grandmother Phillips won Best Cookie of the fair three times and one time she placed third in the national contest. I hope someday I'll win the national contest."

In 1999 she also won numerous awards in other categories, such as preserves, butters, Recipes of Yesteryear, canned vegetables, canned fruits (with her spiced apples winning Best in Show), pickles (winning in sixteen classes, thereby winning the pickled food sweepstakes), and candy (in which she also won the sweepstakes). "Sweepstakes is given in each division to the person with the most blue ribbons," she explains. "Reserve sweepstakes is given to the person with the second-highest number of blue ribbons."

According to an article about Tarbell-Thomas published in *The Des Moines Register,* what distinguishes her from other entrants is that she doesn't compete in one or two categories but in many. "She completely rules certain divisions, such as marmalades, conserves, butters, cookies, pickles, relishes and canned fruits," the paper reported.

In the year 2000 the Iowa State Fair offered $12,000 to winners and corporate sponsors offered an additional $46,736 in prizes. Over the past quarter-century Tarbell-Thomas has won U.S. savings bonds, money, gift certificates, cookbooks, cooking utensils, magazines, fruit jars, spices, T-shirts, caps, sunglasses, aprons, an M&M's watch, engraved plaques, boxes of candy, cases of popcorn, pounds of honey, and free passes to Living History Farms of Des Moines—and more. Most classes offer $6 for first place, $4 for second, $3 for third, light purple ribbons and an additional $5 for reserve sweepstakes, and dark purple ribbons and an additional $10 for sweepstakes winners.

"I use most of my ribbon money to buy ingredients, to pay for entering classes, and to pay for gas to commute to the fair," Tarbell-Thomas says. "Grandma Phillips's bonds were cashed in after her death to settle the estate. Mom and I have never cashed in any of our bonds. Some of Grandma Phillips's ribbons were made into lovely quilts. Maybe someday quilts will be made using mine."

Taking to the Iowa State Fair over the years has meant more to Tarbell-Thomas as she has grown older.

"I have been going to the Iowa State Fair every year since birth and it really is a family heritage," she says. "I grew up with it. I remember Grandma Phillips in the kitchen baking all sorts of things and taking great pride in everything she entered. It was fun to go to her house at fair time and just watch her and sample the goodies. Grandpa Keith Phillips even entered grains and vegetables. The Iowa State Fair was a big part of their lives. A lot of times when people would interview Grandma and ask why she entered things at the fair she would laugh and say, 'It's in my blood.'

"Every year when I get ready for the fair, I always think of Grandpa and Grandma Phillips. Grandma Phillips was always cooking doughnuts early on the morning of entry day. Then Grandpa would always start loading up the car. One time he was going to enter some really nice big potatoes. When they got to the fair, he couldn't find them and thought he had left them at home. He decided to drive back to get them. As soon as he left, Grandma found them with her food entries. They had the Iowa State Patrol looking for Grandpa and they were also announcing on the radio for him to come back to the fair. Of course, he didn't listen to the radio and he made it all the way home before he found out that the potatoes were already at the fair. After he finally entered the potatoes, they were disqualified because they were too big.

"My mom always reminisces about when she and her brothers, along with Grandpa and Grandma, went to the fair and camped out. All the way to the fair they would sing the song 'We're from Iowa, Iowa, that's where the tall corn grows.' When they camped out, Grandma would cook supper and all their friends would come over and eat with them.

"I feel fortunate to have had such wonderful grandparents and to have such wonderful parents. If I had grown up in a different family, I might not know how to make cookies and candy, flaky biscuits, barbecue sauce, homemade uncooked noodles, yeast breads, quick breads, cakes, and non-alcoholic drinks of yesteryear. I might not know the art of canning. I'm not saying that would be bad, because I probably would have learned another kind of art. But growing up with my grandma, I even learned to make candied orange peels, which a lot of people think are yucky, although a few people really love them. I've learned that you can pickle almost anything and everything and nothing goes to waste. I'm not afraid to try new recipes. It can really be fun to cook and you can feel proud of the results.

"Taking to the Iowa State Fair is not just entering things, it's a lot more than that. When families do things together that they enjoy, it brings them closer together. Taking to the fair has also given me more self-confidence. I have been interviewed by newspapers, magazines, and cookbooks, and I've been on television. I won a contest sponsored by the M. A. Gedney Company with my grandmother's recipe for dill pickles. There are jars of pickles with my picture on them for sale in grocery stores. I was sent on a three-day pickle tour of the state and treated like royalty. Norita Solt, from Bettendorf, who won for her sweet pickles, and I were driven around in a limousine. If it weren't for my grandparents and parents and for taking to the Iowa State Fair, none of this would have happened."

State fair rules have changed since Robin received her Suzy Homemaker oven at the age of five and wasn't allowed to take anything to the fair. There are now categories for children as young as three to enter. In 1996, Molly won a red ribbon for having the second-longest ponytail (it was eleven inches). In 1997, she won a red ribbon for having the second-longest pigtails. In 1998, Robin Thomas didn't think Molly's hair was long enough to win with a ponytail or pigtails, so she braided it into twenty-five braids in the car on the way to the fair. Molly won a blue ribbon for the most braids.

By 1997, four-year-old Molly was also competing in food categories. C&H sponsors a division for children five years and younger: "My Most Creative C&H Sugar Cookie." Molly's ladybug cookie won a blue ribbon. In 1998, Molly won three firsts in food categories. One was a cupcake-decorating contest for children five to nine. "I decorated my cupcake to look like Rudolph the Red-Nosed Reindeer, and I got a blue ribbon," Molly says. She won blue ribbons in the C&H Sugar Cookie contest with her bumblebee cookies and in the Pillsbury cookie-decorating contest.

In 1999 Molly won eleven ribbons, in 2000 she won fourteen, and in 2001 she won thirty-four. At the age of nine, she has already won seventy-three ribbons.

"I hope that Molly continues to take to the fair or at least always go to the fair," Robin Tarbell-Thomas says. "I enjoy the fair even more now that I have a daughter. When Molly wins a ribbon, she gets so excited and I feel very proud. Now I know the way my grandparents felt and the way my parents feel when I win a ribbon at the Iowa State Fair. I think my Grandma Phillips was right when she said, 'It's in the blood.' Four generations of winning at the Iowa State Fair seems to prove it."

Four

Ann and Sam Ritter: To Fly

For Ann Ritter, heaven on earth would be a simple place: "I'd like to be able to live on an island that has grass on one half of it and beach on the other part of it, and have enough money to fly our friends over and have kite parties all the time."

The island is almost a necessity if you're going to have kite parties round the clock, Ritter explains, because the ideal condition for kiting is "a wind coming off the water at between five and ten miles an hour. When the wind comes off the water, there's nothing to block it." A land breeze, by comparison, can create incredible turbulence, especially when there are buildings or natural formations for it to swirl around, which is why kite enthusiasts spend so much time heading toward empty shorelines and keeping a close eye on which way things are blowing.

"When you go to a sports bar with kite fliers, it's a lot different than with other people," Ritter says. "They don't want the hockey game on. They want the Weather Channel. They want to know where the wind is coming from and how strong it is."

As for the kites themselves, they're a necessity not just for an earthly paradise, but pretty much for life itself as Ann Ritter and her husband, Sam, have come to live it.

"Someone bought us a sport kite for an anniversary present in 1989," Ann Ritter says. "By 1991, Sam was competing. He'd fly the kite, but it wasn't self-launching. Sam would crash and I'd fetch. That got old fast. He went and found a kite that was self-launching, but that was in the antique days of sport kiting and it was a pretty heavy kite. Then we discovered a kite shop near us in Plymouth, Michigan, that made kites as well as sold them. We started hanging around there a lot. They had a kite team—we were both competing by then—and that's when kites evolved from a hobby to a lifestyle. In 1993–94, every single weekend, that was all we did. Finally we bought a house and life got in the way, but most of our recreational activities still revolve around kiting."

To their collection of dual-line sport kites—the balletic, delta-shaped kites that first caught hold on the West Coast in the mid-eighties—the Ritters began to add a stable of four-line "quad" kites that can be stacked one of top of another and operated as a single unit. The extra lines, Ann Ritter says, give you "control on the top and the bottom. It's more like a helicopter of kites—up, down, backwards and forwards." Soon, too, both collections were being supplemented by single-line kites as big as a queen-size mattress.

"When you count all up all the sport kites, count all the stacks as individuals, we have over three hundred kites," she says, "and we've been adding and adding."

As the number of kites mounted, so did the venues at which the Ritters competed and, increasingly, performed: regional meets; the annual national conventions of the American Kitefliers Association; international kite festivals in places such as Wildwood, New Jersey; and an international sport-kite competition held on the island of Guadeloupe, in the Caribbean. In April 2000 they made their first trip to Europe to take part in another international kite festival, this one at Berck-sur-Mer, below Calais on the northern coast of France. Berck-sur-Mer, Ann Ritter says, was a real eye-opener.

"Over here, because we're so litigious, kiters are really careful not to get in other people's way. In Europe, it's sky anarchy. If you're in the way, oh, well, just launch! They are so much more into kiting over there. There must have been a hundred fifty thousand people watching at Berck-sur-Mer. We performed before more people that weekend than we had collectively in ten years."

With more kites and more venues to take them to, the Ritters also found themselves needing more infrastructure. Hauling their kites from show to show came to require a seven-by-fourteen-foot Cargo Mate trailer—license plate MOR WND—because, with so many varieties to fly and so many possible wind conditions to fly them in, you never know what you will need.

Hauling the Cargo Mate in turn necessitated a Dodge Ram 2500—license FLYQUAD—with a Cummins twenty-four-valve turbo diesel engine because pulling a trailer that size at high speeds takes some serious power. Then there is all the lesser but vital equipment that has to be brought along as well, including the "line laundry"—spin socks, flags, and other pieces that are hung from kite lines for decoration and to make the lines visible to other kiters, as well as for stability when the winds start to roar.

All that, of course, is for the big shows, not for the quieter moments when it's only themselves and a windswept shoreline—often on Lake Ontario, a few hours from their home in Ann Arbor, where Ann Ritter works as a reimbursement specialist at the University of Michigan Medical Center. Sam is a software engineer.

"Last Sunday, it was just Sam and I and our two rottweilers," Ann says. "We put a few kites up and a spinning lighthouse on the ground, and it was wonderful. You get out there. You fly the kites. And all of a sudden everything goes away. It's you and the kites and the weather. You can sit and watch them, watch the tails, and just get lost. A lot of high-tech people do this—doctors, lawyers, a lot of computer people, a lot of type A's. You just unwind."

In the mid-eighties, when a kite was just something you told people to go fly, Ann Ritter was running an Ann Arbor bar called the Second Chance—a place where one-time music idols like Chuck Berry, Jerry Lee Lewis, and the Four Tops would rotate through on what amounted to the senior circuit of rock 'n' roll.

"That's where Sam and I met," she says. "I was managing the club. Sam was working as a bouncer next door. They were being mean to him, so I hired him. We got married a year and a half later."

As she speaks, Ann is standing on the boardwalk at Ocean City, Maryland, where she and Sam have come to take part in their second Maryland International Kite Festival. Ann is here to judge the sport-kite competition, a two-part affair similar to figure-skating events, that will be held later in the day. In the first part, contestants are given a set of required maneuvers a month in advance and then judged on how well they perform each and how successfully they get from one to the other. The "requireds" are followed by the ballet event, four minutes of kite choreography set to whatever music the contestants choose. Sometimes, the competition is individuals against individuals; other times, teams of up to four people are competing against one another. Kiters are vying for points that will qualify them for the grand nationals or to be invited to national and international competitions. A fourth-place finisher in the grand nationals at Santa Monica, California, in 1994, and already something of a veteran of international events, Ann Ritter has done both.

While Ann will occasionally compete in the larger festivals, Sam Ritter has retired from kite competition altogether, but hardly from kites. He's invited to events like this to put on a show, draw a crowd, and entertain visiting groups such as the local schoolchildren who are beginning to mass on the boardwalk. Standing out on the beach in front of them in nearly perfect kite conditions—a sunny day, a sea breeze between five and ten miles an hour—Sam is filling the sky with very large objects and looking like a man who couldn't be having more fun.

"Sam always wanted to be an aerospace engineer or a pilot, but he lost the sight in one eye," his wife explains. "Now, he gets to play all day long. He didn't have such a good childhood, but he's making up for it. He can take a kite down and land it in the palm of your hand."

Already Sam has suspended two Jordan Air Kites above him: a tooth-shaped 252 (the number refers to the perimeter, in inches; think of an object roughly six feet by four and a half feet) and a smaller 200 that looks more like an extra-puffy air mattress you might take into the ocean. Named for Dean Jordan of Gainesville, Florida, who invented them, the kites are mostly nylon and air. Maybe fifteen pounds in total weight, they have no supports, spars, or other sticks; but thanks to an ingenious system of bridle lines, the air forms are "beautifully self-launching," Ann Ritter says, "and these kites love to fly."

Following Dean Jordan's model, Sam Ritter has made both kites and a third 200 that he will launch later in the day—the first time he and Ann will have had all three of their air forms in the sky at one time. The nylon pieces are cut with what amounts to a hot knife from fifty-four-inch-wide cloth that the Ritters buy in hundred-yard rolls. Stitching is done with thread used for sails. The clips, rings, and other necessities for holding the air forms to their lines are the same kind parachutists and serious mountain climbers use.

"Clips tend to fail on you at inopportune moments," Ann says. "We use equipment built for people when their life is dependent on it."

Stitching together an air form 200 might take twenty hours for the kite and another four hours for each of the two sixty-foot tails that help stabilize the kite. (Kite and tails together consume about a hundred square yards of fabric.) For Sam Ritter and other air-form enthusiasts, most of them male, that means a lot of time hovering over their sewing. "You'd never expect to hear men talking so much about sewing machines," Ann says, "but you do."

Under adverse conditions, an air form can be a formidable sky warrior. "In Berck-sur-Mer," Ann says, "the wind was twenty miles an hour, coming off the land. The big kites were doing suicide sweeps. We couldn't put enough line laundry on them to hold them down." Under normal conditions, though, air forms are closer to sky manatees, hanging placidly in the air from seven-hundred-to-eight-hundred-pound lines anchored, in this case, into the sand. Not so the stacked quads.

"The quads," Ann says simply, "are like flying a Winnebago."

Made by Revolution Enterprises using wrapped graphite spars—the same technology that supplanted the old steel-shafted golf clubs—the quads, or Revolutions, are hooked together on the ground by five-foot-long train lines, then pulled into the air, where they resemble an acrobatic, multideck sandwich. (Quad-line kites come in a variety of shapes. The ones made by Revolution Enterprises suggest "the bottom half of a bow tie," Ann Ritter says. A notched trapezoid also comes close, for the geometry-minded.)

Ann Ritter has flown six Revolutions in a stack, as much of an airborne Winnebago as she cares to handle. Sam has been known to put up a stack of sixteen, a train of kites that stretches 150 feet from ground to tip when it's flown off a 75-foot line, and he and his friend Lee Sedgwick once flew a stack of twenty-three Revolutions with shortened train lines between the kites, until the wind picked up—and broke the stack apart.

As the schoolchildren watch, Sam is putting a train of twelve quads through a series of graceful swoops and arches in what is essentially a dance of counterbalancing physical forces. Built along the lines of an NFL offensive lineman, at 320 pounds Sam Ritter has the heft to withstand the updraft pressure on the kites, but only barely. Even in almost ideal conditions, he's being pulled around the beach by the twelve-stack—a tug-of-war that he says is due in part to a lack of technique: "Lee Sedgwick can handle as much kite as I can, and he weighs only about a hundred fifty pounds. He's using all technique, where I use strength combined with technique." In more adverse weather and with more kites in the stack, Sam has had the stainless steel handles he uses to hold the lines bend in his grip.

As members of Team Revolution International, the Ritters are able to buy their quad-line kites for less than the full retail price, a minor offset in an expensive pursuit. "We're fortunate that we're able to afford our habit," Ann says. "We both have good jobs. Kiting has a very high junkie factor."

Like other once relatively tame sports, kiting gets ever more extreme. Kite fighting has long been a popular sport in places such as India, where glass-coated lines are used to sever an opponent's line, and in Japan, where the sky mayhem can be a community activity.

"They have whole villages that fight with Rokkaku kites," Ann Ritter says. "The name means a six-sided kite in Japanese. It's real simple and maneuverable. They have special line they use—one is called 'black death.' They wrap it around and tug, and it slices the other line. The last kite in the sky wins."

Now, she says, the one-line fighter kites are getting a strong foothold in the United States, but with a twist. Abrasive lines made from Kevlar (the same material found in bulletproof vests) and hemp-jute combinations that are popular in the rest of the world are mostly banned in the United States, in part for fear of legal repercussions. "Here, of course, we have to be safe," Ann Ritter says. "So you have to loop over or under your opponent's line instead of slicing. The kite fighters are in their own world."

Power, or traction, kiting—using quad-line kites shaped roughly like airplane wings that propel everything from skiers to buggy riders—is also on the rise.

"It evolved from wind surfing," Ann explains. "You're using a kite to propel yourself around. You have these buggies—these adult Big Wheels—that you steer with your feet. My career ended when I hit a curb, flipped the buggy, and cracked my kneecap. I was going about ten or fifteen miles an hour, if that. They have buggy events in the desert where they're going thirty to forty miles an hour. That would scare the bejesus out of me. I'm accident-prone."

The "new big thing" in the sport, she says, is kite surfing—"the power-kiting guys and the wind surfers are coming together." For the very brave, and the non-accident-prone, there's also kite jumping, in which participants rise and fall with the kites themselves. "A guy in France was going a hundred feet off the ground and coming back down." For the Ritters, though, the future has more to do with entertaining than risking life and limb. "For us," Ann says, "it's the big show kites, the spectacular displays, giant stuff you can see for miles."

The Ritters have their eyes on a four-thousand-dollar, one-hundred-foot-long octopus kite made in New Zealand that's "a showstopper," according to Ann. "The air goes in the mouth and top of the head." Meanwhile, Sam is dreaming of sewing together a showstopper that would be closer to both their hearts: a fifty-foot-long rottweiler that would be inflated by the wind as it rose into the sky.

"The neighbors think we're crazy," Ann says. "They're not sure what we're doing. One day Sam put all the kites out in the yard, and the neighbor said, 'Oh, that's what you've got in that trailer: hot-air balloons!'"

Wait till they see the fifty-foot rottweiler out on the lawn.

Five

Leonard Lauder:
The Beauty of
Small Things

Leonard Lauder, the CEO of Estée Lauder Companies, Inc., is in the library of his Fifth Avenue penthouse. On the library's walls are two paintings by Gustav Klimt that almost every museum in the world would be delighted to own. Tilted against a wall are a Picasso and a Braque that almost every museum in the world would be delighted to own—and would not place on a floor. Lauder and his wife, Evelyn, have one of the finest collections of Vienna Secessionist and Cubist art in the country.

There is a door in the library wall that doesn't look like a door. Lauder, a trim, courtly man with gray hair, opens this door and emerges from a small room hidden behind it, carrying several albums of picture postcards. "Evelyn and I collect art and go hiking together," Lauder says. "Evelyn's personal interest is photography. Mine is postcards. I have the same affection for the postcards as for the Picassos." Lauder has the finest postcard collection in the country. He has about two hundred thousand cards.

By the time Lauder purchased his first Fernand Léger, he had already bought a great many postcards. He grew up in Manhattan and, as a child, often went out walking with his nanny. When he was five, he spent his weekly nickel allowance at Woolworth's, buying five postcards that cost a penny apiece, each showing the same picture of the Empire State Building. "They were so lovely I couldn't resist," he says.

During the late nineteen-thirties and early forties, Lauder went on vacation with his parents to Florida, and attended boarding school in Miami Beach. He opens a leatherette album with Mylar pages. Encased in the "archivally correct" Mylar are postcards showing art deco hotels in Miami Beach, arranged in alphabetical order. "I picked up all these cards as a kid, starting from the age of six," he says. "There's the Hotel Arlington. There's the Cadillac Hotel. On the card, it stands alone. There were buildings right next to it but they aren't shown. They were airbrushed out. We used to stay at the Charles Hotel."

He fast-forwards down the alphabet. "Here's the Roney Plaza," he says. "It used to be restricted. No Jews were permitted, so we didn't stay there. The Roney has been torn down, but most of these other hotels are still standing. The cards are linen-y. Linen went out in the late forties or early fifties and was replaced by chromes—photographic reproductions. These cards had no value until a few years ago, when the world rediscovered art deco and South Beach. To me, this is my childhood collection and I treasure it.

"When I was in high school I joined the oldest ongoing postcard club in America, the Metropolitan Postcard Club. I'm member number seventy-five. I'd swap cards with other collectors. Cards were worth between one cent and five cents. If we swapped, I might owe you ten cards or you might owe me twenty."

Lauder went off to college and to the navy, then came back to work for the cosmetics company his mother founded. He married and had two sons. "I was preoccupied," he says. "I didn't do much with postcards for fifteen years. Around 1965, I was building our company in England and I spent a lot of time in London. One weekend, I stumbled on some postcard dealers who had a stand on the Portobello Road. I became reinterested in postcards and started buying them. When I returned to the postcard scene in New York, the concept of exchanging was disappearing because the value of cards had gone up rapidly. You couldn't swap card for card. You'd wind up swapping value for value, which very quickly became buying and selling. The best way to collect was to go to postcard shows and make the rounds of the forty or fifty dealers who had tables at these bourses, and to buy the best of the best."

At these three-days shows, Lauder says, everyone was looking for something else. "A person would say to a dealer, 'Do you have any baseball stadiums?' Another would say, 'Do you have any dogs?' When I hear of people who collect postcards of cats or canaries, I'm not interested in them. That's never been the way I've collected cards. I collect cards that I think are beautiful—I'll get to that later—and cards I believe are of historical, sociological, or anthropological interest. I'm also interested in communication. The postcard has its place in the history of communication."

The telephone rings. Lauder answers it, looks at a calendar on his desk, and makes a tentative dinner date with a friend. After putting the receiver down and writing the date on a piece of paper, he says, "It's important to remember now that we're at the beginning of the twenty-first century that at the beginning of the twentieth century most people were unlikely to have telephones in their homes. Let's pretend the year is 1905 and I want to confirm a dinner date. I would probably do it by postcard.

"The first American government postal cards date back to 1873. Businesses bought these cards from the post office for a penny and had them printed with advertisements, greetings, or illustrations. In 1898, Congress put privately printed postcards, which had cost two cents [to send], on an equal footing with government-issued cards by cutting their price in half. It was the establishment of rural free delivery around the same time that made sending postcards a way of life.

"Free mail delivery in cities began in 1863, and home delivery was made to residents of towns with populations of at least ten thousand, but it was not until sometime between 1896, when RFD began, and 1906, when RFD was fairly well established, that farmers no longer had to travel considerable distances to the nearest post office to send or receive mail. Many had made this trip only once a week. Now the mail arrived every day, in cities sometimes two or three times a day, so people used the mail more often. You could send a card in the morning saying you expected someone for dinner at seven, certain in the knowledge that the dinner guest would receive the card well before seven o'clock. A penny postcard was a bargain. It was half the price of a letter and required less effort on the sender's part. The price of the penny postcard only went up to three cents in 1958."

Germany and Austria had started to produce beautiful postal cards in the eighteen-sixties, Lauder continues. Other countries soon followed, and a postcard-sending and postcard-collecting craze swept through a good part of Europe. "After 1898, the so-called golden age of postcards embraced America, and that age lasted for about twenty years," Lauder says. "I've read that in 1906 over a billion postcards were sent through the mail in Germany. By 1913, close to a billion postcards were mailed in the United States."

In that halcyon period between the Spanish-American War and the beginning of the First World War, people sent each other commercially produced postcards on birthdays and on holidays. Not just on Valentine's Day,

Saint Patrick's Day, Easter, Thanksgiving, and Christmas, and other current greeting-card-industry holidays, but on Groundhog Day, Lincoln's Birthday, Washington's Birthday, Leap Year, April Fool's Day, Decoration Day, and Labor Day. They sent scenic views from their travels.

"Postcards also became a source of instant news," Lauder says. "If there was a fire in a small town, the local photographer took a picture of it, then went to a studio and produced fifty or a hundred photo postcards of the fire. That afternoon or the next day you could buy a postcard of the event and send it to your mother or your aunt who lived elsewhere and tell them, 'This is where we had the fire' or 'This is where we had the trolley car accident,' and your relatives could see what these disasters looked like. Small newspapers of that era did not reproduce photographs. Larger papers printed only photographs of important events and people, in a separate gravure section of the Sunday paper, so photographs of news events were generally made available by other means, primarily the photographic card."

In 1903, Eastman Kodak manufactured a camera that was designed to take postcard-size negatives. Adults had their own photographs taken and their children's photographs taken and printed on postcard-size stock and dispatched them for a penny. Many professional photographers found it lucrative to produce nothing but postcards.

"Some photographers went to the workplace and took photos of you and your mates," Lauder says. "Each of you would buy one to have. Except for my childhood collection of the hotels on Collins Avenue in Miami Beach, I don't collect touristic cards, although I'll send them from my travels if I spot some pretty ones. I don't collect postcards of movie stars either, but one of my granddaughters loves Shirley Temple and I was delighted to buy some Shirley Temple cards for her. The American photographic cards, known as 'real photographic cards,' to which I am partial, include views of people in the streets. I like scenes showing knife vendors and chestnut sellers. I'm fascinated by the small tradesmen of times gone by. I think the highest-quality American cards were produced by the Detroit Publishing Company.

"Detroit hired William Henry Jackson, one of the best-known photographers in America, as its manager and chief photographer. They got him a railroad car, which had in it a developing lab, and sent him around the country. From 1898 to 1914 he photographed America. Many other photographers worked for Detroit, which produced about sixteen thousand cards. They're numbered. I have most of them in my collection. I've already given away my Detroit duplicates to the New York Public Library.

"Most of the time I remember whether I've seen a card before, and whether I own it, but when you buy collections, as I do from time to time, you invariably acquire duplicates. You also get duplicates when you have a card and you have a chance to buy one in better condition and you upgrade. I have dealers looking for the missing Detroits on my behalf. Raphael Tuck's cards are also outstanding. Without postcards, we wouldn't have the incredible visual record of America that we do. And of a good part of the rest of the world, for that matter."

One of Lauder's favorite categories is transportation. He turns to a photographic card that shows the *Hindenburg,* the famous German airship, under construction. "That photo wasn't taken for a newspaper," he says. "It was taken for a postcard." He turns to a card showing the *Normandie,* a French luxury liner, while it was under construction. "That photo wasn't taken for a newspaper, it was taken for a postcard," he reiterates. He repeats these words as he goes through albums with cards showing more airships, or zeppelins, as they were called ("a moment in aviation history"); cards of the rue des Juifs in Toulon and a deserted street in a Moroccan ghetto; and streets in turn-of-the-twentieth-century Berlin and Moscow.

He holds up a postcard of Adolf Hitler, wearing white tie, in a box at the opera house in Dresden, taken between 1933 and 1939; people in the orchestra section below, wearing white tie, black tie, and business suits, are saluting him. Then Lauder proffers a postcard of the *Titanic* lifeboats, shot by a photographer aboard the *Carpathia.* "When that photographer boarded the *Carpathia,* he expected to take pictures of the Pierrot parties and other festivities on board," Lauder says. "When the *Carpathia* came to the rescue of the unsinkable ship's more fortunate passengers, he shot these historic photographs and turned them into postcards."

He studies another historic photograph-turned-postcard. "That picture was taken in Sarajevo on June 28, 1914, just moments after Gavrilo Princip, a Serbian high school student and nationalist, assassinated the Austrian Archduke Francis Ferdinand and his wife," he says. "You can see the Austrian automobiles and policemen chasing Princip. That assassination was an immediate cause of the First World War. I have postcards of the Russian revolution and of the German revolution right after World War One. It's extraordinary that such records of events and of revolutions exist."

Lauder speaks of another of his cards, which shows a ship that was part of the U.S. Navy's Great White Fleet approaching Japan. "I have a wonderful subcollection of about thirty thousand Japanese cards," he says. "I believe in collecting at great depth. Alone, a card often means little, but as part of a group it has meaning."

"The best of the best." Lauder repeats these words and glances at the

Picasso and the Braque on the library floor. "Those two pictures were done at the same moment in time," he says. "The artists copied each other. Braque was the more creative of the two. Picasso was the better artist. These works of art speak to each other. If you put a Monet and a Lichtenstein next to each other, they would not have a dialogue. I think my best postcards are those done by expressionist artists like Oskar Kokoschka and Egon Schiele, and over forty other artists for the Wiener Werkstaette, and cards done by artists, among them Lyonel Feininger, for the Bauhaus.

"The Wiener Werkstaette, founded in Vienna in 1903, was an arts and crafts cooperative that created fine furniture, carpeting, wallpaper, silverware, and crystal for the home, fashionable clothes, and postcards. The postcards financially supported the other activities of the Viennese Workshop and advertised its other endeavors. These postcards are the top of the top because they are all original lithographs. Artists were commissioned to do these lithographs. They're the twentieth-century equivalent of a Rembrandt etching. They're a reproduction of nothing. The same is true of the Bauhaus cards. If a museum wanted to have a definitive collection of the works of Kokoschka, it would have to own the cards he did for the Wiener Werkstaette. I have collected early twentieth-century posters. A century ago people frequently collected posters and postcards. Posters very often appeared on postcards. Postcards did not become billboards."

Lauder says that he has most of the Wiener Werkstaette cards, but dealers are still searching on his behalf for the ones he is missing. He is ambivalent about completing this collection. "Until recently I was missing one of Eugène Atget's eighty photographs showing tradesmen in Paris that were put out only on postcards," he says. "A while ago I met a dealer who knew of two men in France who had retired from working as flight attendants for Air France. They decided after their retirement to become postcard dealers. I sent them a list of cards I needed. To my astonishment, they had the Atget my collection lacked. I was momentarily pleased. And then I was disappointed. I had no more Atgets left to look for."

Almost as soon as Lauder completes a set of postcards, he starts looking for cards of a different variety. "I'm now collecting so-called rack cards," he says. "They're advertising cards, and of course in my line of work, advertisements are of the greatest importance." He pulls a few cards for Absolut vodka out of a Clinique bag he has brought home from his office. "I'm told that you can find these cards on racks in medium-priced restaurants between the men's and the ladies' rooms," he says. "I don't frequent such restaurants, so dealers buy them for me."

He also plans to collect postcards showing all the works of art displayed at the 1913 New York Armory Show, a pivotal point in the history of modern art. And he has started to collect photographic postcards from black Africa taken between 1895 and 1935.

"Missionaries were sent down there not only with crosses but with cameras," he says. "They captured a world that has disappeared. These cards are real anthropological statements and they give me a great deal of pleasure. As this is a new collection, I don't have to worry that I will complete it anytime soon. For me, the pleasure is in the chase, and for a while in the acquisition. Possession is far less exciting. I don't ever really want to have a complete collection. I prefer infinity to completion."

PART 2
Thrill of the Chase

Six

Alexandra Stafford:
Food of Life

Consider the New Orleans Arena as a piece of urban architecture, and there's little good to be said about it. Built next to the Superdome and clad in green tiles, the arena calls to mind a public rest room turned inside out. Look at the arena as a dispenser of food, though, as Alexandra Stafford is likely to, and much of the ugliness disappears faster than a plate of pecan pralines from Laura's Candies. What's not to like about a place where, for not a lot more money, you can sit in the club level and enjoy a buffet that features a very passable crawfish pasta?

Although she is descended from a long line of New Orleans natives, Stafford was raised mostly in Paris and settled in New York City after college. Marriage brought her back to her mother's native city, and happily so, because Alexandra Stafford loves food. She loves the ritual of it and the taste of it. She loves to talk about food, and she loves the way great meals leave a lingering impression in memory, just waiting for Proust's orange madeleine (or a plate of Casamento's butter-drenched oysters on toast points) to unlock it. And in all those qualities, it is hard to think of a place that could better serve her than New Orleans.

Just as important, Stafford loves to pursue food, and in that regard, too, she seems to have found the ideal home. All the time not taken up in New Orleans with eating and drinking appears to be spent moving between food and drink providers because, heaven knows, one-stop shopping or eating just won't do in the Crescent City.

Maurice's French Pastries is for rum balls, Stafford says, and McKenzie's Pastry Shoppe is for petit fours and chocolate turtles, although both are likely to be picked clean by 4:00 P.M., when Aimée, Stafford's young daughter with "sugar and icing for blood," begins to get a hankering for an afternoon sweet. As for Gambino's Bakery, which advertises itself as "The King of the King Cake," it's really for the best doberge cake going.

"They push the king cake for Mardi Gras–hungry out-of-towners because it ships well, but the doberge is unique, and Gambino's is the king of that one, too. It's an extremely high, double-layered cake with chocolate or lemon icing," Stafford explains. "You go there and ask for a half-and-half—half lemon, half chocolate. The lemon is like a custard, and the cake is very soft and crumbly."

The Mile High Pie at The Pontchartrain Hotel on St. Charles Avenue is even taller than the doberge cake and still more substantial, and it's available in both the Caribbean Room and the hotel coffee shop, otherwise known as the Café Pontchartrain.

"It's on a horrible pastry pie shell that you never touch. Then you have peppermint, vanilla, and coffee ice cream, the whipped meringue on top of that, and a dripping dark-chocolate topping. The coffee shop is a power breakfast spot. The men are three hundred pounds each. They wear white shirts and suspenders, and they have nothing to do, so you know they're politicians."

For something sweet and lighter—and Alexandra Stafford doesn't have an extra pound on her—she favors curbside snoball vendors, although not just any one.

"You have your own snoball stand, just like you have your own waiter at Galatoire's and Antoine's, and you won't go to any other," she says. "Everyone has her favorite flavor. Mine is nectar. It's pink, almond-and-vanilla flavored, on shaved ice. I like condensed milk on it."

The secret to the local snoballs, she says, is the SnoWizard machine: "It's made in New Orleans, and you can use only that. The ice is much finer than Italian ice."

If Stafford has her way, daughter Aimée will make nectar-flavored snoballs topped with condensed milk her absolute and unshakable favorite, too: "I'm trying to train Aimée that it has to be hers—it's a tradition!" In the meantime, she's working on another tradition: sautéed pecan pie à la mode from the Camellia Grill, which on weekends is open conveniently until three in the morning. Stafford remembers having the pie there with her mother on visits to New Orleans when she was young; now, she's indoctrinating her own daughter.

All that, of course, is just for the last course: dessert. For the rest of the menu, Alexandra Stafford has a large green Range Rover and a city filled with food just waiting for her to arrive. Uptown on Annunciation Street, Clancy's, which hardly advertises, has sweetbreads to die for and soft-shell crabs, either smoked or sautéed. At the seventy-year-old Pascal's Manale on Napoleon Avenue, you can sit down for a shrimp loaf—"They cut the center out of French bread and fill it with shrimp floating in oil and seasonings"—or you can stand at the marble slab near the back and eat oysters as quickly as Thomas shucks them, and because he has been shucking them at Pascal's Manale for ten years, Thomas does them very quickly indeed.

"We do a lot of sucking here in New Orleans," Stafford is saying as she attacks yet another raw oyster. "We suck oysters off the shell, and we suck the crawfish heads—"

"And that's why we have so many famous singers and whistlers coming out of New Orleans," Thomas adds before going on to deliver a dissertation-level discourse on oysters and the various pearls they can contain.

No one local goes to Brennan's anymore, Stafford says. "We're not going to pay thirty dollars to have an egg. It's too popular with the tourists—that breaks the spirit." But the Brennan family is everywhere, not just in the longtime landmark that bears its name. One branch of the family runs a new market chain: Foodie's, chock-full of prepared dishes and delicacies. Another branch oversees what may be New Orleans's most famous restaurant these days: Commander's Palace, in the Garden District.

"You dress up the kids for birthday parties and take them to Commander's Palace," Stafford explains, "and they learn how to be proper diners. The service is the best in the city, even above Windsor Court, because they're friendly. And that's the Brennan's training."

For downscale grazing, there's always Mosca's, forty-five minutes or so out of town, housed in a shack that could have been used for the opening scenes of the movie *Deliverance*.

"It's famous," Stafford says of Mosca's, "and it's ugly like hell. You go there for the Oysters Mosca. They're baked in a casserole and breaded, with Parmesan, on top."

For something closer and less ominous, she prefers the Lake Pontchartrain shorefront, where her husband, Raymond Rathlé, grew up. Russell's Marina Grill on the way out has onion mums: "It's a big onion they bread and fry. The onions open up like a mum." Sid-Mar's of Buckton is her father-in-law's favorite for a poor boy half-and-half: "half shrimp, half oyster—the best of both worlds." For fish and seafood to cook at home, she relies on Schaeffer Rusich, where a hand-painted sign promises:

STUFFED CRABS, OYSTERS, ÉTOUFFÉE GUMBO, FISH, ICE, AND TURTLE SOUP. Just a little bit away is R&O's, where the tables are basic, the waitresses are all "Catholic high school y'ats" (from the local idiomatic "where y'at?"), and the line at dinnertime can stretch all the way around the enclosed front porch.

"We go there nearly every Sunday night," Stafford says. "People come for the fried platters, which are absolutely horrible. We'll have a dozen raw oysters, and then oyster poor boys. They're dry and never greasy, and then you 'dress' the sandwich [add lettuce, tomatoes, mayo, and pickles, in local parlance] and add the tartar sauce, and you've made it really fattening. They also have this Italian salad—iceberg lettuce, olives, pimento, artichoke hearts, celery, and a great vinaigrette that stays in your mouth. You get addicted to it."

For those exhausted by all this running around in pursuit of food and drink, there's even a drive-in daiquiri vendor located conveniently midway between city and suburbs.

"The White Russian daiquiri is very strong," Stafford says. "One and you're snockered. They get away with it by handing you the straw separate from the foam cup. 'Drink and drive' is our motto here."

And then there's the last big lunch before Christmas and especially Mardi Gras—"Fat Tuesday," the day before Lent—both of which mean Galatoire's on Bourbon Street in the famous French Quarter and some very serious planning.

"You have someone wait in line the night before at Galatoire's. You make sure they're supplied with drinks while they wait. And then you show up refreshed at eleven-thirty the next morning and take their place, and all your friends come and join you. There might be just ten people waiting out front, but by the time everyone goes inside, it's full."

Stafford is tucking into a trout almondine at Galatoire's as she tells the story—in the first-floor dining room where locals prefer to eat and not even members of the Galatoire family can make reservations, not in the Siberia of the second floor where the tourists congregate. Across from her, Raymond Rathlé has turned his attention to a filet smothered in béarnaise sauce. Fried eggplant sticks are on the table. A shrimp rémoulade is already in the past. Cups of superb chicory-laced coffee and balloons of B&B lie ahead. All around, diners are hopping from table to table, voices are rising in gaiety, food and drink are disappearing at what might seem an alarming rate, and the effect, as it so often is in New Orleans, is of having fallen headlong into a very movable feast.

* * *

Alexandra Stafford's mother was born and raised in Metairie, just west of New Orleans near the lakefront. She graduated at the top of her class at Sophie Newcombe College, took a secretarial course, and set off for Germany not long after the end of World War II to work for the Marshall Plan.

"She met my father on the boat. He was Romanian, twenty-five years older. They arrived in France, and she was supposed to go on to Germany, but, naturally, there was a strike. So he wined and dined her. She went to Germany anyway, and he went every weekend and wined and dined her there, too."

Eventually the couple settled in New York, where Alexandra was born in 1960. A year later, the family was off to Paris, where Alexandra was to live for the next thirteen years.

"By 1961, their interests were really in France. He was a financier, a stock entrepreneur. My parents were art collectors, and they wanted a good education for us"—including a good education in food and the art of cuisine.

"It was really old-fashioned," she says of dinners *en maison*. "We had a waiter with white gloves. There was always an appetizer—a salad and a soup—and then the main meal. It was maybe an hour, but it seemed like forever when you were young. I remember watching the chef do angel hair with caramelized sugar, and the créme anglais—I'd eat so much of it that I got sick."

Sundays—every Sunday—the family would eat out, often at a place called Rampeneau next to the American Church in Paris.

"It doesn't exist anymore," Stafford says of Rampeneau, "but just recently I tried to imitate the artichoke appetizer they had, and I nearly got it! I'm trying to train Aimée to go to restaurants. My husband says, no, you can't take her to Galatoire's. But how else is she going to learn? I remember these great meals in Paris, and I want to give her that."

At home in Paris, English was always spoken at the table during meals, and civility was the norm. In the kitchen and elsewhere, the norm had a way of breaking down.

"We had a Moroccan chef and French help. They all hated each other. They were chasing each other with knives. There was always a tragedy. By the early nineteen-seventies, Mom had fired every one of them, and she started cooking herself. She would go to the PX and buy peanut butter and Duncan Hines cake mixes. It was my introduction to American food, and it was wonderful."

In 1973, just shy of her thirteenth birthday, Stafford was sent to stay with her grandparents in Metairie for the summer—a visit that was to last three years while her parents were selling their Paris home and resettling once again in New York. Naturally, Stafford marks the time with memories of what she ate.

"I remember getting the fresh peach sherbet from Angelo Brocato's, in the French Quarter. They'd use Louisiana peaches, and they'd crank it the old-fashioned way. The place was very beautiful, with these flowery tiles. It's been turned into a coffee-and-croissant house, but there's still an Angelo Brocato's on North Carrollton. It's run-down and rude and uncomfortable and fun, and has delicious Italian ice creams and sorbets."

There was also her grandmother's crawfish bisque: "They'd keep the crawfish heads, and my grandmother and my cousin who lived next door would stuff them with a bread mush. The soup was the original bisque, a heavy one, and then you'd suck the heads and get this tasty mush out of it. My grandmother died not long after I moved to New Orleans, but her bisque was memorable."

Stafford joined her parents in New York and stayed there through her twenties, with food never far from her mind. For three years at the end of the nineteen-eighties, she and several friends produced a four-page weekly restaurant review called "Taste" that at its peak went out to six hundred subscribers—"mostly Yuppies and Europeans," she says—willing to pay thirty-five dollars a year.

"We captured new restaurants before *The New York Times* did, but being a food writer isn't much of a life. You eat, you write, you never see daylight."

Raymond Rathlé got her back to New Orleans for good, but not before Stafford had passed the acid test: "Raymond's sister, Simone, had to check me out, so she invited me to the Windsor Court Hotel to chat. We met in the kitchen, down where then-chef Kevin Graham was cooking for the Grill Room. After a few nervous moments, we sat in his tiny office, cleared the table, and . . . had lunch! I think that did it. We talked about food—New York restaurants, New Orleans restaurants, Paris restaurants, great food. We had a ball, and we still do."

Appropriately, visitors enter the Stafford-Rathlé house today through the kitchen. To the right of the front door is a beautiful food-preparation island flanked by flawless cabinets, counters, and appliances. To the left is a spacious area for breakfast and casual eating. Just as appropriately, half a year after the house was finished, the chairs in the dining room were still grouped around a candelabra that sat on the rug. Who has time to shop for a dining room table when there are so many restaurants to check out? And such a pleasant setting to do it?

"The food here is not all a culinary delight. It's not like going to France," Stafford says. "A lot of our food is fried. Basically, you're ruining a piece of fish and then adding tabasco and mayo. But the waiter-client relationship here reminds me very much of Paris. We stick to restaurants. We return, and the waiters take us seriously because we do. They know what we want, and they're proud of knowing us and seeing us and our families grow.

"New York is a more interesting food town, but there's no fidelity, no tradition. It's all trends: Is the food horizontal or vertical? We make eating more of an event, a get-together. You're enjoying the food and each other. The food reminds us of convivial gatherings, whether at restaurants or at home, and the memory etches a permanent passion for those happy moments."

In its March 2000 issue, *Harper's Magazine* took note of the "last suppers" requested by inmates executed in the state of Texas since 1984. One made six pieces of French toast the centerpiece of his final meal on earth. Others opted for T-bone steaks, barbecued chicken, four fried eggs sunnyside up. David Allen Castillo asked for twenty-four soft tacos, six enchiladas, six tostadas, two whole onions, and five jalapeños, and that was just for starters.

Not to be morbid, but what would her own choice be? Alexandra Stafford is asked.

"The turtle soup with sherry from Commander's Palace," she answers with only a slight pause, "followed by a shrimp rémoulade from Galatoire's, an oyster poor boy 'dressed' from R&O's, the bread-pudding soufflé with whiskey cream sauce also from Commander's Palace, a cup of chicory coffee, and a nectar snoball for a palate cleanser, topped with half-and-half, not condensed milk—if I'm going to die, I want it all."

And then she adds a final request: "pecan pralines from Laura's, for the executioner."

That's a touch of class.

Seven

David Hanschen:
On the Road Again

David Hanschen, a very tall man with a pony tail, has one of the largest collections of precanceled stamps in the world. In 1957, when he was seven, Hanschen started collecting stamps. He noticed that some stamps had two thick parallel lines, or bars, printed across them and, between the bars, the name of a town or city and the state where it was canceled. Such stamps are known as precanceled postage stamps, or precancels; they have been canceled prior to being affixed to mail. The primary users of precanceled stamps are mail-order firms and other organizations doing bulk mailings. They receive a substantial discount over first-class mail rates because the Post Office saves on labor costs when it doesn't have to stamp pieces of mail individually.

Precancels fall into three main classes. In the first are those imprinted by hand. Hand stamps can cancel ten stamps at a time, two across and five down. In the second class are precancels made by feeding stamps through a printing press, a mimeograph, or some other semiautomatic machine. An entire sheet of one hundred stamps, ten rows of ten each, can be precanceled at once. "I'm partial to the printed precancels because they're easier to find and I think they're prettier," Hanschen says. In the third class are stamps precanceled by the Bureau of Printing and Engraving as the stamps are being manufactured.

When Hanschen was ten, he saw a precanceled stamp with the name of a town in Iowa printed between the two bars. He couldn't find it on a map,

and learned that the town had been washed away by a flood. "I was trans-fixed when I realized I was holding a small relic of a lost place," he says.

Hanschen, who lives in Dallas, started collecting precancels in 1959. He bought stamps by the ounce or by the pound and sorted out the precancels. He says that the Post Office first issued cancellation plates just after the turn of the century, and that the use of plates for precanceling stamps dropped off precipitously in the nineteen-sixties. When the main post office in Dallas moved, a postal employee took the precancelation plate home. He sold it to a stamp dealer, who knew Hanschen collected precancels. The dealer sold Hanschen the Dallas plate in 1985 for twenty-five dollars. "I nearly broke my wrist reaching for my wallet," Hanschen says. "It's a beautiful copper-faced electroplate from the early thirties, and it's on my living room mantel-piece. It's twelve inches by twelve inches, and one inch thick, with a wooden back and a metal surface. It hadn't been used since 1940."

After graduating from college, Hanschen spent twelve years as the presi-dent of a venture capital company. He became a stamp dealer for a year in the early nineteen-eighties but gave up dealing because "collecting is much more fun." In 1987 he started law school at Southern Methodist University. "I did three years of law school over a period of five years," he says. "I didn't take a complete course load. I was too old not to have a life. But I probably didn't look at my stamps during those five years. They waited very patiently for me."

Now a divorce lawyer and a visiting family court judge, Hanschen is active in the Precancel Stamp Society, which has about a thousand members in America and Europe. "There are one hundred and fifty serious active col-lectors," he says. "There are probably twenty of us who have gone over the top in our fervor."

Quite a few people have traveled around the United States getting post offices to hand-cancel stamps for them. What sets Hanschen apart from other precancelers is that he drives around the country on weekends and vacations in his 1982 Mercedes-Benz with his own printing press.

"The guy at the place where I do my copying sold me a little proof press for a hundred twenty-five dollars," he says. "It weighed two hundred pounds. I replaced the solid steel base of the press with an aluminum one, which reduced its weight to seventy-five pounds. Two hundred pounds was heavy to carry and also dragged the trunk of my Mercedes way down. I take a supply of ink with me, and I have a glass plate for the ink. I roll out the ink until I get the right consistency and transfer it to the printing plate. Then I take the stamps I want to cancel, put them face down on the plate, and I go to work printing, just the way Benjamin Franklin did. My press is no more sophisticated than the one Franklin used in the eighteenth century. It's slow, and I can only do one sheet at a time. I take the printing press with me because many post offices don't have one. The trunk is full of precanceling stuff, so I put my luggage in the back seat. I also pack a folding chair, so I can sit and work outside if I'm not allowed in a post office."

Eight hundred cities and towns have about fourteen hundred of the hundred-stamp plates that will print a full sheet—the sort Hanschen is after. Hanschen, who has read extensively on the history of precanceling, knows where these plates are supposed to be. "If I'm lucky, the places I go will have the plate and they'll dig it out," he says. "I've learned enough of the language that they kind of think I'm with the Post Office. I frequently take the Dallas plate with me when I hit the road."

Each year Hanschen attends the annual precanceled stamp convention. In 1999 it was held in Lexington, Kentucky. He drove on to Missouri, where he knew of five post offices that had been issued plates. Joplin didn't have its plate, nor did Carthage, Springfield, or El Dorado Springs. His last stop was the old main post office in Jefferson City. He introduced himself to the clerk in charge of the stamp stock. He asked her about a precanceled printing plate and showed her the Dallas plate he had brought along. He believed their plate was somewhere in the building. The clerk went off to the vault, where the plates are usually stored. When he heard her say "Oof," he knew she had found what he was after.

"The only thing that would have caused the clerk to say 'Oof' was picking up this heavy plate. It weighs about thirty-five pounds. It hadn't been used since the nineteen-thirties, so it must have been sitting in that vault for over sixty years. She didn't know what it was or how it was used. After I saw it, I asked to see the post office's printing press. She said they didn't have one. I already knew the post office wouldn't have a press. The psychology is to present a problem and then provide the solution. So I told her I'd brought mine. I also brought in stamps to precancel. At this point in the conversation there's a quantum shift in reality. Now she's talking to a guy who has a printing press in his car. Postal people are very regulation oriented. I have to be very gentle with them. And I often have to refer them to the proper section of the *Domestic Mail Manual*—the Post Office rule book. I carry a photocopy of the five pages of the D.M.M. that pertain to precanceled stamps. It specifically authorizes collectors to print precancels.

"I have let postal employees in other places believe the Dallas postmaster gave me the Dallas plate, but that wasn't necessary on this occasion. The stamps I brought to precancel are those that could have logically been precanceled in Jefferson City, in other words any stamps produced after the post office got its plate in 1920. I know the issue date of the plate from three sources: the authorization date revealed by the Bureau and/or the issues of stamps on which the plate was first used, and the typestyle used on the plates." Hanschen drove home a happy man.

"I've had the full spectrum of responses on my quests," he says. In Artesia, California, the plate had never been used. "The postmaster himself told me he didn't know what I was talking about, but he was extremely cordial and suggested we look around. I always try to talk to someone in a fairly high-up position because they have the authority to go all over the premises to try to find the plate. Many underlings don't. The postmaster let me go behind the counter—a sacred area—and I found the plate on a dusty shelf."

"Bring it back when you're done," he was told. Hanschen precanceled two full sheets of stamps to have a full device impression, plus several hundred more denominations in blocks of four.

The opposite extreme occurred in Tarboro, North Carolina. Hanschen went into the post office and a man, possibly the postmaster, literally slammed the door in his face. "That was that," he says.

An in-between-the-two-extremes experience was Bettendorf, Iowa, where the postmaster did find the plate but appeared terrified. She came outside with Hanschen, rolling her office chair with her and carrying out all her morning mail and work. Hanschen parked five feet from the loading dock. The postmaster sat outside and watched as he printed for three or four hours.

Another in-between experience was Tallahassee, Florida. "I knew from the records that a plate had been shipped there," Hanschen says. "I went by once and the person I needed to talk to, Star Nelson, the clerk in charge of the stamp stock, wasn't in. I called her up, described what I was looking for, and was told the plate was kept in the vault. I told her I'd return the following year. I did. She was terribly nervous that I would drive away with the plate. 'How about I give you my driver's license and my car keys?' I asked her. She locked them up in her desk. Three or four hours later I was finished, so I went back inside the post office, carrying the plate. Ms. Nelson had gone home. One of her colleagues telephoned her and, as good luck would have it, she was there. She returned to the post office. She was very apologetic. I'm lucky she hadn't gone out for the evening because I had to get back to Dallas the following day."

In many post offices, the people in charge believe they don't have the plate but are willing to look. In York, Nebraska, in the summer of 2000, the postmaster checked his vault. The plate was there. The man admitted he'd been in charge of the post office for twelve years and had never noticed it. In

Spring Valley, New York, however, the post office personnel were very friendly but they had, indeed, thrown the plate away years ago. Hanschen has driven to all forty-eight contiguous states searching for plates and has over 250,000 miles on his Mercedes. The car has broken down only once, "in the Oklahoma outback, on the way to the Ponca City post office."

When Hanschen precancels sheets of vintage stamps, he breaks them into blocks of four. He keeps one stamp from each block, sells one to a friend in Massachusetts, one to a friend in California, and holds the last one for anyone else who wants it. "I don't make money this way," Hanschen says. "I may be on the road for a week or more; I pay for gas, hotels, and meals. The fourth one is likely to sit in a box in my house for a while until I get around to selling it." Hanschen also buys precanceled stamps. "I paid one thousand dollars for [a block of] four twenty-five-cent Leon, Iowa. When I break it apart, I'll want three hundred dollars apiece. That means my copy will cost a hundred dollars. I prefer to keep one and trade off the other three for things I don't have."

One of Hanschen's best pieces of luck to date concerns a stamp from Phenix City, Alabama. In 1980, Chet Hibril of Center, Texas, who repaired band instruments for high school students, came to the Precancel Stamp Society convention in Dallas. He had two volumes of Bureau of Printing and Engraving precancels. There didn't appear to be anything of value in the collection, but Hanschen suggested that Hibril catalog it. Afterward, Hanschen heard through the philatelic grapevine that Hibril had found a two-cent Jefferson stamp from Phenix City. Hanschen knew that the Phenix City one-center was a common stamp that, like many precanceled stamps, sold for a nickel. He also knew that a two-center had been printed in March 1959 and sent down to Phenix City and that no one had ever found a copy of it. The conclusion precanceled-stamp collectors had reached was that it didn't exist.

"The first thing I did was call the Phenix City post office and ask for the name of the man who had been postmaster there in the late fifties," Hanschen says. "I reached the retired postmaster, Dub Green. I asked him if he had received a shipment of precanceled two-centers in 1959 or 1960. He said he had, and that they were for the use of the local Catholic boys' orphanage. I asked if they had ever been used. He said the orphanage had got off one mailing. Then it merged with an orphanage in Selma, Alabama, and returned all the unused precanceled stamps to Washington for credit. So I called Chet and said I'd like to buy his collection. Chet hesitated.

"Another collector had heard that Hibril had the Phenix City two-center and had offered him a thousand dollars for it. Hibril had turned him down.

Chet started talking about building a garage in which to do his musical repairs. I finally said, 'Chet, how much would it cost to finish the garage?' He said twenty-two hundred dollars. I told him I'd buy his collection for twenty-two hundred dollars and he'd have a certified check for that amount the next day." Hibril agreed.

Hanschen kept the Phenix City two-center and sold all the other stamps in Hibril's collection to half a dozen people for seventeen hundred dollars. The man who had originally offered Hibril a thousand dollars for the Phenix City two-center then put an ad in *Linn's Stamp News,* offering twenty thousand dollars for another copy of it. "Chet's turned out to be unique," Hanschen says. "I was probably an idiot for not selling it. That man is no longer collecting and there's no one else around with that kind of money. From a financial point of view, I can't ignore the fact that I'll never get that high a price for it, but that's all right. I've gotten my five hundred dollars' worth of enjoyment out of it. I've climbed Mount Everest with that stamp.

"Collecting precancels is the most complicated type of stamp collecting because it requires the greatest amount of knowledge and research. If I wanted to collect American stamps and had millions of dollars I could probably buy ninety-seven percent of them in a week. I wouldn't have learned anything, I'd just have written a check. If I don't get any action out of collecting, it's boring. With precancel collecting, I don't think it's the pride of ownership that matters to me, I think it's the thrill of the chase.

"Precancels afford an enormous amount of action, a lot of bang for your buck. I'll sell precancels only if I get replacement copies that are in better condition. Occasionally I'll swap something. I have four or five hundred volumes of precanceled stamps in three-ring binders. I added a third story to my duplex so that I'd have additional space for my collection. I spend at least a couple of hours a day on this. My enthusiasm has reached the point of lunacy. But without enthusiasm or passion for something, why bother?

"Frederick Sommer, the photographer, was my friend and mentor. On his tombstone are inscribed some wonderful words: 'Enthusiasm is the duty of understanding before the night fatal to remembrance.'"

Eight

Barry Popik:
First Words

Sign on to the list server maintained by the American Dialect Society, and you'll be entering a world where what often seem small distinctions—of usage, roots, provenance, and the like—matter greatly.

In a typical few hours of e-mail traffic, a woman named Anne laments the use, especially on American television, of the unnecessary conditional subjunctive construction, as in: "If she wouldn't have helped me, I would have been dead." A man named Peter responds that "the big no-no is the use of 'wouldn't' in an if-clause, when it should be used only in a result clause." Soon, Larry is weighing in with the observation that the unnecessary conditional subjunctive might be tied to the "more general disappearance of the pluperfect, especially in colloquial speech," but by then, attention has drifted to the exact usage of the word "parse" and to dialect variation in North American swearing.

Names reappear with some frequency in the Dialect Society discussions, and places, too. The members tend to be from academic institutions in the United States, Canada, and the British Isles. But no name appears more frequently than that of Barry Popik. Popik is all over the ADS list server like white on rice, like a cheap suit, like ticks on a hound dog—all oddities of American usage that he would gladly run down for you and almost certainly find, because when Barry Popik sinks his teeth into discovering the first usage of a phrase, you can pretty much assume it's a done deal.

Popik is the guy who showed that "Big Apple" predated Harlem in the nineteen-thirties, the guy who proved that "Windy City" was in use a decade

before commonly supposed. It was Popik who crossed the *t* on the provenance of "hot dog," Popik who found that "hello" was in parlance, at least
in and around New York City, long before Thomas Edison spoke the word
into the mouthpiece of his new telephone. Not—as Barry Popik would be
quick to tell you—that anyone in authority appears to care in the least.

Popik seems to have found word sleuthing at just about the right moment in
his life. Raised in Spring Valley, north of New York City, he attended Rens-
selaer Polytechnic Institute, in Troy, New York, and the Touro Law Center
in Huntington, New York, from which he graduated in 1985. Eventually,
Prentice-Hall, the publisher, tendered a job in its legal department, and
Popik took it.

"I had no offers after law school. I took the lowest job at Prentice-Hall,
at $19,100 a year. Legal secretaries start off at more than that. On the side,
I was writing plays and screenplays that weren't going anywhere."

By 1988, even the little good news was turning bad. His sister married
that year and moved with her husband to Scarsdale, in suburban Westchester County, leaving behind an apartment on East Fifty-seventh Street, in
a building that was just going cooperative. Popik pulled together his life
savings and bought the apartment. Soon thereafter the building owner filed
for bankruptcy, precipitating a legal maelstrom that for years would leave
in question the value, if any, of Popik's investment.

This, then, was the state of Barry Popik's life on the evening in 1988
when he left work at Prentice-Hall and stopped by the New York Public
Library Annex, on West Forty-third Street. Ahead of him in the sign-up line
was a University of Missouri–Rolla professor named Gerald Cohen, and the
two of them fell into conversation about the topic Cohen had come to the
library to research. In 1971, Charles Gillett, head of the New York Convention and Visitors Bureau, had transformed the city's motto from the
short-lived "Fun City" to "Big Apple." Now, the columnist "Dear Abby"
(Abigail Van Buren) was appealing to her readers to help solve the origin of
the name, and Cohen had joined the chase.

Gillett had borrowed the name from a dance craze of the late nineteen-
thirties, and for some time it appeared as if a musical connection would win
out. New York's Governor Mario Cuomo, among others, weighed in with
the opinion that the name had originated with African-American musicians
in Harlem earlier in the thirties, and indeed a Harlem watering hole that
opened in either 1934 or 1935 had been christened the Big Apple.

The editor of the journal *Comments on Etymology,* Cohen wasn't convinced. Using the archives of the prolific word-sleuth Peter Tamony, Cohen traced the phrase to John J. Fitz Gerald, the racing editor in the late 1920s of the New York *Morning Telegraph,* the forerunner of today's *Daily Racing Form.* In 1991, Cohen published a monograph noting that Fitz Gerald had used the phrase "Big Apple" on seven occasions in and around 1928.

For Popik, who had changed jobs in 1990 and become a judge with the New York City Parking Violations Bureau, Cohen's explanation seemed scholarly but still incomplete. Had he pushed back far enough through the archives? Exhausted every lead? "I said, We know 'Big Apple' is there in 1928, so why don't we go backward," Popik recalls, and so he did—through the *Morning Telegraph* and through another New York newspaper of the day, the *New York Evening Graphic,* where Walter Winchell also had used "Big Apple." The further back Popik went, the more it became apparent that Gerald Cohen had the source right but the date wrong: in the first-usage game, one is nothing without the other.

"The *Telegraph* is not on any database. I read every issue on microfilm at the New York Public Library. The scanner was broken all the time; the paper was jammed. This was a day a week for half a year or a year. I looked in 1927 and 1926. I didn't expect to find it, and there on December 1, 1926, was 'In the Paddock with John J. Fitz Gerald.'" Fitz Gerald wrote:

> So many people have asked the writer about the derivation of his phrase, "the Big Apple," that he is forced to make another explanation. New Orleans has called it to his mind again. A number of years back, when racing a few horses at the Fair Grounds with Jake Byer, he was watching a couple of stable hands cool out a pair of "hots" in a circle outside the stable.
>
> A boy from an adjoining barn called over, "Where you shipping after the meeting?"
>
> To this one of the lads replied, "Why we ain't no bullring stable; we's goin' to the big apple." The reply was bright and snappy. "Boy, I don't know what you're goin' to that apple with those hides for. All you'll get is the rind."

Note, above, the phrase "another explanation." For Popik, the question was: Where was the first? That he found in a February 18, 1924, issue of the *Telegraph:* the first installment of a short-lived column titled "Around the Big Apple with John J. Fitz Gerald." The logo of the column showed an apple with what was then the world's tallest building, the Woolworth Building, prominent in the skyline.

There was still the issue of how the stable hands came to the phrase, just as there was at least one earlier association between "Big Apple" and New York City to sort through. Popik's best guess is that Fitz Gerald first heard the phrase in January 1920, a few days before he sold a horse to the same Jake Byer mentioned in the 1926 write-up. The issue, though, is when the phrase first began its passage into common usage, and that, Popik says, is a closed case, with a nice bonus. On the very day he came across Fitz Gerald's 1924 column, Popik also stumbled over what he considers the first use of the phrase "Great White Way," used to describe a Broadway covered by snow, not one bathed in lights.

"I copied everything and sent it to the [New York] *Times*," Popik says of his "Big Apple" breakthrough. "Nothing. No response. I sent it to the *Daily News*. Nothing. I sent it to *The New Yorker*. Nothing. It wasn't in *The Village Voice*, the *New York Press*. Nothing. I wrote to the mayor. Nothing."

Emboldened by failure, Popik broadened his attack. Working through records of the New York City Department of Health, he learned that J. J. Fitz Gerald had resided during the last three decades of his life in a welfare hotel at West Fifty-fourth and Broadway, just around the corner from the Ed Sullivan Theater, where *Late Show with David Letterman* had set up shop. Visions began to dance in Popik's mind: a plaque would mark the building; a street sign, meanwhile, would designate that stretch of Broadway as "Big Apple Boulevard." Ideally, too, the proximity to the Letterman show would give the whole project visibility.

"In September 1995, I went before a committee of the community board. I said, 'I'd like a plaque, a street sign. There are things we should do to honor this guy.' They said, 'We're going to adjourn this. You've got to get the plaque. If you do that, we'll put up a street sign. Otherwise, no one will know what the sign is for.'"

The street sign, though, was running into problems of its own. "Boulevard" struck some committee members as grandiose. Eventually, a compromise was reached. "Boulevard" would be stripped back to "Corner." A building plaque would provide the details. Final approval was reached in February 1997, and Popik set the dedication date for May, on the ninth anniversary of the "Dear Abby" column that had launched his and Gerald Cohen's inquiry.

"I wrote to all the newspapers, the TV stations, everyone. I wrote to every staff member on the Letterman show. I told the police station that there might be a crowd, so they sent a policeman. It was raining. No one came. It was just me and the policeman."

*   *   *

And so life has gone for Barry Popik.

For more than a century, it had been assumed that Chicago was dubbed the "Windy City" by New York City newspapermen trying—unsuccessfully, it turned out—to run down the crown jewel of the Midwest in the competition for who would host the Columbian Exposition, the world's fair that was to mark the four-hundredth anniversary of the discovery of the New World. The reference was assumed to be a slap at the boisterous nature of Chicago's politicians—"the nonsensical claims of that windy city," as Charles Anderson Dana, editor of the New York *Sun,* put it—not to the strong breezes that blow in off Lake Michigan.

Popik dug through old issues of *Puck* magazine to learn what satirists were calling Chicago in the last decades of the nineteenth century. He also paged through *Sporting News* and *Sporting Life* to see what shorthand sportswriters used. Up to 1885, Chicago had been referred to as the "Garden City." By late 1886, he found, "Windy City" had begun to creep into the sports press, but that didn't solve the problem of its origin until Popik came across the Louisville *Courier–Journal* in the Library of Congress.

Throughout much of 1885, the newspaper's editor, Henry Watterson, had been taking shots at Chicago based on its weather, not its politicians. ("The Chicagoans," he wrote on July 3, 1885, "call a stable a barn. This is doubtless the effect of the lake winds blowing through their whiskers so much.") Then, in 1886, Watterson comes out and says it: Chicago is the "Windy City." Bingo. Popik wrote up his findings and submitted them to the magazine of the Chicago Historical Society. No dice. He wrote to the *Chicago Tribune* and to every Chicago alderman, again to no avail. When the American Dialect Society held its annual convention in Chicago in 1999, he refused to attend.

The American Hot Dog Council didn't change its story, either, after Popik sent it what he considers conclusive evidence that the term "hot dog" didn't originate among food vendors at New York's Polo Grounds baseball park in the first decade of the twentieth century, as the council contends, or even with a 1906 "Tad" Dorgan cartoon about a six-day bicycle race at Madison Square Garden, as the *Dictionary of American Regional English* states. "Hot dog," Popik found, was being used by Yale students in the middle eighteen-nineties—they started calling lunch wagons that sold frankfurters "dog wagons"—and spread from there to Harvard, Cornell, across the continent to Berkeley, and to points in between.

Unlike the Chicago Historical Society or the Windy City's aldermen, the

Hot Dog Council at least put Popik on its mailing list. Now, he says, every July during National Hot Dog Month, the council sends him the wrong information.

An occasional laurel has fallen Barry Popik's way. New York City officials may have stiffed him on credit for tracing "Big Apple" to its root, but Charles Gillett recognized Popik's work at a 1992 meeting of the American Name Society. Soon enough, his mentor Gerald Cohen has assured Popik, he'll be in the "golden Rolodex"—as the go-to guy whenever the first usage of a word or phrase falls into question.

Already, Popik has made his presence known in the agate type of such resource works as the *Random House Historical Dictionary of American Slang* and *The New Dickson Baseball Dictionary,* as well as the online version of *The Oxford English Dictionary*. Citations are forthcoming in the *Dictionary of American Regional English* and elsewhere.

Popik hopes to get back to his plays and stories. After having been wedded for so many years to the parking ticket bureau and its scofflaws (a term, by the way, he has traced to a Prohibition-era drinking contest) and to his databases and microfilm readers, he also has aspirations of starting a family. In the meantime, if he has trouble convincing authorities of the value of his work, Barry Popik has few reservations on that subject in his own mind.

"Words are important because they become issues. It's important to get these things right. It leads us to who we are and who we're going to be. Why is 'African American' better than 'nigger'? Why is 'Jew' better than 'kike'? Because of the associations the words bear. People need to understand that, and that's why you need people like me."

And when everything else just seems too glum for contemplation, Popik can always walk crosstown from his apartment to Broadway, just north of the Ed Sullivan Theater. There, fifteen feet up the pole at the southwest corner of the intersection with Fifty-fourth Street, are four green signs. The two at the top mark the intersection itself: WEST 54 and BROADWAY. Beneath them is the crown jewel of Barry Popik's word sleuthing: BIG APPLE CORNER. And below that is a final marker, SENOR WENCES WAY, honoring the longtime neighborhood resident and Spanish-born ventriloquist who made his own unique contributions to the American vernacular.

"S'all right?" Señor Wences was forever asking his puppet-in-a-box Pedro on the old *Ed Sullivan Show.*

"S'all right!"

Nine

Cathy Henderson:
Buried Treasures

Most Fridays, Cathy Henderson, forty-six, a librarian in Austin, Texas, goes through the approximately two hundred garage sale ads in the *Austin American–Statesman*. The ads appear in alphabetical order by location. She lives in the area designated Central and doesn't venture to places like Pflugerville, Dripping Springs, or Round Rock. "To go further afield I'd have to learn a whole new map and that would slow me down," Henderson says. "I like to move as efficiently as I can from one sale to the next. There's plenty for me centrally. My ambition isn't to hit each and every sale every weekend."

Almost every Saturday she is in Austin she is out of her house by 7:30 A.M.: most sales begin at 8:00 A.M. She consults a plastic-coated map of central and downtown Austin if she is unfamiliar with a street address, then drives to the first destination.

"I'm looking for nothing, just for what catches my eye," Henderson says, and promptly qualifies this statement. "I generally look for jewelry, decorative objects, art, books and CDs, and accessories. I don't buy furniture. I already have too much furniture. All my friends know about my garage-saleing and ask me to shop for them. Right now, I'm looking for a manual typewriter for a friend."

She parks her white Volvo station wagon and surveys the "stuff" on a lawn outside one house. She leaves empty-handed. "They're trying to get too much for their junk," she observes. At the second address, the goods for sale are displayed on the lawn and in a garage. She picks up a golf shot-glass for fifty cents ("a Christmas present for a neighbor"), a Gorbachev skullcap with a twenty-five-cent price tag ("a joke present for friends"), and a few crocheted pot holders (twenty-five cents apiece). "Those are for a friend who sells old linens at an antique mall in Lockhart. She'll charge three dollars for them."

At a third sale she buys a five-cent mushroom slicer ("nice") and, for fifteen dollars, a sterling silver dragonfly pin ("real nice"). "I like jewelry, but I never buy it brand-new. I only buy it at garage sales," she says. "I once saw eight place settings of sterling silver someone had bagged up and was selling for a hundred dollars. I passed it up. That was a bad decision, but some days you just don't feel very acquisitive. My long-range view is what you get you were meant to have and what you miss you weren't meant to have."

At the next two sales she finds nothing that strikes her fancy except a funky pocketbook she doesn't buy ("Three dollars? Too expensive") but at the following house she pays a dollar for a bad copy of a Salvador Dali painting ("for a friend who really likes his work") and fifty cents for a 1975 edition of *The Columbia Encyclopedia* ("It'll be useful to keep at the library").

She pulls up to a house where three young men are out on the lawn and continues on her way, saying, "Guys' sales usually aren't worthwhile, because guys tend not to buy very much and they tend not to get rid of what they buy." She goes past another house she describes as a "repeater."

"Some people run a weekly business out of their homes," she says. "They try to sell stuff over and over again. At these perpetual garage sales there's too much to avoid: plastic cups from fast-food restaurants, old clothes, and FTD vases." As she is driving along she spots an unadvertised sale outside a church, where she buys an acid brush for twenty cents. "I don't know exactly what I'm going to do with it, but as my father says about things that have no apparent utility, 'I might could use that someday.'" She cites a doctoral dissertation that says there are between six million and nine million garage sales in the United States every year. She calls eBay "the world's garage sale"—she is convinced it is better for sellers than for buyers, that some people first try to sell their wares on eBay, then, if that fails, take them to thrift stores or, another rung down the price ladder, offer them up on their lawns, "which makes garage sales the cheapest bet for buyers."

Cathy Henderson was born in Pennsylvania and moved to Houston with her family when she was thirteen. "My mother took me to garage sales on

Thursdays and Fridays when I wasn't in school," she says. "I'm pretty sure garage sales shifted to the weekends when more women went to work. I don't go on Sundays. I don't know why, but Sunday sales aren't as good."

As she goes from garage to garage and lawn to lawn she spends a quarter for a Slinky ("A friend asked me to buy any I saw for her to use in a mobile she's making"); a dollar for an ivory bracelet and ten cents for a headband (both for herself); fifty cents for a letter opener, also for herself ("I have a few and I don't really collect them; I do accumulate a number of things"); a dozen corks for a nickel apiece ("They'll be good for vinegar or flavored-oil bottles"); two dollars for a power bracelet, semiprecious stone beads strung on elastic ("Interesting, I've been wondering when they would show up at garage sales, I'll probably give it to my oldest sister"); a mint-chocolate spoon for a quarter ("I'll put it in the staff lounge at work for anyone who wants to stir their coffee with it"); a plastic storage unit for five dollars for another artist-friend ("I don't buy furniture but that doesn't count as furniture"); and three items for a nickel apiece: a storage jar, a brush, and a cooking ring. She is looking for wavy-edged TV trays for an artist-friend in California ("She paints new images on them and she's told me the straight-edged ones don't inspire her") but doesn't find a wavy-edged TV tray today—or a manual typewriter. "And probably by the time I find a manual typewriter, my friend won't need one anymore."

She has had success on countless other Saturdays when she takes "commissions" for "clients"—friends whom she never charges more than she pays for an item. "I'm especially happy if I can get something they wanted for less than they said they'd pay—a slide-projection screen for two dollars when they said they'd pay ten dollars, an enamel colander that someone was willing to pay up to five dollars for, which cost only fifty cents." For her best friend from high school, a veterinary pathologist who lives in Virginia, she has often been able to pick up old Steiff stuffed animals. "They relate to the subject of her work, but, more importantly, she had to leave a large childhood collection of them behind in Cuba when her family emigrated to the United States when she was five," she says. Henderson doesn't talk to other garage-salers ("Talking slows you down"), and she calls it quits around noon. "At noon the returns diminish for the amount of time you put into it. But I did get a couple of bargains at noon a few times. A twenty-six-inch strand of pearls with a gold clasp and a fourteen-carat-gold and opal ring. Some sellers forget to put out the jewelry so you can sometimes get good things late." Generally, Henderson has seventy dollars in her wallet but spends less. On the rare occasion she comes across items that add up to more, she goes to an ATM.

After stopping for coffee and a piece of cake, Cathy Henderson returns to the house she shares with her husband, Jim.

"One thing about Cathy's garage-saleing is I hardly ever have to go to a store," he says, pointing to the Coach belt he is wearing. "If I need a belt, she'll find one for a quarter. But Cathy, please, no more ties."

Henderson's house looks like a non-garage-saler's vision of a garage-saler's house. A Camel sign, a stack of baskets, a silver apple on a coffee table ("It didn't quite make it onto the Christmas tree, it also didn't make it into storage with the other Christmas ornaments"), some masks on a wall, and an old spindle from a weaving mill—garage sale trophies all—decorate the porch. A collection of carved cowrie shells, Native American miniatures, a pre-Columbian face, a Haitian bus, and a large number of wineglasses are in the dining room.

"I have a bad habit of buying wineglasses when there's no room to house them, but they get broken often enough in the dishwasher or when we have parties," she says.

"We could use a little more breakage right about now," her husband puts in. "Cathy goes about collecting sets of things, like Griswold skillets from Erie, Pennsylvania."

"It's a way of limiting myself," she says. "I won't buy cast iron if it isn't Griswold. It's one way to keep down the number of pots and pans I buy and I'm sentimental about Griswold because the Griswold manufactory was in Erie, Pennsylvania, where my aunt lived."

One prominent item in the kitchen—a birthday present from a close friend at work, with whom Henderson sometimes goes garage-saleing—is an Our Lady of Garage Sales votive candle, with prayer. The prayer reads:

Our Lady, I offer this candle that you will guide me in my quest for the best garage sales. Help me leave my warm bed early to secure the best deals, and keep the best items hidden from my competitors. Insure I will know the difference between treasures and trash, and that I will always negotiate the lowest price. And with your great power, keep me from risking my retirement fund on tchotchkes! Amen.

The official directions for its use are:

Light candle on Friday night before retiring. Repeat prayer once while checking out garage and estate sales in classified ads. Repeat prayer three times while driving around searching for posted sales. *Good Luck.*

"If the candle works as traditional votives do, you're supposed to light it, say the prayer, snuff the candle, and then go out on the garage sale rounds," Henderson says. "I've never done that and, frankly, I'm still doing pretty well even without Our Lady's blessing."

The candle-giving friend coined the phrase "Drink-and-a-Thrift Thursdays"—when, Henderson says, "We'd leave work a little early, go to thrift stores, and then stop for a beer. The phrase was a wordplay on the title of the popular late-night TV show *Dinner and a Movie*."

Every year or two, Cathy Henderson herself holds a garage sale, but only if a number of other friends are interested in going in on it. "It's a way of recycling back out into the community of garage sale–goers items I no longer have a use for or an interest in—books I've read, clothes I no longer wear, videos I've watched, that sort of thing. I don't like to have too many sales because they're a lot of work *and* they prevent me from going to other people's garage sales." She donates many things she doesn't need to the Association for Retarded Citizens of Texas.

"I'm not too cerebral about why I go garage-saleing, but I'll track it back to my high school debate coach dissuading me from pursuing a career in archaeology," she says. "He said it didn't pay enough. Archaeology as treasure hunting had a real appeal for me, so now I do my treasure hunting at garage sales, where any found treasure can be kept and is affordable, as opposed to having to turn it over to the state or nation because it's priceless. I suppose, in short, I'm my own museum curator, in the seventeenth- and eighteen-century traditions of the *Wunderkammer,* "wonder cabinet" or "cabinet of curiosities"; such rooms were themselves the progenitors of our contemporary museums. I can stand to have all these things in my home because I view them individually as objects of interest or beauty and not just pieces of a decorative whole. I really do like objects. So treasure hunting, I think, is a pretty good reason to get up by seven A.M. each Saturday morning, if not otherwise obligated to other tasks.

"Each weekend is a fresh opportunity. My garage sale philosophy is, 'It's the searching and hunting and gathering that's fun.' I like the process of going out and possibly discovering something very nice for not very much money. I'll often come back without having bought much, but what's important is going out and seeing what's there."

Ten

Henry Sakaida:
The Go-Between

The date is Memorial Day, 1983. The place, a suburban cul de sac in San Gabriel, California, about fifteen miles east of downtown Los Angeles. Inside the home of Tadashi Sakaida, a former American rear gunner named Harold "Lew" Jones of Unionville, Nevada, is meeting with one-time Japanese fighter pilot Saburo Sakai. Jones and Sakai had encountered each other once before, under far different circumstances: during the summer of 1942, in aerial combat over Guadalcanal.

A business consultant in Japan by the early nineteen-eighties, Sakai has brought along his flight helmet, still pockmarked with bullet holes from the dogfight that left him permanently without sight in one eye. Jones, who with his wife would go on to open a bed-and-breakfast in Unionville, notes that when his SBD Dauntless dive-bomber finally made it back to base, crewmen counted 232 bullet holes in the fuselage.

"I thought you were gone," Jones tells Sakai.

"This is just like a dream," Sakai says.

Forty-one years earlier, as Jones was manning his twin .30-caliber machine guns, Sakai had approached so close that the rear gunner could see his face as the Zero flashed by.

For Henry Sakaida, Tadashi Sakaida's son and the person who researched and arranged this reunion, it was a moment never to be forgotten.

"All these local stations were there. The cul de sac was packed with people. It was so exciting. Here's an American dive-bomber, and he goes up and shakes hands with a Japanese Zero pilot who he had traded fire with. The Zero pilot was blinded in one eye by this guy's gunfire. For them to shake hands after all those years—this had never been done before. It was just so wild, and I had engineered it."

By day, Henry Sakaida helps run a wholesale nursery business based in Rosemead, California, that was begun and is still overseen by his father. By night and by weekend and in nearly every other moment he can squeeze out of an already packed life, Sakaida makes history come alive. He puts a name and, where he can, a face on memories of life-and-death struggles more than half a century old. Sakaida takes relics collected on faraway battlefields in a war fought before he was born and turns them inside out until they talk to him and tell him where they came from, and then, again when he can, he follows the relics backward in time to find the people whose lives the objects were once a part of. Sometimes, too, he becomes a part of those lives himself. Henry Sakaida is a guy who just can't leave a question alone.

When Sakaida was still a junior high student, he came into possession of several Japanese aviation magazines. "They had stories by these World War Two pilots," he says. "I couldn't read Japanese, so I'd bug my father and say, 'Read this. Read this.'"

Tadashi Sakaida, whose own parents had emigrated to Selma in central California before World War II, had spent his war years at the Japanese-American relocation camp at Manzanar, at the foot of the Sierra Nevadas in eastern California, and had no near relations in combat on either side. But he knew how to satisfy his son's curiosity. Tadashi put Henry in touch with a war history center in Tokyo and translated into Japanese his request for information about Zero pilots, and from there Henry took off on his own.

By the time Sakaida was in college at San Jose State University, he was corresponding regularly with former combat pilots and military aviation historians in both the United States and Japan. In 1971 one of the historians, retired Air Force Colonel Raymond Toliver, wrote Sakaida that the American Fighter Pilots Association would be hosting a group of former Japanese Zero pilots at a meeting at the Miramar Naval Air Station—the famous "Top Gun" school in San Diego. Did Sakaida want to stop by? He did, and it was there that he met Saburo Sakai, whose reunion with Harold Jones he would arrange a dozen years later. Sakai and Sakaida remained friends for the next three decades, until Sakai's death in September 2000 at age eighty-four.

Four years after the Miramar meeting, Sakaida was sitting in a Tokyo coffee shop when he was introduced to another ex-Zero pilot, Sadamu Komachi.

"We were talking," Sakaida remembers, "and then, just before he left, he said, 'Oh, by the way, Henry, can you do me a favor?' 'What?' I asked. 'When you get back to the States, can you do some research and find out about the guy who shot me down over Guam in 1944?' I thought, My God, what a strange request! I eventually solved it, but that was many, many, many years later, in 1992."

Unfortunately, Wendell Twelves, the retired steel company administrator from Springville, Utah, who downed Komachi's Zero in June 1944, died three months before his former foe could meet him in person. For Henry Sakaida, though, Komachi's "strange request" helped give further shape to a lifetime's avocation.

TAPPING THE HERITAGE: FROM ROOTS TO RICHES reads the headline for an article in the July 1977 issue of *Income Opportunities* magazine. The article goes on to describe how Sakaida and two other Asian-American friends from San Jose State several years earlier had launched a mail-order company that sold martial arts training aids, books, and other accessories. The name of the company had been Sakaida's inspiration: Divine Wind, a literal translation of the Japanese word *kamikaze*.

"I started the company after reading a book called *Think and Grow Rich*," Sakaida says. "I became blindly optimistic. I didn't know what the hell I was doing, but I was inspired. We rode the crest of the martial arts and Bruce Lee fad, and grossed about $120,000 the first year, but like all fads, this one went up and then petered out. No one got rich, but I used the money to pay my way through college. When you're blindly optimistic, you don't know it's not going to work, so you do it and, miraculously, it does work."

The same might be said of Sakaida's pilot searches. Some are a snap. His record, he says, is ten seconds: "One of my contacts in Japan has a friend whose brother was leading a dive-bomber attack at Okinawa. The brother never came back. I was asked to determine what had happened. I have this computerized list of all U.S. Navy victory credits. Any pilot who ever claimed a victory—his name is there, his unit, his location, and so on. When the Japanese person said his brother was lost on such and such a day in such and such a place, bingo, I could tell him the unit, the name, the location, even the hour and minute."

Often, though, the searches require wading back through the murk of time and cloudy memory—and bulky official records—to events that many people would just as soon forget in search of answers that not everyone wants to hear.

Sakaida's "toughest" case, he says, began as a neighborhood matter. A friend in Rosemead, Minoru Fujita, had been a gunboat commander with the Japanese navy's Eighth Submarine Base Unit at Rabaul, on the island of New Britain, in the Solomon Islands, when the base was attacked by Allied air forces units. Fifteen minutes into the bombing, a Corsair dove down from fifteen thousand feet to eight thousand feet, where it took a direct hit on its right wing from a 70-millimeter antiaircraft gun. The pilot bailed out at two thousand feet, floated down into the sea-snake- and shark-infested Bay of Rabaul, and was captured.

The only one at the base with even rudimentary English, Fujita was put in charge of the prisoner. His name, he remembered four decades later, was Keefer. He was perhaps Australian. Rabaul had no seasons, Fujita said, no way of marking time, so he wasn't sure of the date although he thought it might be 1943 or 1944. At the prisoner's request, the two had said the Lord's Prayer together—Fujita having learned it at the same Christian church in Japan where he had taken early English lessons. And then "Keefer," suffering from a gaping wound on his upper left arm, had been taken away. Had he survived? Fujita asked Henry Sakaida. Alive or dead, who was he? The questions had haunted him ever since.

"I did all this research, and I hit all these dead ends," Sakaida says. "It was extremely frustrating. I became obsessed with it. I'd lie awake at night and think, This guy has a name. He actually existed. I've got to find him."

Almost five years later, an Australian aviation historian whom Sakaida had contacted for help came across a document listing the names of Allied and civilian prisoners kept on Rabaul by the Japanese navy, and there was the answer: Minoru Fujita's unknown soldier had been a New Zealand flight lieutenant, not an Australian. The date had been January 15, 1945, not a year or two earlier. His real name was a letter shorter than Fujita had heard or remembered: Francis George Keefe, born in Auckland in 1916. And he had died of blood poisoning and other complications at Naga Naga, a settlement near Rabaul, on January 30, 1945, fifteen days after he was shot down, at age twenty-eight, the same age as Fujita.

On the day an article about the search and discovery appeared in the *New Zealand Sunday News,* Minoru Fujita received a phone call in California from Keefe's older brother, John O'Keefe. (The younger brother had dropped the O.)

"John O'Keefe had heard Frank was tortured," Sakaida says. "He was very anti-Japanese, but when he learned more about the case, he invited Mr. Fujita and his wife to stay with him."

After traveling to the New Zealand War Cemetery at Bourail, on the main island of New Caledonia, to place flowers on Frank Keefe's grave and say a prayer for him, the Fujitas flew to Auckland and spent a week with John O'Keefe and his wife.

Not every search has so happy an outcome. On June 23, 1945, Captain Yasumasa Miyasaka was in charge of a detail digging underground fortifications in Chiba prefecture, east of Tokyo, when he looked up at the air battle going on overhead and saw a pilot bailing out of a burning American P-51 Mustang. By the time Miyasaka got to the potato field where the wounded pilot had come to earth, many of his men were already there, threatening to finish off the enemy. Miyasaka got the soldiers away and bandaged the pilot's wound with strips from his parachute before a truck came to take the prisoner away. A few days afterward, a hospital official assured Miyasaka that the pilot was still alive. Another forty-six years later, Sakaida had to tell Miyasaka, by then the president of a Japanese sake brewery, that he had been lied to.

The pilot Miyasaka had asked Sakaida to research—the one Miyasaka hoped had survived the war and might still be alive—was Second Lieutenant Jack Scanlan, a native of Louisville, Kentucky. Not long after he had been taken from Miyasaka's care, Scanlan was released to a mob and beaten to death. At the war crimes trials held in Tokyo in 1948, the colonel responsible had been sentenced to forty years of hard labor. Sakaida was able to track down Jack Scanlan's family, but they chose not to respond.

More commonly, Sakaida gets to deliver good news about bad times. In February 1945, a Japanese nurse named Mayumi Shirakata had helped to save the life of another downed and injured enemy pilot threatened by a mob—an auburn-haired American she knew only as "McCormick." When she told her story on a Japanese television show thirty-five years later, the station contacted Sakaida and asked for his help in tracking "McCormick" down.

"Luckily, they gave me the date of the encounter. I looked up the American loss records for that day, and there was a Forrest McCormick missing in action. Once I had his full name and unit, I wrote to his commander, Captain Marshall Beebe, and Beebe took it upon himself to make quite a few calls. He actually found McCormick. I just took credit for it."

Forrest McCormick, it turned out, had spent the duration of the war at the Ofuna POW Camp near Tokyo. At war's end, reduced from 170 pounds to about 100 pounds, he had been sent home to Oklahoma, where he married and worked on his father-in-law's ranch for five years, before going back to school and finding permanent employment with the U.S. Postal Service.

"The old lady in Japan never knew what happened to him," Sakaida says. "She said she had always prayed for the guy. I was able to contact her and say, 'Guess what, the American pilot you saved—he sends his best regards!'"

"People all over the world are the same," Sakaida goes on. "They don't want to hurt anybody. You take these young kids eighteen, twenty, twenty-two years old, and you put a gun in their hands and say go out and kill. But they really don't want to do that. When they meet their opponents, they shake hands like they're long-lost friends. The lesson to me is that there's no personal animosity. It's the governments that get them involved in war. People are basically good."

As the pool of World War II veterans on both sides of the conflict ages and diminishes, Sakaida has found himself dealing more and more with the objects they brought home and the ones they left behind, especially Japanese battle flags.

"They're the most common souvenir GIs brought home. They'd take it right off the bodies of the dead soldiers. When the Japanese went off to fight, they'd get a flag and have their families, friends, and neighbors sign it. A lot of GIs don't understand the spiritual significance of the flags—they're the last physical connection people have to their fathers. When you return one to a family, they're very emotional."

Recently, Sakaida says, a pilot who had sent him a flag to return followed that up with a black-and-white photo of a Japanese grave.

"It's just a post in the ground with a bunch of Japanese kanji writing [the ornate characters associated with Japanese script] on it. I have the person's name. He told me that he took it [the photo] on New Guinea when they raided the air base. He found it while cleaning his house and thought I might be interested in it. Now, I want to find the family so I can send them this original black-and-white photograph.

"A lot of these GIs have these battlefield pickups. I've returned letters, photo albums. The GIs are eighty, eighty-five. They've lost interest in the objects. They're no longer important to them. But they hate to throw them in the trash, so they call me and say, 'Hey, can you return this?'"

The greatest challenge Sakaida has ever faced in returning an object, he says, was with one he bought himself: a Japanese navy flight jacket that he purchased over the phone in 1979 for $250. When the jacket arrived in California, he found the words "Flight Leader Tsurumaki, Thunder Corps" written in kanji on the back, and with that, the chase was on. More than five years would pass before Sakaida would learn the full story: In February 1945, a twenty-one-year-old Zero pilot named Shigeki Tsurumaki had made an emergency landing on a mountainside near Shanghai. To avoid capture by the Chinese, he had abandoned his flight jacket and taken to the hills, where he was finally rescued by a Japanese army patrol. His jacket, meanwhile, fell into the hands of an American officer, who brought it home to Maryland as a souvenir. In 1987, with the help of friends in Japan, Sakaida was able to return the jacket he had purchased eight years earlier to Tsurumaki.

Sakaida is quick to point out that nearly all the "cases" he has solved have been solved by means of collaborative efforts. Although he's not fluent in Japanese, he has a foot in both cultures, and he even retains a faint smattering of Russian from a high school language course. Sakaida makes ready use of military libraries on both sides of the Pacific; the National Archives in Suitland, Maryland; a wealth of associations in the United States and Japan built up over thirty-plus years of pursuing his curiosity; and the work of other authors. (Sakaida himself has published five books of his own on World War II aviation in the Pacific, mostly for those who follow the minutiae of such matters.) His own "national archive," he says, can be found in his Temple City home, not far from the Rosemead nursery and his parents' home in San Gabriel.

"I've got boxes and boxes of files. It goes from my room to the attic and from the attic to the garage." His wife is interested in his work, he says, "but she basically leaves me alone," as do his teenage daughter and son. "I'll tell my daughter, 'Hey, I solved this one!' And she'll say, 'That's great, Dad.' My kids have no interest in World War Two or anything I'm doing.

"I think that when I croak, I'll turn all my files, all my books and references, over to the Marine Corps Aviation Association in Quantico, Virginia. They built a new library there a few years back. Many of the books I have are rare. I'd hate to see them tossed out or sold at a garage sale. They need to be preserved and utilized by future generations."

Until then—and that seems a long time away—Sakaida will continue to act as the go-between, a kind of bridge between World War II and modern memory: a place where those who fought the war, those who survived it, and those who must deal with it still can go for solace and for what we know today as closure. Sakaida says his own closure has been at issue, too.

"When I was in fifth grade, we had a dog. It disappeared one day. It always bugged me, that mystery—what happened to our dog? I searched high and low. I wouldn't say it haunted me, but I never got my own closure. It's not that I would have had that intense closure that veterans of World War Two and Korea and Vietnam talk about, but it's an open mystery. If I found out that the dog had been run over by a car, I could have put it away. But I didn't know what happened to our dog.

"There's no money in this. This is for personal satisfaction. I wouldn't have the heart to charge money for this. How do you charge for bringing closure to someone? You can't do it. It wouldn't be right."

PART 3

Going to Extremes

Eleven

Gig Gwin:
Worldly Riches

It's cheaper and easier for Gig Gwin to go to faraway places than it is for most people: he owns a travel agency. Gwin has, however, traveled a lot more than is necessary even in his line of work. He is the first, and thus far the only, travel agent who has been to every country on earth.

When Gwin was a boy, his father was a poultry industry professor at the University of Maryland. The family lived in College Park. Every summer Gig went with his parents and two sisters to a meeting of poultry science people, held at a state university; the Gwins stayed in college dorms. He enjoyed this travel at an early age. When he was in his teens, his father took a job with Ralston Purina in St. Louis, Missouri, as director of poultry marketing.

Gig Gwin (his first name is Graydon) dropped out of college, had fun bumming around Sacramento, California, and, in 1964, at the age of twenty, was drafted into the army. After the American embassy in Saigon was devastated by a car bomb on March 31, 1965, he was dispatched to Vietnam. "We flew on a prop plane and puddle-jumped across the Pacific," he says. "We stopped to refuel in Hawaii, on Wake Island, and on Okinawa." He was stationed at Tan Son Nhut Airport outside Saigon as an MP, guarding a Hawk missile unit. Discharged in April 1966, he flew home. He went to college on the GI Bill and studied Asian history at the University of Missouri–St. Louis: he had enjoyed Vietnamese culture and liked the country's people. He graduated in January 1970 and took a job that April with TWA as a reservations agent in New York City.

"It was great to get a glimpse of the travel industry from the airline perspective," he says. "I had to learn geography, and I had the opportunity to use my passes to fly to Alaska, Puerto Rico, and Japan." When he and thousands of other TWA employees were laid off at the end of the year, he went home. Early in 1971 he got a job with Maritz, a large St. Louis incentive travel company—one that helps large corporations increase their sales through incentive programs like group trips.

"First I was a travel director," he says. "That has to be the neatest job in the world. I researched destinations and escorted business-incentive groups, making sure they had a wonderful time on the trips they had won. One week I was in Acapulco, the next in Portugal." Gwin's title changed as he moved up the corporate ladder—to travel planner, product manager, and travel specialist. "I started collecting countries because I was being paid to go to them in the line of duty. Right off the bat I set as one of my dreams to pick up a few countries every year. Life was good."

In the fall of 1979 he wanted to run his own show, so he left Maritz and formed Gwin's Travel Planners. By then he was married, with two young sons. His father had retired. Father and son went to junior college together: they took a two-year night course in travel and tourism geared toward how to run a travel agency. They graduated in 1982. His father, who already had three degrees, including a Ph.D., worked for Gig for eight years without drawing a salary, before his second retirement.

Gig Gwin's travels, more or less suspended during his night school years, resumed. He had averaged some ten countries per year in the nineteen-seventies. "It was easy in the early stages," he says. "You could pick up five countries from the back of a ship. On a Caribbean cruise you might spend a day in Martinique sightseeing, sail on to Dominica, and Guadeloupe, St. Martin, and St. Thomas. I tried to spend at least half a day in every country." By 1982 he had been to over ninety countries.

After that he picked up the pace, going farther, going faster. He went to the United Arab Emirates, India, Nepal, and South Korea in 1983, the year his third son was born. In 1986 he went to Chile, Costa Rica, Nicaragua, Honduras ("It was at the time of the contras and I was shot at by soldiers in Tegucigalpa"), Belize, El Salvador, Guyana, Yugoslavia, East and West Berlin, Czechoslovakia, Hungary, Romania, Bulgaria, Macedonia, Serbia, Bosnia, and Slovenia.

The pace quickened in 1987 and 1988 as he journeyed to many places in Europe, Africa, and Asia. "Three days after my mother died in April 1988, my father told me he didn't want to stay in the house where they had lived, so we went on a Travel Agents' Familiarization Trip—it's called a

FAMTRIP—and I picked up Kenya, Burundi, Zaire, Rwanda, Ethiopia, Tanzania, and Zanzibar," he says. "Three years later came that magical day when I flew from Montego [Bay] to Santiago de Cuba. It was difficult to go to Cuba for political reasons. As an American you weren't supposed to go there. My first goal was the western hemisphere. Cuba gave me all the countries in my backyard—Central America, South America, North America, and the Caribbean."

Nineteen ninety-one was also the year that Gwin boarded a boat in Corfu and spent a day in Albania, his second-to-last country to see in Europe. "I went on an excursion of beautiful Greek and Roman ruins and saw picturesque valleys near Sarandë and artesian natural springs, but the poverty was overwhelming."

In 1995, Gwin bought into a group tour that took him to seventeen countries in Africa, most of which he didn't enjoy, but all of which he needed to complete his I've-been-to-every-country-on-earth list. He feels altogether differently about Tanzania's Serengeti Plain, which he ranks as the world's "ultimate sightseeing trip" because of its incredible animals and birds. He describes himself as a "safari junkie" who has done seven safaris—"and I'll do seven more."

Gwin earns free tickets as a high-volume travel agent—his clients include the St. Louis Cardinals and the St. Louis Rams, GSA of St. Louis, and a division of Ralston Purina—but he earned them primarily on TWA, which had its corporate headquarters in St. Louis. "I can't go free to Djibouti"—one of the African countries he saw in 1995.

That year he flew 127,130 miles. In 1996 he flew 90,020 miles. In 1997 he vowed to finish racking up countries within three years. In 1998 he flew 106,221 miles, but his most time-consuming trip was by ship to Tristan da Cunha. It is an island in the Atlantic Ocean with a population of about two hundred people that Gwin describes as "perhaps the hardest place in the world to reach," with just two supply ships per year going there and only occasionally "an adventure ship" of the sort he was on.

About twenty of the hundred people aboard the adventure ship *Explorer* that went from the Canary Islands to Ascension Island to St. Helena to Tristan da Cunha were members of the Travelers' Century Club. About sixty were birders, and the rest were "just people who wanted to go on that sort of a trip for thirty-four days." Not everyone considers Tristan da Cunha a country (the dictionary says it is a British territory), but the Travelers' Century Club, an organization based in Los Angeles, does.

According to the Travelers' Century Club, countries include "an island or island group situated at least two hundred miles from the closest continental portion of its administrating country." By TCC definition, Hawaii and islands like Tristan da Cunha are countries. To those who are skeptical about Hawaii's status as a country, or Alaska's (also a country according to another TCC definition), Gwin points out that he has been to about two hundred countries that are universally acknowledged as countries and to perhaps a hundred additional ones that are not. "No harm in that," he says. To qualify for membership in the Travelers' Century Club a person must have been to at least one hundred countries.

Gwin qualified for membership in 1983. "I wanted to get to one hundred," Gwin told the *St. Louis Post–Dispatch*. "It's kind of like a golf score. You break one hundred and you say, really what I want to do is break ninety. Then you break ninety and you say, what I really want to do is break eighty."

In 1998, Gwin and ten other TCC hard-core country collectors were among the one hundred people on another adventure ship, the *World Discoverer,* that went to Pitcairn Island in the South Pacific. "It was settled by mutineers from the H.M.S. *Bounty* in 1790," he says. "There were only forty-three people on the island when I was there, many with the surname of Christian, probably descendants of Fletcher Christian, who led the famous eighteenth-century mutiny against Captain Bligh on the H.M.S. *Bounty.* The weather is dreadful. We had a terrible storm when we arrived. We were on Zodiacs—rubber boats with large outboard engines on the back that are great for landing on beaches without harbors or piers. We all had life jackets on, but people were screaming and I wondered for a while if I would survive."

The following year, Gwin flew to Pago Pago in American Samoa, went from there to Western Samoa, and took an adventure ship, the *Akademik Shuleykin,* a double-hulled converted Russian spy ship, with thirteen other TCC members to Atafu, one of the three Tokelau islands. "That was one of the great days of my life," Gwin recalls. "The natives told us a cruise ship had never docked there before. The only ships that came regularly were supply ships every three or four months. The island's elders declared a holiday, closed the school, and put on a feast for us. They said prayers and made speeches—they speak some English because they're administered by New Zealand. They served fresh vegetables and tropical fruit, roast pig, huge crabs, and spiny lobsters. We provided the beer. I like to think we were respectful of the native hospitality because we were pretty professional travelers. The following day we went snorkeling in a clear blue lagoon with five-hundred-pound green sea turtles."

Gwin is a glass-is-half-full, type A person who enjoys most of his travels. He aims to have fun wherever he lands, and usually succeeds. He is an avid golfer, and while in Lesotho in 1989 he played golf on a course in a verdant jungle whose putting greens were made of sand. While visiting Tonga in 1997, he had an audience with its monarch, King Taufa'ahau Tupou IV, and established common ground: the king, who was at one time the world's heaviest head of state at 461 pounds, told Gwin that he had been by train to St. Louis.

Sometimes the trips that are not altogether comfortable leave pleasant memories of hardships viewed through a glass brightly. In 1997, Gwin flew from Siberia through Beijing to Tokyo. He paid twelve hundred dollars for an upgraded cabin on an oceangoing ship, the *Ogasawara Maru,* bound for the island of Chichi-Jima, one of the islands in the Ogasawara group.

"The ship was modern but my cabin was a mat on the floor in a large space with several hundred of the thousand Japanese students who were bound for Chichi-Jima to go scuba diving and to take nature walks. I was going because it was on the TCC list. I lay down to sleep. The mats were about two and a half feet by five feet and they were close together. I'm five feet eleven. Every time I stretched, I hit the person next to me. I was on Chichi-Jima for five days. I would never have had to go to that speck of an island from a work-related point of view. And I have never had a client ask to go to Nauru, an island republic in the Pacific Ocean which is famous for its phosphate—its bird droppings. And no client has ever proposed going to Niue, another speck in the Pacific. On Niue I explored an underwater cave. That tiny bit of exploration eventually qualified me for membership in the Explorers Club, another of my goals."

On January 1, 1999, there were 313 countries on the TCC list. Gwin had 12 left to see. Some, like Christmas Island and Rodrigues, were simply remote. Two of the last 3 were dangerous. He spent nine days in Iran, then crossed into the no-man's-land claimed by Afghanistan ("I stopped walking when Afghan soldiers raised their rifles, and walked back to Iran") and spent only minutes in Iraq, on the western border of Iran. The TCC had decided that, to qualify as a visit, the shortest visit would suffice—"even if only a port of call, or plane fuel stop."

Gwin is looking forward to returning to Afghanistan for sightseeing if and when peace returns, and also to Iraq. "I'd love to see what used to be the great Babylonian Empire," he says. "For me this is about more than ticking off one country after another." He also hopes to return to North Korea, another country he believes he has yet to see properly. "In 1998, I visited a room in Panmunjom where the truce ending the Korean War was signed," he says. "The room is split down the middle by the border and I simply walked to the North Korean side of the negotiating table."

The last of the 313 countries currently on the TCC list he saw in 1999 was Lampedusa, in the Mediterranean. He spent a happy September day on the resort island celebrating his final country in Europe and the world with good Italian food and white wine on a topless beach.

The world's most traveled travel agent says that the last four years of flying (he estimates he has flown over two million miles in thirty years of country-viewing), cruising, and riding trains and buses, and the occasional horse, mule, donkey, camel, elephant, ostrich, and turtle, have taken their toll. "I went to over fifty countries between 1996 and 1999," he says. "Some were dangerous, some were emotionally draining, but I'd made a commitment to see every country and I wasn't about to back down when the going got rough."

In a rare serious tone Gwin says: "The last four years were hard on me but that was my choice. They were also hard on my wife. She wasn't getting a whole husband. And on our sons. They weren't getting much of a father. They were hard on my company. I have sixty employees and my company didn't have a proper chairman and that dramatically slowed its growth. I'm going to spend more time at home and at work. My wife has never wanted to visit the weird countries and for the most part she'll travel with me only when the boys are along. They may be college age, but she still worries about them when she's away and they're at home. We've done lots of really neat things in the last year. We've renovated part of the house with our own hands. Life is good."

Twelve

Jim Dreyer:
Far Shores

The night of August 1, 1998, found Jim Dreyer standing in the shallows of Lake Michigan, a few miles north of Two Rivers, Wisconsin. Due east, 43.2 miles away, lay Big Sable Point, Michigan. Dreyer was about to attempt to get there by swimming, an unprecedented feat.

"I'm standing there, the water lapping at my feet, this endless expanse in front of me. No one so far as we know had ever done this. And I remember thinking, Wait a minute. I've never asked anyone if this could be done."

Over the next two years, Dreyer would swim across all of the Great Lakes but the most daunting—Lake Superior. He would try and almost succeed in crossing Lake Ontario both ways on one swim, with a 26.2-mile marathon run and 130-mile bike ride thrown in. Not only would he perform feats no one had performed before, he would perform ones no one perhaps had even thought of trying. But the first venture into the unknown is always the hardest, and for Jim Dreyer, that was Lake Michigan.

"Out of everything I've encountered, Lake Michigan was the worst experience in terms of what can go wrong. The strategy was to start at night when the lake is calmest. Then the next day, when the winds came out of the west as they usually do, they would push me along. Where we were wrong was the wind direction.

"The first night, conditions were great. I swam seventeen miles. Then we started getting a southeast wind blowing me northwest, way off course. There was a point the second night when land had been spotted. We were about fourteen miles out. And we were actually getting pushed backwards. The crew was saying, 'Jim, you've just got to swim harder,' and I was almost asleep.

"Finally, I asked how much farther. I figured I had two, three miles to go. It was pitch-black. I said, 'How much farther?' And they said, 'Just nine more miles.' It was so deflating.

"I discovered in Lake Michigan that you can swim in your sleep. It's a very happy state of mind, but you can swim away from your support ship. Now I've got glow sticks, and they have night-vision goggles that they can borrow. But they lost me twice in Lake Michigan. It's black. You can't tell the water from the sky. You're swimming in this black void. I also went through a lot of the swim where I couldn't see. My goggles leaked, and my eyes swelled shut.

"When I got seven miles out from the Michigan coast, the water temperature dropped from the low seventies to fifty-six degrees. The east wind had pushed all the warm water to the center of the lake.

"There were about three hundred people on the beach when I finished. I could hear them the last half-mile. My father had passed away in 1993. I spent a lot of time talking to him at the end. I really feel he was with me. The first thing I did after kissing the sand was write in it, 'Thanks, Dad.'

"I swam for forty hours and fifty-six minutes. A 43.2-mile swim had become a 65-mile swim. My shoulders got extremely tired, and I had hypothermia. A half hour after I was out of the water, my body temperature was at ninety-three degrees. But I thought I was safe. The paramedics were taking me away on this trailer attached to an ATV [all-terrain vehicle], but they forgot to attach it. As the ATV pulled away, the trailer flipped over and dumped me."

Of all the remarkable things about Jim Dreyer's swims, this is maybe the most remarkable: Until he was in his early thirties, swimming used to scare him to death.

"I had a lifelong fear of the water," Dreyer says, sitting in the living room of his home in Byron Center, Michigan, south of Grand Rapids. "When I was three, I had a near drowning. The family had a cottage northeast of here. Easter Sunday I'm out on the dock, all dressed up in a snowsuit, fishing, when I fall in. My sister saved my life."

In March 1996, two and a half years before he swam for sixty-five miles and almost forty-one hours across Lake Michigan, Dreyer showed up at a fitness facility run by the local Johnson Controls factory, intent on finally conquering his fear of water.

"I remember the terror," he says. "I had to swallow a lot of pride. I was going to teach myself to swim, but the lifeguard approached me—he was very tactful—and said, 'Jim, I'm getting tired just watching you. I can make this a lot easier for you.' His name was Mike Landis. He ended up being my swimming coach and is to this day."

It takes something of a village to support Jim Dreyer and his aqua-marathons. The support boat that accompanies his swims generally carries eight to ten people: the captain, his two-man crew, a cousin who works as an emergency medical technician and serves as Dreyer's medical adviser, his training partners (for swimming, running, and biking), a photographer, and someone from the local *Grand Rapids Press* to document the crossing for the record.

In water, Dreyer has to be fed every half hour: six ounces of beefed-up Gatorade, two ounces of water, and six ounces of baby food (he prefers Gerber) alternated with a power gel. Dreyer treads water as he eats and drinks off a feed stick—a pole with sports bottles clamped to its end—extended from a dinghy that trails behind the support boat. In calm weather, it all goes like clockwork, and the dinghy protects Dreyer from the nauseating diesel fuel burned by the larger boat. In eight-foot seas, the dinghy is pitching one way, Dreyer is pitching the other, and if he grabs hold of anything for support while he tries to eat, he's disqualified.

Out of water, the work is almost as hard and more constant. Dreyer's regular regimen, what he calls his "maintenance training," consists of a weekly twelve-to-eighteen-mile run on the dunes of Lake Michigan or on the beach for strength training, hour-long bursts of high-intensity sessions on his bike trainer, and regular pool time.

"It's hard for me to train in a pool because distance for me is double dig-its, but with the help of an engineer, I've devised this underwater parachute' that you drag behind you from your ankles. I can do that in a pool—it's like pulling a small building around with you."

On weekends, there's also a regular mini-triathlon: a swim of three to five miles, a run of five to ten miles, and twelve to twenty-five miles on the bike. That's only maintenance training, though. Intensive training is some-thing else altogether.

"It's all-consuming," Dreyer says. "It's like maintenance training, but I ramp it up. The amount is so much more. I'll do two to six hours of train-ing a day with a twenty-four-hour training period on the weekends."

Dreyer warmed up for his bike–run–double swim of Lake Ontario in the summer of 1999 by swimming ten miles, running sixteen to eighteen miles on beach sand, biking sixty to eighty miles, and jumping back in the water for another fifteen-mile swim.

To keep his body going through all the training and the ordeals it leads up to, Dreyer works with a sports nutritionist and swallows lots of pills—twenty-one every morning, another twenty-four each night, for everything from essential fatty acids to protein supplements, vitamins, minerals, and speciality products to combat arthritis and ease the pressure on his joints.

"I've got a list as long as my arm of the things I take," he says. "We've got it really fine tuned. Day to day, besides the supplements, I eat like a normal person: no red meat, high carbohydrates because I burn those like crazy, high protein because that's what rebuilds your body. I don't count calories at all—I'm burning them up—but I do track my protein and carbohydrate intake."

Keeping his mind prepared requires a separate and just-as-intense effort, Dreyer says. If the Great Lakes had been meant to be crossed by human swimmers, they presumably would have been regularly crossed long ago.

"The fear can be very intimidating. I used to say I was going to overcome it. I've since learned you can't overcome it, but you learn to control it instead of letting it control you. And you do that by facing it. I call it mental conditioning, and it's very important. I'll go out when the water is extremely cold—the low forties. You can't stay long, but it's learning to fight the elements, the cold and the rough waters. Sometimes it's like swimming in the spin cycle of a washing machine. You also have to go out at night when you're tired. I'll go out and swim all night by myself—it's really hard to find someone to train with you when you're doing that.

"It's just doing it, facing it, but to this day it's still scary to go out to the lake in the dark. We're not night animals, and we're not water animals, but you're doing both. I settle down after I get going, but as I'm going out there, my heart is racing."

On the official swims, not the training ones, the mental effort is no less important. It's not just a matter of starting the swim, Dreyer says. It's a matter of imagining himself finishing it as well.

"Usually, because I'm so goal-oriented, I keep the goal in mind. I visualize myself coming out of the water, being successful. I do it so thoroughly that when I do finish, it's almost like I've done it before. And it's knowing the kids are behind you. I visualize them, too."

*   *   *

The "kids" Jim Dreyer mentions are the children helped by Big Brothers/Big Sisters. Dreyer first got involved in the program in 1988 when he started dating a woman who was the Big Sister to a nine-year-old girl.

"The girl had been raped by her uncle when she was five. He was in prison by then, and she was living with her mother. There were a lot of different men around. You just hated to bring her home to that. Even at that age, she was running with a rough crowd. We spent a lot of time with her on weekends. By the time we moved to Chicago in 1993, she was making the honor roll regularly. She wanted to be a schoolteacher. Even her mother couldn't believe it."

Dreyer, who operates a one-man marketing business out of his home, began doing fund-raising for Big Brothers/Big Sisters in Chicago and continued when he returned to Michigan. His Lake Michigan swim was done, in part, to raise awareness of the program. Soon, though, he became the event he was managing. "After my Lake Michigan swim, volunteer inquiries rose thirty to forty percent. That's when we knew we were onto something good. I hadn't intended to make the swims a series, but after I did Lake Huron the next summer, inquiries rose another forty to fifty percent."

The Big Brothers/Big Sisters connection also helps garner much-needed corporate and individual sponsorship for Dreyer's aqua-marathons. The diesel fuel alone for his 2000 crossing of Lake Erie ran to nearly seven thousand dollars. There's always the chance, too, that the attention his feats draw in the regional newspapers and on TV and radio might help him reconnect with the girl, now a young woman, who first connected him to the Big Brothers/Big Sisters program.

"We tried to stay in touch with her," he says, "but it was tough. Her mother moved a lot. I keep hoping she'll find me."

For all the support Dreyer gets and all the motivation he has, in order for his events to succeed someone finally has to wade into very large bodies of water—lakes carved eons ago by glaciers, lakes with waves so formidable that they can sink oceangoing freighters, lakes that can reach depths of more than nine hundred feet—and start swimming toward a far shore he's not likely to see for more than a day, even if everything goes right. And everything doesn't always go right.

Dreyer was less than a mile into his first attempt to cross Lake Huron in August 1999 when he hit nine-foot waves, building to thirteen feet, and got turned back by the Coast Guard, which had come out to help a boat that had bottomed out on the rocky reefs off the Michigan shore. The next day, he set out again from Port Hope, headed to the Point Clark Lighthouse fifty-one miles away, in Ontario.

"I got thirty-four miles across the lake. Conditions were good. I was having the swim of my life—seventeen miles to go; the crew could see the lights of Canada. I was thirteen hours ahead of pace. The storm came out of nowhere, this gale-force wind. We were in twelve-foot waves, heading east, and the gale was coming out of the south, hitting the support boat. They couldn't feed me in those conditions. We fought it for an hour and a half. The support boat isn't small—it's forty-six feet—but it nearly capsized for a third time before they called it off. At that point, I'd been swimming for twenty-one and a half hours.

"I remember Mike Landis saying, 'Jim, you've got to get on the boat. We're going to capsize!' It was one of the strangest things anyone has ever said to me. We didn't know we were safe until we were tied to the dock. It was a white-knuckle ride all the way."

Three weeks later, on September 5, 1999, Dreyer was back, in the dead center of Lake Huron, swimming in near-perfect conditions when another storm kicked up and began throwing four-to-five-foot waves in his face.

"I drank a ton of water," he says. "I must have got into something really bad because the last twenty miles of the swim I was throwing up. Swim. Throw up. Swim. Throw up. After the swim, I had an IV for a while. I couldn't take solid food for nine days. I lost twenty-two pounds, and it was all muscle mass. I don't have weight to lose."

The nausea, though, wasn't the worst of it.

"We knew we were going to run into heat problems. We said, Let's put a thin dive skin on. It's like a fleece. It was real comfortable, but it didn't fit good. From about the halfway point on, I could feel it ripping my skin with every stroke. It took all the skin off my back, my sides, a lot of it off my stomach. You try to separate yourself from the pain by focusing on your goal and just knowing you won't quit. I always tell myself quitting is a *choice*."

The dive skin wasn't the worst of it, either.

"Out of everything I've experienced," Dreyer says, "the boat mix-up almost did me in. We knew my support boat could not make it all the way into the Canadian shore—it's too shallow and rocky—so we had arranged for a smaller boat to come out with my nutrition supply. We're three and a half miles from the shore when a bunch of boats come out, but the one I had arranged for never made it. It's dark. I'm cut up. I've been swimming for fifty hours, against the current for the last seven, and there's no boat for nutrition. My legs are paralyzed, I'm swimming just with my arms, the current is getting worse and worse, we're just not getting any closer to the lighthouse, and my coach is swimming in with me and going into hypothermia. Onshore are three thousand people—a great turnout—and I remember honestly not knowing if I was going to make it."

Eventually, Dreyer says, the mistake was discovered, and the Coast Guard was sent out. By then, though, it was eleven at night and too dark to spot anyone. At Dreyer's urging, Mike Landis, his swim coach, went in ahead of him. Ten minutes later Dreyer finally could stand, neck high, in the water in the Canadian shallows. Once again, he had set a world record for crossing a Great Lake, but this time there was a known standard to swim against. Dreyer beat it by over seven hours. Unfortunately, he'd come in on the wrong side of the breakwater from where the crowd was waiting.

Dreyer came back in the summer of 2000 with his eyes set on two of the remaining three Great Lakes.

"Every year, I try to raise the bar a little. You've got to. The media want the world records. Lake Erie and Lake Ontario are narrower than Huron and Michigan. They've been crossed a few times. So I thought, Well, we've got to keep this interesting, so what if I did Erie and Ontario consecutively? I couldn't get in my car and go to the next one after I'd swum the first one— that wouldn't be right. And I couldn't swim the Niagara River to get from one to the other—there's that falls. I thought, Well, I'll run and bike instead.

"But the transition is so tough. Exerting yourself horizontally [in the swim] then vertically [in the run and bike ride] is hard on the circulation. It's like jumping out of bed and getting dizzy. I knew the transitions would be key, but I couldn't know how tough it would be. You just can't simulate swimming a Great Lake."

Dreyer set off from the Pennsylvania shore of Lake Erie on July 23, 2000, headed 26 miles to the tip of Long Point, a finger of land that sticks out into the lake from the southern coast of Ontario. From there, he planned to run 26 miles, bike another 112, and then plunge into Lake Ontario at Toronto. Even though he encountered a strong Lake Erie current nine miles off Canada and the estimated fifteen-hour, 26-mile swim became a nearly twenty-hour, 30.4 mile one (his support boat uses geosynchronous plotting to measure distance), the first leg of the extravaganza went well, Dreyer says.

"I ran out of the water, dropped to my knees, and wrote a big 3 in the sand. It was my third world record. Then I changed my clothes, grabbed some solid food, and started out on the run. But I started too quick and didn't acclimate enough. They had to call my cousin in twice to give me oxygen. I told my running partner, Bob, 'I feel great. I just can't stay conscious.'"

Dreyer slowed his pace, he says, and ran another 14 miles before taking a bathroom break at mile 17.

"I was never the same again. I zigzagged into the bicycle transition area, and I passed out. I was cramping up into a fetal position. It was clear I couldn't do it. That was it, but I'd set a second world record: nobody had ever run a marathon after swimming a marathon. Lake Erie was the only lake I didn't get sick in or fall asleep in. For an event I passed out in and had dehydration in, it went pretty well."

A month later, Dreyer returned, but with a different strategy. This time, he would swim Lake Ontario round-trip, from Niagara-on-the-Lake, Ontario, just across the U.S. border from New York, to Toronto and back again, a little over 62 miles in all, if he could hold to course. To avoid the transition problems of moving from horizontal to vertical exertion, he decided to do the 26.2-mile run and the 112-mile bike ride—a ride that actually became 130 miles when the lead car took some wrong turns—first, then head into the swim. "My theory is, get me to the water, and I will finish it."

The run and ride completed, Dreyer set off from the New York–Ontario shoreline at nine o'clock on the evening of August 25, 2000. By seven the next morning, he was two miles away from Ontario, within sight of the Toronto skyline, when the current changed, and he found himself swimming on a treadmill.

"I finally fought my way into Toronto at seven at night and made the turn at Leslie Street Point. A lot of people were there to cheer me, the world record was set. Now I'm going out, and for the first eight hours, the current that had been trying to keep me out of Toronto was with me. But about three-thirty in the morning, things started changing. The waves came up quick. At first they were at my back. I felt like I was surfing. Then they came around to the side. Just as the first light came, they moved against me— eight-to-ten-foot waves.

"They couldn't feed me. We were getting pushed backwards. By the time the swim was called off [at 9:23 A.M., on the morning of August 27], we'd lost 2.3 miles."

In all—the biking, the run, and the swim—Dreyer had completed 212 miles. At the end, he was within 13.6 miles of his double crossing. By comparison, the so-called Iron Man triathlons sanctioned by USA Triathlon entail a total of a little over 140 miles: a 26.2-mile run, 112 miles of biking, and a 2.4-mile swim.

"Basically, USA Triathlon told me, 'We have people do double the running, we have people do double the biking, but we've never had anybody do even a double-digit swim in combination with the other Iron Man distances.'"

Nothing as intense as Jim Dreyer's regimen comes without a cost—other roads not taken, ones abandoned because there was no time for them.

"I'm divorced," he says—from the woman who first introduced him to Big Brothers / Big Sisters. "You're always training. I feel that was a contributing factor—not the only one, but a contributing one. I wasn't involved in a relationship all through Lake Michigan and Huron. But I'm dating someone now. Cheri is enjoying the ride. She finds this exciting. She has children, but I'm not always able to spend time with them. It's something that's probably kept me from having children of my own. But this is what I love to do. I've always wanted to make a mark in sports."

Dreyer dreams these days of warm-water events—for example, circumnavigating the Hawaiian Islands in a shark cage. But in the meantime there's the last of the Great Lakes to conquer: the aptly named Superior, graveyard to many ships, including the *Edmund Fitzgerald,* the American freighter that sank during a November 1975 storm, killing twenty-nine sailors. The most likely route—from the Minnesota-Canadian border near Grand Portage, past Isle Royale National Park to the thumb of far northwestern Michigan at F. J. McLain State Park—covers 62.3 miles that could easily become 90 with storms and currents.

"It's a monster lake," Dreyer says. "The *Edmund Fitzgerald* was snapped in half like a twig. But I've been doing a lot of research through the Great Lakes Research Laboratory in Ann Arbor, and I've been working with the National Weather Service in Marquette County, Wisconsin, too. I can't say I'm convinced it's humanly possible until I do it, but I believe that given the right window of opportunity, it might be. The lake is at its calmest mid-July to mid-August and at its warmest mid-August to mid-September. To try to get the best of both worlds, I'm shooting for mid-August."

Dreyer's best guess, he says, is that he'll have a one-week opening to start the swim—seven days in which all the external elements necessary for success have the best chance of coming into alignment. Near the end of the summer of 2000, he tested Superior and found it almost too accommodating.

"When I went up there to train for three days, the lake was like glass. It was as if it was trying to lure me: Come on, try me. But if it's humanly possible to swim it, I'm sure I'm the human to do it."

A first full-scale attempt to conquer the lake, in August 2001, was called off after thirty-six hours in the water, with both swimmer and support boat being pushed far to the south by waves of up to eight feet. Naturally, Dreyer isn't discouraged.

"My sports nutritional specialist says to me, 'Everyone has a limit. We just haven't found yours.' I am curious to know what it is."

Thirteen

Peter Holden:
Macs Without End

Peter Holden is sitting in a McDonald's a few miles from his home in Falls Church, Virginia. Holden has been in more McDonald's restaurants in the United States than anyone else alive—10,509 of the 12,804 that currently exist in the United States. It is the first time he has been to this particular McDonald's at Loehmann's Plaza. It opened only recently. "This isn't opening day here, but I *have* managed to catch opening day at eleven McDonald's so far," Holden says. "It's a challenge because I always put my career first." He is the logistics and planning director of a corporation in Warrenton, Virginia, that converts paper documents into electronic files.

A tall, slim man in his mid-fifties, Holden is wearing a blue shirt that has a Coke, a Big Mac, and some french fries embroidered on it ("That's the Big Mac Extra-value meal," he explains) and a Ronald McDonald quartz watch. The shirt and the watch were gifts from Jack M. Greenberg, chairman and chief executive officer of McDonald's Corporation, whom Holden met in 1999. McDonald's appreciates his loyalty. Holden orders two crispy McChicken sandwiches with mayonnaise and a diet Coca-Cola. "I prefer Big Macs, but the McChicken sandwiches are on a two-for-one special tonight at this store and I can't pass up a bargain," he says. "I'll eat french fries only if they're free or close to free. My cholesterol is one sixty-nine. That must be genetic good luck."

In his years of passing under the golden arches, Holden has eaten far more exotic items than chicken sandwiches and Big Macs. On his list of the unusual items he has sampled at McDonald's are Oscar Meyer hot dogs, McHoagies, Italian McSubs, Lemon Mendota Springs Sparking Mineral water, chicken fajitas, sweet-potato pie, cappuccino, espresso, eclairs, chocolate biscotti, Black Forest cake, hot dog McNuggets, flurries, after-dinner mints, McTurtle sundaes, and Mega Macs. "I've tasted some very local items," he says. "I've had hominy grits in the South. Because they're a vegetable, I am already unhappy. If I wanted to eat the equivalent of white mushy granules, I could go to White Sands, New Mexico, after a rainstorm and lick the ground. I've had cheddar melts on whole wheat rolls in the Midwest. They came with onions and I asked for them without onions—I loathe onions—but dark brown bread makes anything boring.

"McDonald's carries experimental items from time to time. The McLean, a low-calorie burger, was a sop to people on diets and it failed. The Arch Deluxe didn't fly because people didn't like its taste and, although it started out cheap, at ninety-nine cents, it ended up too expensive—two dollars and fifty-nine cents. Right now McDonald's is selling the Big 'n' Tasty. That may be its sixth or eighth 'Whopper stopper.' I hope it crushes Burger King's Whopper. I rarely go to Burger King unless I want to check it out or they've distributed free coupons. Why patronize the opposition?"

Holden bought some shares of McDonald's in the late eighties or early nineties. "If you had bought a hundred shares for $2,250 when McDonald's IPO'd in 1965 and you never touched them, you'd have 74,360 shares worth $2,230,800 today."

Holden, a born list-maker, has a list of McDonald's he has visited in out-of-the-way places like airports; train, bus, and subway stations; Home Depots and Wal-Marts ("I've eaten at over five hundred McDonald's in Wal-Marts"); amusement parks; universities; high schools and hospitals; military bases; ice-skating rinks, bowling alleys, casinos, and zoos; riverboats, boardwalks, and ferries; and national parks.

"There's a sign on each table at a McDonald's I went to over ten years ago near the edge of the Grand Canyon. I'm paraphrasing the sign from memory, but it read something like, 'Please excuse our prices, but our McDonald's is located fifty-five miles from the nearest food, supply, and labor sources. In order to offer our customers the McDonald's experience, our menu prices may be higher than those to which you are accustomed at home.'"

The cost of eating at McDonald's does vary from one restaurant to another. According to Holden, Manhattan's prices tend to be higher than those in small towns in upstate New York, reflecting the city's higher rents, taxes, labor costs, and zoning regulations. "I have a difficult time collecting

McDonald's in Manhattan because of the parking problem," Holden says. "I don't believe in paying to park. I also don't like people touching my car or wasting time getting in and out of garages. That can use up forty-five minutes. I could be visiting two or three McDonald's in those forty-five minutes. I sometimes park in front of fire hydrants. I once got three parking tickets in Manhattan in less than three hours, but I talked my way out of them a year and a half later."

When Holden is at home or on the road, he eats—or rather drinks—his breakfast ("juice and a chocolate Ultra Slim-Fast") on his own. When he has lunch at his desk, he brings sandwiches from home. When he's out and about in Warrenton at lunchtime he goes to one of the five McDonald's in the area. For dinner it's back to one of those five McDonald's "or minimalist food at home, peanut butter and jelly sandwiches, bologna sandwiches, or hot dogs."

Holden is a bachelor who isn't interested in cooking. When he is on the road, he will eat as many lunches and dinners at McDonald's as possible. "If it isn't possible to find a new McDonald's near my business appointments, then a revisit to a store already on my list is in order." He likes to be at McDonald's at closing time—customarily 11:00 P.M. Sundays through Thursdays, midnight on Fridays and Saturdays. "When a McDonald's closes for the night and the employees don't want the surplus food, they'll give it to whoever is in the restaurant. I've gotten free pies, salads, sandwiches, and drinks."

In Aspen, Colorado, where he lived for a month in February 1990, Holden frequented a McDonald's that closed at eight o'clock in the evening. "This local option outraged me," he says. "I had to eat earlier than I wanted to."

His visit to another McDonald's was a happier one. On October 16, 1991, he was driving from his home in Virginia to his parents' house outside Chicago. "I was on Route 20 and it was almost eleven o'clock," he says. "I was thinking, I'm not going to make it to this McDonald's in Clyde, Ohio. I'm going to have to go all the way back to it someday and I like to drive by a different route from Virginia to Chicago every time I go home. I roll into town and there's traffic and stoplights and the clock is ticking but the golden arches are lit up—which doesn't mean the store is open, although it's a good sign. It's eleven-ten when I pull into the McDonald's parking lot but there are still lights on inside. I see the doors are opening and closing, and there are people in the store. I go to the counter, I'm out of breath, I'm all excited. I ask the manager how come the store is open. He tells me to turn around. I do and I see a Whirlpool factory. 'The shift gets off at eleven o'clock,' the manager says. 'We decided to keep our franchise open so the workers could get something to eat after work. It was a good business decision. We make money, the workers don't go home hungry, and we close at eleven-eighteen.'"

Sometimes Holden goes on a McDonald's spree, as he did on October 26, 1975, when in one day he went to forty-five McDonald's in the metropolitan Detroit area. He cannot eat forty-five meals in a day, so in Detroit he drank a lot of diet Cokes and bought snacks, like cookies and pies, for future consumption. "I eat the snack later," he says, "because otherwise I consider it unethical to count the store." In October 1975 he set his record for most new McDonald's visited in one month: 246. In 1975 he also set his record for most new stores visited in one year: 643.

Holden doesn't add a McDonald's to his list without documenting it. He makes a purchase, obtains a receipt, and writes a brief description of the store in a notebook. At the McDonald's in Loehmann's Plaza, he noted the restaurant's beech-wood trim, its half-wood walls ("beech planking on the lower half, flat latex paint on the upper half"), two Coca-Cola fountains, real flowers on the tables, gray floor tiles, and ceiling fans. It was not a McDonald's with exciting decor—he prefers the riverboat McDonald's in St. Louis—but it was a large step up from a drive thru–only stop.

"Drive thru–only McDonald's are becoming more commonplace because they're less expensive to operate," he says. "But I want the experience of eating inside. I don't like to eat in the car. That's the car experience, not the eating experience."

Peter Holden has been collecting one thing or another since the age of seven. He has collected coins, stamps, baseball cards, and stock certificates. He divides his many collections into retired ("The collection is either finished and no longer generates interest on my part, or the collection is for sale or trade and is no longer worth my time"); passive ("The collection is pursued based upon extra time, money, or opportunity"); and active ("Time, money or opportunity are allocated whenever possible and at times to extremes. I do everything to extreme in moderation"). He says that stamps and baseball cards are retired, but "I'll work them up into saleable condition." Coins and stock certificates are passive.

Holden believes in "running parallel collections." One of his active collections is state capitols. "I've been to every state capitol except Juneau, Alaska. I'm waiting for them to build a highway so I can drive there. I suppose if I were on a business trip to Anchorage, I'd puddle-jump to Juneau, but I'd rather drive. I've driven over 1.7 million miles in my parents' cars, friends' cars, my cars, and rental cars. I have the receipt for every tank of gas I've ever purchased." A second active collection is visiting every national park, monument, historical site, scenic trail, "and other jurisdictions administered and managed by the Department of the Interior." He estimates that he has visited over three hundred on the present list of "about four hundred." A third active pursuit is traveling along every state and interstate highway. "I've driven a few miles on every one that exists, but there are a couple of new ones in the works."

A fourth is climbing the highest mountain in every state. "'Mountain' isn't the proper word for some states' highest points of elevation," Holden acknowledges. "I've ambled up to the highest point in Florida. It's three hundred forty-five feet and it's in Walton County. It happens to be the lowest highest elevation of any state in the country. I've got seventeen left to climb. Most of them are over eleven thousand feet. The tallest mountain in the United States is Alaska's Mount McKinley, at 20,320 feet, and I'm not going to attempt it until I'm physically fitter, and I'll only go with an expedition for safety's sake."

A fifth active hobby is collecting souvenir glassware and porcelain from the early twentieth century. "Almost every place had a salt-and-pepper shaker set, a creamer, or a goblet on which was written 'Souvenir of Coney Island' or 'Souvenir of Manhattan, Kansas,'" Holden says. "These pieces were made between 1895 and 1935, but they have historical meaning to me because I saw them years later. I like the fact that they look like relics of an earlier age."

Still, there is no question in his mind: McDonald's is Holden's favorite collection. "I like eating at McDonald's," he says. "Some people say the food doesn't taste very good. I like it because it always tastes the same. I can close my eyes and I'm eating the same Big Mac."

It's also inexpensive. "I don't drink or smoke," he says. "Money spent on alcohol or tobacco would be a diversion of resources from my collections." He generally sleeps only four to six hours a night, and can get by on fewer hours, if necessary. "The less I sleep, the more things I can do." One thing he likes about his McDonald's collection is that it is the country's best, and he believes he can keep it the country's best in his lifetime.

Holden went to his first McDonald's—in Palatine, Illinois—in June 1958, when he was in grade school. It was near the first McDonald's opened by Ray Kroc, McDonald's founder, in 1955 in Des Plaines, Illinois. He didn't start documenting the McDonald's until he'd already been to over one thousand. He started tracking them in the early nineteen-seventies. "Because I didn't document the first thousand I visited before 1974, I don't count them unless I revisit them and take the proper notes and obtain a receipt," he says. "I have two hundred revisited ones on my list of 10,509. Quite a few of the ones on my list, including the McDonald's in the Philadelphia Naval Shipyard, have closed, so no one will ever be able to collect them."

What Holden appears to enjoy most about his collection of McDonald's is that it is a collection without end. "I may climb every mountain in the United States someday, but I'll never have eaten at every McDonald's," he says. "I've 'finished' eating at the McDonald's in many states a few times, but they keep opening new restaurants so I keep having to go back. I'm glad."

While Holden has been to 706 McDonald's in Canada, he has yet to go to a single one of the thousands of McDonald's in Europe and in Asia. "I plan to collect the McDonald's experience by eating at every McDonald's in the world," he says. "It's just a question of when. One day I will climb Mt. Everest. I will certainly be eating my way to and from the mountain as well as shooting more slides of my adventures. I believe in independent travel and frugal travel and adventure, and go, go, go until your time is up."

Fourteen

Marietta Phillips:
Bossing Around

The photo is three and a half inches square, taken with a Kodak Instamatic camera. A table lamp illuminates what appear to be off-white cinder-block walls. There's a hint of a sofa. In the foreground, slightly off center, stand four people. Robert Vanacore and his cousin, Pam Springsteen, are on the outside of the group, left and right respectively. Beside Pam, dressed all in black and with his arm around her waist, is her brother, Bruce Springsteen, a.k.a. "The Boss," one of the most durable and popular music acts of the last quarter-century. Next to Bruce, sandwiched between him and Robert Vanacore, with her head leaning into Springsteen's shoulder and her long dark hair cascading down the front of a white T-shirt, is Marietta Phillips.

The time is May 27, 2000, shortly before midnight; the setting is a backstage room at the MGM Grand Hotel in Las Vegas, where Bruce Springsteen has just finished performing. For Phillips, who was thirty-six years old at the time, this is the moment toward which her life has been building since childhood, ever since she first heard Springsteen and his E Street Band.

"I was thirteen," Phillips recalls. "It must have been an AM station on the clock radio in our kitchen. My buddy Joe Provenzano and his older brother, Jerry, talked about Bruce all the time. When I heard him on the radio, I said, 'Hey, this is the guy!' A lot of his earlier music just really reflects the struggles of adolescence, trying to decide who you are. That's pretty heady stuff for a thirteen-year-old."

The next year, age fourteen, Phillips bought her first Springsteen album,

Born to Run, the third one he had recorded and the one that put him almost overnight on the national rock map, especially after simultaneous appearances on the covers of *Time* and *Newsweek*. Phillips picked up her second Springsteen album, *Darkness on the Edge of Town,* in June 1978, on the day it came out. What had been a scattered teenage interest in the music of Bruce Springsteen was starting to become something more. His music, words, and life were beginning to run together for her, just as his art and her life would begin to do a slow merge.

"*Darkness* was a great album," she says. "You saw the magic, the passion of Bruce Springsteen. It was all raw material."

Phillips had been born on Long Island and raised there, in Los Angeles, and elsewhere after her parents divorced. When Springsteen's "Darkness" tour, named for the album, rolled into the Capital Center in Landover, Maryland, late in 1978, she was a high school junior, living with her mother in nearby Alexandria, Virginia.

"I had tickets to see Bruce at the Capital Center, and my mother wouldn't let me go. It was a school night. It's one of those things where I was wrong to obey my parents. There comes a time in your life when you should rebel, and I didn't. I should have gone. I should have seen him in 1978. It was probably one of the worst fights of my teenage years. It was horrible, horrible."

On November 23, 1980, Marietta Phillips finally saw Bruce Springsteen live, at the same Capital Center she hadn't been allowed to go to two years earlier.

"I was pretty much a goner after that," she says. "That was the Thanksgiving break of my freshman year in college. I had posters and stuff in my dorm room. When people thought of Marietta Phillips, they thought of Bruce Springsteen. No one could believe I hadn't seen him live until then."

By then, too, the coincidences connecting Phillips to Bruce Springsteen were beginning to mount. There was, for example, the date of the concert where she first saw him perform.

"November twenty-third is my grandmother's birthday. That's part of the tale as well. When she was visiting me during my freshman year in college, my grandmother said, 'Have you ever heard of a guitar player, David Silverspring?' I said, 'No.' She said, 'Are you sure?' I said, 'Silverspring?' She said, 'Do you know you're related to him?'"

"David Silverspring" is, of course, Bruce Springsteen, and "related" stretches the point. In an e-mail that even Phillips can't decipher, her mother tried to clear up the family ties for her: "Aunt Gloria's father and Bruce's mother were brother and sister. You are related to Aunt Gloria and all the

Vanacores on Grandpa's side. Grandpa's mother and Aunt Gloria's mother were sisters."

"I'm not really related as a cousin," Phillips struggles to explain. "It's a cousin of a cousin of a cousin thing—an Italian thing." Still, the "Italian thing" that her grandmother had first alerted her to would be enough to get Marietta Phillips backstage at the MGM Grand twenty years later. Some things get better with waiting, but not everything. "My one regret when I first met Bruce was that I couldn't call my grandmother up and tell her. I just lost her a year and a half ago."

Bruce Springsteen released albums in 1980 and 1982: *The River*—"He went on tour for that, and that was when you started to be nervous about whether you could get tickets"—and *Nebraska,* a solo acoustic album that he supported mostly by playing club dates. Then, in 1984, came the album for which he is still best known, *Born in the U.S.A.,* one of the top-selling albums in history, followed by the American tour, later global, that established Springsteen as one of the top draws on the world rock circuit.

"I probably saw close to fifty shows on that tour," Phillips says. "Bruce has an uncanny timeliness. He's gone on tour at perfect times in my life. That summer I'd just graduated from college. All these cities where he was playing were two, three hours apart. It was just really easy. If you hooked up with a couple friends and they paid for gas, there was no reason not to go.

"I love the fact that a Bruce Springsteen show feels familiar in my life; it feels like home. You always hear people say that you walk out of a Bruce show and feel like you've just been to a party with twenty thousand of your best friends. I love that. I love that bond. I wound up sitting next to Sting on this last tour. I felt this incredible comfort striking up this dialogue with him. We were here, doing this together."

Marietta Phillips's concert going would tail off dramatically in the late nineteen-eighties through most of the nineties, in part because Springsteen broke up with the E Street Band in the fall of 1989 and in part because Springsteen himself went into a kind of self-imposed blackout following the breakup. After recording *Tunnel of Love* with the E Street Band in 1987, he would not put out another release for half a decade, by far the longest lapse since his first album appeared in 1973. It would be 1995 before he'd record again with his old group.

Phillips herself was on the move, too, and not getting closer to anywhere

Bruce Springsteen was likely to perform, with or without backup. She was in graduate school, getting a master's degree in social work at the University of Southern California, when the call of the Far North began to get to her. A series of summer vacations spent in Alaska only heightened her interest. After getting her master's degree in 1992, Phillips moved to Anchorage—"just for three months here to see if I wanted to stay"—and that sealed the deal. But if Phillips saw Springsteen less and less, his impact on her life grew stronger still as she established herself as a clinical social worker.

"I go back to his songs," she says, "his characters, the people he sings about—they're the people I see every day. His music is about looking inward and finding the courage to take a stand, to take the life you've been given and create a life of your own. Bruce didn't teach me that; it's a life perspective I just connected with. But how my life evolved personally, ending up in social work—it all just kind of fused."

In February 1999, Phillips was back in the New York City area, attending her grandmother's funeral, when word began to leak out that Springsteen and the E Street Band were reuniting for a global tour set to begin in Barcelona in April and return to the states in July.

"I'm back up here in Anchorage after the tour has been announced, and I think, My God, how am I going to do this? I live in Alaska. I'm adult now. I don't have the time or money to fly around and see him. I caught twenty-six shows on this tour. I amazed even myself that I was able to pull this off."

Certainly the scope of the tour helped. In all, Springsteen and the E Street Band played eighty-seven nights between April and November 1999, took three months off, then returned to the road at the end of February 2000 for another four months. Of necessity, Phillips leaned toward the shows west of the Mississippi: Phoenix, Arizona; four in Los Angeles in October 1999; Fargo, North Dakota; Tacoma, Washington; two in Anaheim, California; the fateful night in Las Vegas.

Technology also made the ticket quest easier this time around than it had been when Phillips had last seriously pursued the touring Springsteen, in 1984.

"I remember being on Long Island back then, at my grandmother's house. I had to drive down to central New Jersey to meet this guy so I could buy tickets from him to go to the show in Philadelphia. I can't even remember how I hooked up with him. Now there's the Internet and e-mail. There were Web sites where we had ticket exchanges. Scalpers would get on there, but we would ferret them out. Tickets were outrageously expensive already."

Frequent-flier miles helped, too.

"I got from Anchorage to Fargo and back, and all it cost me was the rental car out of Winnipeg, for thirteen dollars a day. I flew to Seattle, and Seattle to Vancouver with Alaska Airlines miles. Then I did Vancouver to Winnipeg with an Air Canada voucher I had from the year before. I rented the car, drove three hours to Fargo, got there about five, and hooked up with some friends and we went to the show. Afterwards we had breakfast at about midnight and hung out until four. I had to leave at seven to get back to Winnipeg for a noon flight. I crossed into new territory for that show: I had to go through customs four times."

Finding a ticket for the Fargo show was relatively easy: the Dakotas are not a population center. New York's Madison Square Garden, where the tour was scheduled to close with ten shows through July 1, 2000, was a more daunting challenge, especially the final show.

"The obstacles were these," Phillips says. "It was the closing night of the tour. Bruce had not played with the E Street Band at Madison Square Garden in thirteen years. Closing night means a lot of tickets are going to get pulled for VIPs. And the illegal stuff with scalpers is always harder in New York than in other cities. It was just a hard ticket.

"Tickets for Madison Square Garden went on sale Saturday, March fourth, at nine A.M. East Coast time, which means that at five A.M. in Alaska, I get up, pick up the phone, log on the computer, and punch in the Ticketmaster number. Then I lie back in bed, and it's four hours of listening to redials. I also have the cell phone going. My friend CC [Camille Conte] is trying to get tickets, too, and we're calling back and forth. Around one o'clock, I finally get through to a ringing phone, and the recording comes on and says, 'If you're calling about the Springsteen concert, it's sold out.' We knew it was going to be sold out at Ticketmaster, but you just have to try. It was probably one of the most stressful days of my life."

Eventually Phillips was able to pick up tickets, via canceled credit-card orders, to five other Springsteen performances at the Garden, but not to closing night. The quest wasn't over, though. Back on the Internet, she traded an extra seat she had already picked up for Springsteen's Toronto concert—"the New York of Canada!"—for an extra seat at Madison Square Garden on July 1, 2000. After all that work, she got to see Springsteen and the E Street Band bring the tour to an end from row 17 on the floor of the Garden, in what are known with rueful rock humor as the "jail-bait rows," the ones eighteen and under. Phillips had met Springsteen in person less than two months earlier.

* * *

"I'd seen him in Anaheim the weekend before I met him," she says. "The following Saturday he was going to be in Las Vegas, but I said, That's it. I'll do Anaheim. Then I'm going to Madison Square Garden, and I'm done with this."

All of which might actually have happened if Phillips hadn't placed a call to Las Vegas just before the Anaheim show. "I called my cousin Victor and said—I'd never put this in such a forthright way—but I said, I'd like to meet this guy." She was in her rental car in Anaheim, leaving the show, when Victor called back and said that if she wanted a ticket for the Las Vegas show, she had one. Bruce's mother, Adele, was going to be there. So was his sister Pam. Afterwards, they'd probably all go backstage to see Bruce.

Probably?

"I can't say, If I'm not going to meet him, I'm not going. That's not in the spirit of this thing. That would be starting to cross the line. I really believe you have to surrender yourself and let things happen."

And so the next weekend Marietta Phillips did just that: surrendered herself, cashed in still more frequent-flier miles with Alaska Airlines, flew to Vegas, rented a car, drove to her aunt Gloria's house, and set off on foot with Gloria and her son, Robert, down the famous Strip for the MGM Grand, to let things happen.

"It was one of the best shows of the tour. Bruce came out wearing a cape, like Elvis. It was a great, great show. I'm sitting next to his mom. Sometimes at his shows I'm in this trance—this hypnotic thing is going on. This show, every time I'd get embarrassed about being this crazy woman, I'd look over at his mom, and she'd be crazier than me!

"He did this song called 'Be True.' It's about not idolizing him, about loving someone from a human place rather than hero worship. It was sort of setting the tone for what was to follow. I'm trying to enjoy the show, but it's also, I'm going to meet this guy in a couple of hours—the critical moment you've been thinking about much of your life.

"The show ends. We're all standing there, and Bruce's mom turns to me and says, 'So, you want to go back and meet him?' I go, 'Oh, all right.' Pam just kind of cracked up. So we go back there, and it's just hysterical. When they've just come offstage, they keep people away even when you have passes. It's when the stalkers are there. But they just wave us through. I'm with his family, his cousins. It's all cool. He goes, 'Hi, Ma,' and she gives him a big hug.

"Everyone is standing around in a semicircle. I was just really comfortable. I plopped down on the couch, and my aunt Gloria just started in. 'Now this one,' she says, pointing to me, 'she came down from Alaska.' I don't know how Bruce perceives this stuff. I don't want him to think I'm just some geeky, stalky fan, so I just sort of smiled, and he said, 'Oh, is that right?' And I just chimed in and said, 'One thing I love is watching you enjoy the band,' and he just goes off about the guys in the band.

"I said, 'What do you walk away and remember about a show? The fans remember the set list, when you did this, did that. I've seen you sometimes, and it's like you're pointing to someone in the crowd, someone you remember.' I just think he's someone who appreciates his fans as people. I'm proud of that. I'm proud that I was around in 1978 and 1980 and helped create that legacy."

It was roughly in here, Phillips remembers, that she gave Springsteen two CDs by Fred Eaglesmith, a friend and a performer she thought Springsteen would like. Then she got out the Instamatic camera with which the photo would be taken: Pam and Robert on the outside, herself and Bruce at the center. Time was running short.

"I thought, I've got to say something, so I said, 'Listen, I just want you to know that you've meant a lot to me over the years. I've had a lot of great moments that have come from the music and from you.' I'm sort of gushing. He's walking with me toward the door, and I turn around and realize that we're alone, the dressing room is empty. He's been trained to usher people to the door, a kiss and hug, hello and good-bye.

"This isn't a crush thing, a sexual thing, even though there's a lot of sensuality and sexuality there. It's never been a hero-worship thing. What Bruce has brought to my life is artistry, poetry, and music. I believe he walks the walk as well as talks the talk. If it had all been a myth, all illusion, so what? I never wanted to have the experience where I met Bruce and he was an asshole. If it was an illusion, I could have lived with that. I didn't want it to be shattered. I wasn't ready to meet him twenty years ago.

"After I got out of his dressing room, I said good-bye to my cousins and went to find my friends who had also flown down from Alaska. It was shortly after midnight, Saturday night, Memorial Day weekend, Vegas. I couldn't find them anywhere, so I was just wandering around the Las Vegas Strip with my cell phone, trying to figure out who I could call at that hour. *That* was when it started to sink in. *That* was when it became an event. It was so surreal, wandering around under the Eiffel Tower, then the pyramids, then the Empire State Building, thinking, okay, I was just hanging out with Bruce in his dressing room."

Fifteen

Roger Swicegood: Song of Myself

For **Roger Swicegood** the unexamined life is simply not worth living. Swicegood sends out a three-to-six-page typed single-spaced newsletter almost every month to some twenty friends, relatives, and casual acquaintances, chronicling his daily life in Summerville, South Carolina, where he was born, in awesome detail.

The price of gas, for example.

7/27/97: Gas is down to 96.9 cents a gallon. I don't know when it was this low.

3/31/98: I noticed that gas has gone up. It was 93.9 yesterday and 96.9 today.

2/27/99: I saw gas today for 74.9. That's the lowest it's been in a while.

7/17/99: I noticed that gas was above a dollar again. I went out about six for medicine for Imogene and to buy gas at $1.019.

1/21/00: Several days ago I bought gas for $1.179 and now it's $1.199. I don't see why we have to dance to the OPEC's music.

Nothing is explained to casual acquaintances whom Swicegood suddenly puts on the *Swicegood News* mailing list: he once undertook an explanation of its cast of characters, but never finished it. By perusing issues of the newsletter from January 1997 to December 2000, however, a dutiful reader will pick up a good deal about the author and his family. Roger Mason Swicegood, one of the eight children of Carrie Bell Swicegood and John Willis Swicegood, was born on January 22, 1921. From the newsletters it is clear that he respected his mother.

7/9/99: Friday isn't a good time to eat out. It must be family night . . . all the kids screaming. The parents seem to ignore them without calling them down once. It was after seven and those kids should have been in bed. When I was that age and much older we went to bed at six. . . . dark or daylight, my mother used to say. It was the only way she could survive eight children.

Swicegood graduated from Summerville High School in 1939, and wound up spending three years in the navy.

12/7/98: I know where I was 57 years ago today. I was sitting on the front steps of this house. . . . Someone came out of the house and announced that the Japs had just bombed Pearl Harbor. I was working at the Navy Yard at the time, but that day changed my whole life. . . . My little small-town life expanded: travel, education, people and opportunities. I was in the Navy within 7 weeks. Mom was at the railroad in the early morning darkness waving as the train passed North Maple. From Columbia we headed for Norfolk . . . and 12 weeks of boot camp.

He attended an array of universities and schools including Indiana University, Duke, the Parsons School of Design, Mexico City College, and the Universidad de la Americas, before and after his first and second tours in the navy. He has a Bachelor of Fine Arts degree and an M.F.A.

From 1956 to 1983 he lived in Charlotte, North Carolina, primarily teaching Spanish and art to junior high school and high school students, and then teaching foreign students English as a second language. He spent summers in Mexico, where his close friend of fifty years, Joe, still lives. Upon retiring, he moved back to Summerville.

Since 1983, Swicegood, a bachelor, has shared the house his parents bought in 1941 with his younger sister, Imogene Williams, a widow with four children (Jimmy, Kathy, Cindy, and Johnny), nine grandchildren, and (at last count) six great-grandchildren. Swicegood lives upstairs. Imogene, a retired nurse and retired hospital director, lives downstairs. Imogene's maid,

Martha, comes five mornings a week and prepares breakfast and lunch for Imogene and helps her with her hair.

Swicegood likes to keep a close eye on—and hand in—dinner, but in the summer of 1997, after seventy-six years of excellent health, he was diagnosed with throat cancer. Until then a three-packs-a-day smoker, he underwent chemotherapy and radiation. Although Swicegood has been fitted with a prosthesis, he still has difficulty speaking. Happily, a near-army of close relatives showed up to help him and Imogene through the tough times. His sister Marilyn, who lives in Goldsboro, North Carolina, helped with the cooking. So, occasionally, did Lucile, the widow of Swicegood's brother George. Lucile lives next door to Roger and Imogene. Swicegood's brother Dan, whose home is in Greenville, North Carolina, came to stay for many weeks and drove Roger to and from radiation treatments at a hospital in Charleston, South Carolina. Characteristically, Swicegood concentrated on food in his chronicle of those days.

7/11/97: Marilyn made a roast, potatoes and carrots for dinner. Very tender with onion gravy. For dessert she put slices of pound cake under the broiler and then put chocolate ice cream on them.

7/26/97: Lucile brought over a tray of fried squash. It's one of my favorite things. Next week I'll be cooking again.

7/28/97: I'm going back upstairs, Dan's going home, Marilyn's not coming back unless needed, and Imogene says we'll share the cooking. I pretty much have my strength back.

8/7/97: Soon I want to move back upstairs where I belong. I know I'll enjoy sleeping in my full-sized bed even if I do need a new mattress. I can sprawl more. I have three pages of another letter done downstairs, but I think I'll finish on this one . . . and Imogene can enjoy smoking all over the place except when I'm cooking dinner.

9/3/97: I've been working on curtains for my dinette for several days and have one window finished. . . . there are 5 windows. I'm making cottage curtains in 3 colors: yellow, burnt sienna and burnt umber. It's something to do instead of reading or watching television.

Restored to self-sufficiency, Swicegood was again driving a fair amount. A frequent destination is "the Pig," as he refers to Piggly Wiggly, the supermarket he favors, and Wal-Mart. He does most of the shopping and usually prepares dinner for himself and Imogene. Food is the predominant topic of the newsletters.

8/27/97: I don't like buying stuff for one meal, but Imogene wanted things for dinner tonight. I like to go once a week, and I don't like fixing things I don't know how to make and don't plan on learning. It was a dish with green chiles. . . . With melted cheese all over the top it looked okay. . . . I've lost taste buds to radiation and have no sense of smell at all. When I say "that smells good," it means nothing.

9/25/97: I made quesadillas for dinner along with pot roast and mashed potatoes. I have a Campbell's recipe book with lots of recipes I like. A whole list of pasta dishes. I can handle pasta several times a week.

10/3/97: I shopped for Imogene. She's going to try Jump Start and needed lots of fruit except for apples and oranges. I got pears, peaches, grapes, bananas, and celery. I got skim milk for her to mix with the stuff. There's no meat on the diet plan anywhere unless it calls for a sensible dinner after morning and noon Jump Start stuff.

Imogene's diets are short-lived.

10/5/97: Imogene is cooking chicken and dumplings . . . not my favorite meal. She wants me to make chicken salad out of part of the chicken and also make a ham salad. . . .

10/24/97: Marilyn brought dinner with her. Chicken in plum sauce (Japanese or Chinese) from this month's *Better Homes and Gardens*. Tomato bisque, salad of tomatoes and cucumbers, and green peas. Le Sueur, of course. For dessert we had the apple pie I made last night as I fixed dinner for tonight.

11/28/97: The dinner yesterday was fantastic. . . . I had a piece of the cake Jenny made (Marilyn's recipe). The ham was too salty. A Hostess is cheaper, three times cheaper, and people eat it. Kenny soaked this one for 16 hours and it was still too salty. Much more than the standard Thanksgiving dinner was served.

12/2/97: I've decided that I want to make an uncooked fruitcake. I almost know how. It'll go in the freezer. I remember Aunt Lily put icing on hers. She cut pieces like I do the fruitcakes from Georgia. Before those fruitcakes I wouldn't touch one. . . . I waited too long to send this letter.

12/11/97: Today I made my first no-bake fruitcake. I didn't have a recipe, so I made it up as I went. I'll do a baked one. I have enough stuff for one or two. It should be frozen solid by the morning. I hope it's okay.

Nineteen ninety-eight began on a somber note. As Swicegood and a number of his relatives were eating dinner on January 1, they received a telephone call informing them that Swicegood's brother John Willis "Bill" Swicegood, seventy-three, a widower, had died suddenly. There were now only four Swicegood siblings left.

On January 20, 1998, there was an uncharacteristically reflective entry in the *Swicegood News*.

Last year the doctor asked me when he told me I had cancer if I wanted to live to be 77. I said I didn't know, that it wasn't that high on my priority list, and that no one in my immediate family had lived to be 77. (I'll be 77 in two days.) I told him that quality of life meant more to me than life itself.

The following day's entry was more cheerful.

1/21/98: A new Swicegood arrived on the scene yesterday by C-section. Billy and Shannon (Bill's son and daughter-in-law) are the proud parents of 7 lb. 11 oz. 21 inches Jonathan Davis.

Swicegood soon resumed dispensing helpful household hints ("If you ever need the juice of two lemons and only have one, put it in the oven for 10 minutes at 200 degrees and you'll get twice as much juice") and writing about trips to the post office; difficulties encountered in getting the newsletter copied and mailed; the cost of medical bills (he is blessed with good health insurance); gardening (he loves flowers); sewing projects (he designs sweatshirts and other garments for family and friends); his displeasure at buying cigarettes for Imogene ("I hate to buy cigarettes for Imogene. They may think I smoke through my stoma"); and eating.

3/27/98: Imogene brought good food for the shower. . . . Except for the chicken casserole and the little quiche pastries, I ate it all. The shrimp salad, though different, was very good with olives, celery and perajil, or parsley. There was a cheese dish and also a spinach soufflé. Kathy made the Italian cream, which was great as always. I've had it by three or four different people.

4/17/98: A good report from the doctor . . . no signs of cancer. . . . Imogene is giving the rehearsal dinner here on Friday night after the rehearsal. She's planning for baked ham, potato salad and other stuff and a dessert. Martha is working late on Friday and coming Saturday morning to fix breakfast for the people who stay here. I think they could go to a restaurant.

6/25/98: A nice long letter from Joe today. . . . I baked a cake today, and it turned out super . . . chocolate caramel nut. It was something to do inside. I think I'll make an apple pie tomorrow. Yesterday I baked Nutty-butter bars, and they are good.

7/4/98: Joe called this morning. He was in the Chicago area. . . . He sounded great. He thinks I sound like someone he knows . . . someone who growls, I guess.

I baked a pecan pie . . . just out of the oven. It was something to do during the rain. I didn't have much luck with the cake I baked earlier. It fell apart, so I didn't ice it.

Once in a while there are references in the newsletter to the outside world.

8/24/98: On the radio today a caller said that the people were tired of the Monica-Bill mess, and the host, not Rush, yelled back that the people were not tired of it. I know I am, so I turned the noise off. I was tired of it the day it was announced. She let it be known that she wanted to get next to him. Rush called her innocent. An innocent girl would have had her blue dress cleaned. Saving it as evidence put her in a different category. . . . Innocent 21-year-olds don't come out of southern California.

On November 15, 1998, Swicegood was saddened to report the year's second death in his immediate family. "Bubba"—George William Swicegood, the only son of Swicegood's sister-in-law Lucile—passed away after seven months of grave illness at the age of fifty-four. Swicegood had spent a fair amount of time with his nephew, a self-employed carpenter, and five days prior to Bubba's death he had written in the newsletter:

> 11/10/98: Lucile told me to get the keys to [Bubba's] shop and take any small item I wanted. All the big stuff has been sold for $1200. It would take $10 thousand to replace the items.

Bubba was buried "next to his mother's spot, her name is already on the tombstone," but Thanksgiving was celebrated. Martha took out all the Christmas decorations, as she customarily does, and Swicegood decorated the house for the holidays. He put live poinsettias in the Summerville cemetery where his parents and other Swicegoods are buried, and on December 31, 1998, he baked two pumpkin pies. Martha would come in the morning to make the hoppin' John, a southern dish of rice and black-eyed peas, considered a must for New Year's dinner (for luck) and collard greens (for money).

In one newsletter, Swicegood had written that Lucile, who owned the back of the lot on which her house stands, had sold it for fifteen thousand dollars to a West Virginia paper company. Lucile's displeasure with this entry was also recorded in the *Swicegood News*.

> 3/14/99: Lucile got on me yesterday for mentioning the sale of the back lot. I don't think anyone on my mailing list would break into her house looking for money, and I didn't plan to post it on the telephone posts on West 2nd North. If it had been in the millions, I would think it would be of some concern. She sounded angry as if she was sure to be robbed because of something I wrote in my newsletter. It was family news. It was less than half the property my father bought for $600. I have the bill of sale from Mrs. Masterman. She'd be an idiot to keep any great amount of money in the house. The most I ever have is $100.

A happy event of 1999 was a visit from Joe.

> 6/1/99: May was memorable with Joe's visit. Something he hasn't done in years and years . . . I was delighted that he got along so well here and fit in as if he belonged.

When Swicegood isn't cooking and reporting on home-cooked meals, he and Imogene eat out—at IHOP (the International House of Pancakes),

Shoneys (his favorite place for a late breakfast, where "almost all of the 30 percent of obese Americans eat Sunday breakfast" ("I don't think the company makes a profit on any of them. I think obesity is a qualification for employment at Wal-Mart"), Perkins, Appleseeds, Hardee's, Ye Little Old Fashioned, and KFC, and he critiques these and other restaurants and their patrons in the newsletter.

6/8/99: Imogene and I went to China Palace V last night. I meant to take Joe there. I know he likes some Chinese dishes and they have a sampling of all in their buffet. I don't understand why anyone would go there for fried chicken, fried okra, French fries and other American dishes. I saw a fat woman send her thin husband back three times to load her plate with fried chicken and nothing else. I didn't take any of the fillers like rice and pastas and still left half the stuff on my plate.

By September, Swicegood was lamenting his and Imogene's evacuation from Summerville as a consequence of Hurricane Floyd.

9/14/99: Well, we're ready to go. I went to the Pig for cigarettes for Imogene and to the bank for some cash. . . . We may not get back until Thursday. Kathy got us rooms in Union, which is near Pacolet.

9/16/99: We're back. The trip up was awful . . . 7 hours on the road to Union. It took about 3 to get back. . . .
    Floyd did knock lots of green pecans off the tree by the garage. I drove over them putting the car in the garage and it was very bumpy. I've done that when they're ready to pick up. I do like making pecan pies. I guess I'll learn how to make cheesecake. It's one of Imogene's favorite desserts and Kathy likes them, too, and sends some over when she makes them. I don't know where she got the idea that dessert always comes after dinner. Even in restaurants she orders a dessert, but I think desserts are for special occasions, not an after-dinner treat. A mint would do then but not cake and ice cream or pie.
    The governor says he takes full responsibility for the delay in opening I-26 both lanes to Columbia. What does that mean? They're just words. His responsibility won't give me back one of the hours I spent sitting in the car. $100 an hour might make him responsible, his words change nothing.

Soon enough, though, Swicegood and Summerville settled back into everyday life.

11/15/99: Today I was told that I was volunteered for candied yams for Thanksgiving dinner . . . two trays of them no less. I don't think 30 servings of anything should be made. There'll be too much food that way. I think "a dish to pass" is all that's necessary. Except for turkey and ham and some of these pigs take a pound of each for their plates.

12/14/99: I read the letter about the bragging letters in Ann Landers today. A lot of people don't like them. My monthly letter doesn't brag; it complains and reports happenings to the Swicegood kith'n'kin.

12/17/99: Today I bought Imogene's Christmas present: a mouse sander by Black & Decker. It's what she wanted.

The year 2000 was marred by Swicegood's coming down with an extremely painful case of shingles, so he wrote fewer newsletters that year, but he felt well enough to go to Mexico from October 10 to November 9 to visit Joe.

Upon his return, he stopped to look back on the origins of his newsletter and on his reasons for writing it. "I've been writing letters since eighth grade," he said. "I wrote only to my mother from the Philippines and Japan—back then I had no way of copying the letter—and included a stick of chewing gum for the censor, who said, 'Thank you, I needed that.' I started writing letters to relatives at home when I went to Mexico. I can remember writing about the big earthquake of 1957 and the big earthquake of 1985. It got too hard to type through five or six sheets of carbon paper so I started to have my letters copied. I write my newsletter to keep the family informed, and because I like doing it. When I was fourteen years old, it was hard to get half a page down on paper because nothing was going on then in Summerville or in the family."

PART 4

Pleasures Small and Large

Sixteen

Cathy Runyan:
Got Her Marbles

Cathy Runyan lives with her second husband, Larry Svacina, and a million marbles in an underground house built into the side of a hill in Kansas City, Missouri. She built the house in 1982 while married to her first husband because she was unhappy in their previous conventional suburban house-with-lawn.

"Some people spend their whole lives taking care of their lawns," she says. "I like dandelions. So I bought ten acres and moved further out in the country where the seeds from my bright yellow dandelions wouldn't take flight and bother anyone else's manicured lawn."

All that can be seen from the road is her double-car garage and front entrance door, but the gravel of the driveway outside the entrance to Runyan's energy-efficient house is mixed with marbles. The license plate on her car also proclaims her passion: MARBLS. "The license plate reassures first-time visitors that they've come to the right place when the '92 Ford Taurus clunker is in the driveway," she says. "It would read MARBLES if the state of Missouri allowed more than six letters on a vanity plate, as the state of Kansas does."

Visitors have two options after entering at ground level through the front door. They can walk down a flight of eighteen steps or sit and slide down on an adjacent eight-foot slide "We needed a wide entrance to avoid a claustrophobic feeling and I thought the slide would be fun." Sliders land on two beanbags placed on a large inflatable rubber tire at the bottom.

Runyan, a dynamic blonde in her late forties, uses the word "fun" often, both as an adverb and as an adjective. In 1985, she self-published a booklet called "Knuckles Down!" Its subtitle is "A Fun Guide to Marble Play."

Runyan was one of five children. When she was growing up, her four brothers and their friends were not keen on having her play basketball, baseball, or football with them. "Marbles was the one thing I could get in on," she says. "At eight, my grandfather gave me marble-shooting lessons. I was good enough to beat the boys. I still have the shooter—the eight ball of marbles—that belonged to my paternal grandfather." She amassed a wealth of milkies, cat's-eyes, and black beauties from the boys in the neighborhood. She was an ardent collector of the vividly colored and intricately designed marbles until her early teens, when she started high school and put them away.

She married in 1972 at the age of twenty before completing college, gave birth to three girls and two boys between 1973 and 1982, and had little time to think about marbles. She chose to stay home with her children but was a den mother, Brownie leader, and room mother, and was active in the La Leche League. Runyan, a Mormon who tithes, also served in lay positions in her church: as a pianist, chorist, and member of the Women's Relief Society. In the early eighties she supplemented the family income by caring for a neighbor's child before and after school and waitressing at a friend's restaurant evenings when her husband was home.

One day in 1983, when her oldest daughter had to do a fifth grade report on a game her mother had played as a child, Runyan took part of her marble collection out of storage. Her daughter did a presentation about marbles at her school, Runyan was asked to do another presentation for her daughter's class, and other classes started calling. It troubled her that her children knew nothing about the games she had enjoyed during her childhood, and that she had forgotten so many of them.

A search of the Kansas City Library system turned up just a short paragraph about marbles: like tag and leapfrog, it is one of the oldest games children around the world have played. There wasn't a single book on how to play marbles, and when Runyan telephoned all the toy stores she could think of in Kansas City she discovered they hadn't sold marbles for years. Youngsters, it seemed, were primarily playing video games and watching television. It also bothered her that marbles appeared to be near extinction.

Runyan began to research her book. By then she was waitressing part-time at a Days Inn, and she asked the older guests there, as well as residents of the nursing and retirement homes where she was a volunteer, to recall the marble games of their youth. "Knuckles Down!" was the result.

The booklet explains various marbles games (like Picking the Plums, Black Snake, and Ducks in the Pond) and marble terms like knuckling down—"This refers to the most important rule in marble play and describes the correct way of shooting with the knuckles to the ground until the shooter marble leaves the player's hand"—and fudging—"This is the polite way of saying a player is cheating because he has let his hand advance over the ring or taw line before shooting. The penalty is one lost turn." It introduced the game to a new generation and drew Runyan back into marble collecting.

She bought big jars of marbles for a dollar at garage sales or antique stores, went through them, kept a few, and gave most away. She spoke about marbles at Kiwanis and Rotary Clubs. For ten summers she was a referee at the National Marble Tournament in Wildwood, New Jersey. While there, she bounced along the boardwalk wearing a pair from her collection of "moon" shoes—fad footwear from the nineteen-sixties that have two metal spring coils attached to the heel and toe and give walkers the appearance of walking on the moon.

In 1987, she called around to see where marbles were still being made and went to several marble factories in Ohio and West Virginia. The industry that had flourished in the region in the thirties and forties was barely hanging on. Champion Agate Company, one of the surviving companies, had a warehouse filled with old marbles. "They cut me a deal," Runyan says. "Their floors had caved in under the weight of the marbles. They let me have them. All I had to do was pay for the shipping. The ten pallets of marbles, a bit over a million marbles according to poundage, were pretty common clearies or puries—translucent glass of various colors—and Chinese checker marbles, which are solid colors. I've used them as my gravel giveaway marbles for kids, like groups of Cub Scouts, who come to the house. Over the years I've helped five thousand Cub Scouts earn their marbles belt loops and marbles physical fitness pins. If ten Cub Scouts come to the house and each takes fifty marbles, there go five hundred. I periodically toss out a fresh supply."

Roger Howdyshell, the owner of Marble King, another company in West Virginia, gave Runyan two special marbles. One, smaller than the candy sprinkles used for decorating cakes, was among the five hundred smallest marbles ever made. They were originally intended for a NASA expedition and experiments on spheres. When NASA told Howdyshell he couldn't have them back, he kept them all—until he met Runyan. His second gift to her was a peewee ("a marble one-half inch or smaller") white lutz, handmade in Germany in the late nineteenth century.

Before Howdyshell's death, Runyan had decided to give away "kindness" marbles. "The idea is to put a kindness marble in your left pocket in the morning and do something kind during the day," she explains. "That can mean letting a person who has only one item [go] ahead of you in the checkout line at the grocery store, or thanking a mailman for the steady service he provides. When you do something kind, you may transfer the marble to your right pocket. I try to have a kindness marble in my right pocket every night. I gave Mr. Howdyshell a kindness marble. He was buried with it in his right pocket when he died in 1991. Roger's widow and I put a few more in the coffin."

Because Runyan gave children marbles, they named her "the Marble Lady," as that was easier for them to remember than her name. In 1991, the Marble Lady became the first woman ever allowed to play in the National Rolley Hole Marble Championship in Clay County, Tennessee. In some places, like Kansas City, Missouri, there are tennis courts in public parks, but in towns like Celina, Moss, and Livingston, Tennessee, marbles is virtually the only game in town, and grown men play on dirt marble yards seven nights of the week nine months of the year.

In 1992, Runyan went to Tinsley Green, England, home of the British World Marble Tournament, as an alternate player on the American team with six men, all of them from Tennessee and Kentucky. The team won. "No one got sick, so I didn't play, but my way over was paid and I refereed in tournaments in which the American team wasn't playing," she says. "I was the first woman to referee at a world championship. While I was in England, I shot marbles at Stonehenge and in Trafalgar Square. I called my children long-distance so they could hear the bells of St. Mary's and the American operator asked if she could please listen in, too. My parents were staying with the children and had to wake them because of the time difference, but they didn't mind. The bells were so beautiful."

In the nineteen-eighties, Runyan started collecting marbles again. She bought primarily American machine-made marbles from the nineteen-twenties to the nineteen-fifties for between ten cents and five dollars, rather than nineteenth-century handmade ones from Germany, because that was all she could afford. When she went to marble conventions, some of the more prosperous collectors laughed at her.

"It's Cathy with her machine-mades," those buying the high-dollar marbles told her.

"Shoot me, I like them," she said. "I'd learned from years of going through thousands of nickel-and-dime marbles what the rare ones were.

The marbles I bought then are worth hundreds of dollars today. I was ahead of the curve."

Runyan kept her household and marbles budgets separate. If she was paid forty-five dollars for giving a marbles presentation at a dinner or earned money from booklet sales, she used it for travel expenses (plane tickets to Wildwood and hotel and food bills), for giving away kindness marbles to organizations for the developmentally disabled and others with low budgets, and for buying marbles to add to her collection. She had formally separated from her first husband in 1990, and divorced in January 1992. "I was afraid my husband would want half my marble collection, although he'd repeatedly called it dumb and I'd bought no marbles with his salary," she says. "I was lucky. He wanted the camper."

As a single mother, Runyan waited on tables, cleaned houses, cared for other people's children, and did substitute teaching. She gave marbles presentations when she was invited to give them, and sold her own blood for plasma "when I really got desperate." She parted with a few "major" marbles "to keep a roof over my children's heads and food in their mouths." She thought for a while she would be single for the rest of her life. "Who was going to take on five kids?" she asked. "I didn't have a dowry. And my kids have always been more important to me than anything. Four out of the five have been high school valedictorians. Four have graduated from college, one is in college. I'll get my degree when I choose a major."

Cathy Runyan met Larry Svacina in 1987 at a National Marble Convention in Amana, Iowa. Svacina had played marbles in grade school and had bought marbles from an early age, while going to antique stores with his mother. "If I was good I'd get a handmade marble for a quarter or fifty cents. My grandmother had been given a marble by a farmhand in 1882 when she was two. I'd always seen it—it was a sulphide with a bird inside it. My mother had some sulphides with animals inside them. Kids like animals. That's what I bought. Sulphides are clear marbles with clay figures inside. The air bubbles that form around the figures give them a silvery appearance."

Like Runyan, Svacina, fifty-nine, "got away from marbles" when he went to high school. That was when he "got interested in sports and girls." In 1970, he walked into a small antique store outside Denver and saw a marble with the number 1 inside it. "I'd never seen any with numbers in them," he says. "I bought it for fifty cents and that started the collection going again." Sometimes it was difficult to find the marbles he wanted, so he branched out into buying board and box games played with marbles, paintings with kids playing marbles in them, picture postcards with kids and grown-ups playing marbles, and figurines with marbles in them. In 1993, Runyan says, "Larry discovered I wasn't as young as he thought I was and that I wasn't married. We had our first date with a group of marble collectors here in Kansas City after a big marble auction." They were married a year later.

"At least you know I'm not marrying you for your marbles, because I've got marbles, too," Svacina said.

"Larry had bought some of the marbles I'd sold after my divorce, so when we got married I got them back," Runyan said.

Their friends pointed out that when they married they merged two collections, thereby giving them the largest and the best collection in the country.

"If you spent enough money, you could obtain examples of much of what we have, but not nearly all," Runyan reflects. "Some things are one-of-a-kind, no longer available, or very rare, and some things just aren't for sale by anyone. That's not to say no one has something we don't have. Of course they do. But other collectors tell us no one has the extent and depth and breadth of the total marble and marble memorabilia collection that we have."

The underground house is filled with his, hers, and theirs marbles and marble memorabilia: jewelry, trophies, medals, advertising pieces, and historic documents. The family room and two marble rooms (one with a round marble table at its center) gleam with some of the best spheres in their personal collection of fifty thousand valuable marbles.

The most valuable? "The two birdcage marbles," Runyan says. "Our chicken sulphide inside a half onionskin—never before seen. Our triple cat sulphide. My Vitro collection of Peacocks, Sweet Peas, and Black-eyed Peas. My collection of sulphides with missing parts—a head or major limb totally missing. No one else collects these to my knowledge, so I can usually get them very reasonably because most people see them as defective. I, being the strange person that I am, see them as a fun human connection to people from the past. They connect to real people who were tired on Monday mornings or Friday afternoons, or who were perhaps distracted in their work by problems or worries about their families or finances, and these defective figurines were accidentally inserted into the clear glass marbles.

"My dolphin prototype from David Salazar, one of the outstanding contemporary glass marble artists. My millefiori from the Perthshire Paperweight Company in Scotland. I believe only four of these were made and I received one as a gift. And then there is one large End of Day with Mica—

looks like pieces of silver glitter scattered over small pinpoints of every color of the rainbow. Some of these marbles now sell for five to seven thousand dollars apiece.

"We've bought some terrific marbles since our marriage. Wonderful sulphides with figures of eagles, rare sulphides with double figures such as two birds, double human figures—a man and woman dressed in colonial-type clothing with a muzzle-loading gun. And some large gorgeous onionskins, solid cores, swirls, and divided core swirls."

A few years ago Runyan, who continues to buy many of her clothes in thrift shops and to be thankful she lives in a house that is inexpensive to heat and cool, was asked what she would do if that house containing the Runyan-Svacina marble collection were destroyed by fire.

"I said I would mostly be grateful that the experiences and friendships I have gained through my passion for marbles couldn't be burned along with them," she says. "Marbles, in and of themselves, are so pretty. When I look at simple tigereyes, custards, and corkscrews, they make me smile. I get excited when I think about whose pockets were they in, who played with them, what happened to those kids. I sometimes think about where I would roll if I were a marble. I'd like to roll into some of the famous art museums in Europe when there aren't a lot of people around, and just be able to sit down and look at what's on the walls. But the highest value of marbles in my life has been to provide me with a way in which I can be of service to others. I'd like to think that even without marbles I could have achieved this, but I can't imagine a more fun way of doing it.

"Marbles have led me to my wonderful husband and I hope that I will leave this world a little bit of a better place for having been the Marble Lady."

Seventeen

Peggy Dickson: Bird Brains

"If you have never heard a roomful of birds with the giggles, you are missing out on pure joy," Peggy Dickson promised.

Walter, a blue-and-gold macaw, started the giggling off, his prominent tongue clucking inside a huge black beak that is said to be capable of snapping a broomstick. Almost immediately, Beauregard, another blue-and-gold, picked it up. Before long, the nanday conure Charlie joined in, along with Polly, a Quaker parakeet; Margo, a yellow-naped Amazon with the look of a linebacker and a tendency to mutter; and Peggy Dickson herself, a nearly sixty-year-old human who had been the very first to giggle as she rubbed Walter's beautiful blue neck.

And there, of course, is the problem, always, with bird giggles and bird chatter and bird intelligence generally. Is it real? Or are birds just great pretenders?

"I don't believe they only mimic," Dickson says. "Yes, there's a lot of it involved, but how did I learn to talk? I mimicked, and it brought me such rewards that I went on to learn language on my own.

"We've been very chauvinistic as humans in assuming we are the only ones who think, talk, figure things out, or have emotions."

Peggy Dickson's ascent into the world of birds began with a single, small indulgence.

"Nine years ago, I gave myself three finches for my birthday. I went to the pet store to buy food for our German shepherds, and I saw three red finches that I thought were the most exquisite things I had ever seen in my life. There was a Society finch in the group that was all alone, so I had to take it, too. And right then and there I should have known that I was in trouble."

Soon, hanging plants, birdbaths, and millet feeders were taking over the narrow sunroom at the back of Dickson's modest suburban home in Alexandria, Virginia. Two Java finches ("they look like little sleek penguins") joined the reds and the Society finch, as did some tiny strawberry finches, which had babies, which before they fully feathered had eyebrows that blew in the breeze when their parents flew over. The eyebrows, in turn, opened up whole new areas of fascination with avian anatomy and appointments, none of which was lost on Dickson's husband, Sam.

"Sam kept saying, 'Please don't go to the pet store. What is wrong with you?'"

For those who keep pets, though, pet stores are hard to avoid. It was during a visit to buy food for the baby finches, Dickson says, that she fell in love with lovebirds. At first, she tried to resist temptation, or at least put herself out of temptation's way.

"I had to call ahead to pet stores before I went and ask if they had any hand-fed lovebirds, and if they had one, I'd say, Well, call me when it's sold."

But the love of lovebirds wasn't to be denied. Before long, Dickson had her first of the species, a blue named Precious, and with that, another line in her already thin avian defenses fell. "Then I went to buy more dog food, and a whole batch of them cuddled up against me. There was one that I couldn't resist, and I said, 'I'll give it to Sam!' So I wandered in with this green lovebird and gave it to Sam, and he said, 'Oh, she's wonderful!'"

Thus, Buggs came to join Precious, and thus the Dickson flock grew and grew. But there was one line yet to be crossed: big birds. Lovebirds are larger than sparrows but considerably smaller than city pigeons. Big birds get into the two-plus-pound range, and Peggy Dickson says she had no intention of having them under her roof: "one, because I knew they could bite, and, two, because I knew they were likely to outlive me. The blue-and-golds can live seventy-five to a hundred years, and when you're already over fifty years old yourself, that doesn't make much sense."

All that was before Dickson met Sybie, an Alexandrian parakeet and a big bird despite its diminutive-sounding breed, at a store in the Virginia countryside. Just as Precious had breached the lovebird barrier, so Sybie busted the big-bird resolve.

"She was very much like my mother," Dickson says, "very dignified and very opinionated. I went by her cage and read the card, and in an effort to be polite, I said, 'Hello.' And she clamped her body right next to me and said, 'Who? Who?' And I tell you, it was haunting. I came by her cage again as I was leaving, and she said, 'Who? Who?' once more. The cage card said she'd been sold, so I assured her that she was going to have a wonderful home.

"That was a Friday. By Saturday night, she had haunted me to the point I couldn't stand it. On Sunday, I called and asked about the bird in the center of the store, and the woman said, 'She's a mean vicious bird.' It turned out a North Carolina breeder had given a deposit on the bird and hadn't come back. The woman said, 'You can have her,' and I thought, Oh, sure, that's just what you want—a screaming, biting bird." A few hours later, Dickson was at the store, buying the screaming, biting bird.

"They had named her Sybil, for her mood swings. I wasn't going to get into that. So I told her, 'Okay, Sybie, you're going to have cantaloupe and kale and all sorts of good things to eat,' and her eyes were changing as I talked—you can watch them change—and her whole body was becoming the body of a lighter bird."

Other big birds followed. She met Walter while she was cleaning his cage. (By then, Dickson had gone to work part-time for Victor, who owns her favorite bird store.)

"He got on top of the cage, leaned over, grinned at me, and pulled my hair. All Walter could say was, 'Hello, hello.' He'd say it all the time. There was a blue-front Amazon in the store, Buddy, and once when Walter said 'Hello, hello,' Buddy answered: 'What do you want, Walter?'

"I went in one day, and Walter wasn't in his normal space, and I panicked. I said, 'Victor, I'll take that bird because I couldn't stand not to see him every day for the rest of my life.'"

That was August 20, 1994, and Dickson has seen Walter almost every day since, because that is another aspect of keeping birds, especially big ones: there's almost no time off.

Peggy Dickson's daily bird schedule goes roughly as follows: Sleep to 8:30 or 9:00 "if I choose to"; wake up and take out the frozen Hanover yellow corn because the birds will eat only Hanover brand yellow corn and only if it hasn't been refrozen; thaw the kernels under warm water; and then wade into the feathery world waiting in her sunroom.

"I uncover Polly first, and she says 'Yum' and 'Good morning.' By then,

Charlie is aware that food is coming, so he's screaming, and everyone else has to join him. After I feed them, I get my coffee. Then Polly comes out, and I clean her cage—take the paper out, throw it away and change it, take the old seeds and water and throw them out. Many mornings I give the birds a bath with a plant mister. They spread their wings when I mist them to get water on all their feathers. As I'm cleaning Polly's cage, Walter is sitting in there, screaming, 'Come out, come out, good-bye!' Two or three hours later, they're all back in their cages, and I can do something else."

Twice a year, too, she takes all the cages apart—nuts, bolts, and all—and scrubs and washes everything with Clorox. It is, Dickson says, both an all-day job and a very necessary one. Tuberculosis and other diseases are rampant among both domestic and wild bird flocks these days. The cleaner she keeps everything, the less chance there is of a local outbreak. ·

Dickson at first said that her birds have probably cost her "an easy ten thousand dollars over the nine years, and probably a good bit more." Overnight, she corrected that figure via e-mail: "I told Sam I had estimated that we have spent $10,000 on the birds in nine years, and he laughed, saying '$10,000 for the first year!' The actual figures are between $5,000 and $9,000 a year, depending on the size of the birds purchased that year."

But while the birds themselves are expensive—a hand-fed and properly socialized blue-and-gold macaw like Walter or Beauregard can run upwards of $1,750—the small things add up, too. A twenty-five-pound bag of seed sells for about $30 and lasts about six weeks. Dickson buys walnuts, a favorite of the big birds, by the fifty-pound bag; pine nuts in the shell are another favorite. Milk cartons of pellets run $6.99 each. Then there's the big container of dish soap that she runs through every two weeks, new cages and avian gyms, not to mention bird-vet bills.

In terms of time, the cost might be greater still. Dickson guesses that she's had "a minimum of fifty, maybe seventy birds in this house over the last nine years—birds who have been good friends." Some are just passing through; others are in for the long haul. The breeding birds, especially, eat up hours, both for the preliminaries (despite their name, male and female lovebirds need lots of introduction) and in the aftermath: hand-feeding the babies takes a good quarter an hour for each bird, each day.

"The longest I've been away from home is two, three days, max, in the last nine years," Dickson says. "If I had nothing but little birds that don't need so much interaction, it would be one thing. But these big guys—if they don't come out every day, they're going to sicken and die. And by the time the bottom of the cage builds up two or three days in a row, you almost need a flamethrower to clean it."

Emotionally, the love of any animal doesn't come without a price tag, either.

Dickson's first nanday conure, Pooh, was, she says, "the sweetest little guy I ever ran into: very loyal, very gentle, and very consistent in his love." As she tells the story of Pooh's wasting illness—of the days at the vet's office, of the shots she had to give Pooh at home—it's clear the loyalty and love ran both ways.

"I'd given my son shots for allergies when he was young, but it was nothing like giving a bird a shot. There's not a lot of body to a nanday conure. I'd say to Sybie, 'Keep an eye on Pooh,' and I'd go back to get a fresh washcloth. I'd come back, and Sybie would be clamped on the side of the cage, watching Pooh in the little hospital I set up in her cage."

Eventually, Pooh had to go to a real animal hospital, run by the vets who tend to all of Dickson's birds. "I went to see Pooh at the hospital every day she was there, from Monday morning until she died. I believe her last day was a Wednesday or Thursday—I'd spent the entire afternoon with her while the vets did a barium series to see what her crop was doing."

That night as every night while Pooh was hospitalized, Dickson talked with the technician in charge of the case before he left around 11:00 P.M. "She seemed better, the technician was encouraged." The next morning, about 6:45, the first vet to arrive at the hospital called to say that Pooh had died during the night.

"Keep in mind that Sybie is here. I truly believe most animals have ESP, but I know birds do. Sybie paced and paced. Finally, I let her out, and she walked into the living room and looked under every piece of furniture. She'd never done that before. Then she sat on the legs of one of the chairs in the sunroom for hours, just grieving."

Which raises again the issue of bird brains and the interior lives of avians: Was Sybie moved by a sense of loss? Or was she simply confused because something that had been there suddenly wasn't?

Peggy Dickson will cite you chapter and verse in favor of the former view. The time, for example, when she heard the music box that Granny, an umbrella cockatoo who lived with Dickson for more than a year, loved to play. "I said to myself, what the heck is that? It was one of those senior moments when I just forgot about the music box, and Walter said, 'Music box.' He's never said it since."

Or the way Beauregard's eyes light up when he's trying to figure out new uses for the block of wood that hangs by a rope in his cage.

Or the way her birds use the nighttime as a kind of study hall to run over the lessons they've learned. "If you go out there, they're quietly talking to themselves, reminding themselves of the things they want to say. They're practicing, repeating what they've heard during the day."

Such matters are in the air as Dickson introduces a visitor to Margo, the muttering yellow-nape Amazon. Margo has just about completed the shift from her hand to the visitor's hand when she suddenly bends over and takes a peck at the stranger.

"No biting!" Dickson says in a sharp voice.

"Beauregard," Margo answers, with as sheepish a look as a yellow-nape Amazon can muster.

"No, Beauregard did not do that," Dickson insists. "You did that."

"Good girl," Margo counters, halfway between what seems a statement and a question.

"Yes," Dickson agrees, "you're a good girl."

And there the matter drops. Maybe, the visitor thinks, it was simply a case of stimulus-response, or of Margo repeating a chain of sounds she had used in similar situations to positive results. But a particularly clever first grader probably couldn't have gotten herself out of trouble any more deftly. Nor could any parent of a first grader have handled Margo's little breach of etiquette with a much better combination of sternness and leniency.

"I would have been so much better a mother if I had had the birds first," Peggy Dickson says. "But I'm so much better with the birds because I was a mother first."

Eighteen

Harry Kloman:
Matters of Fact
and Fiction

In 1970, when Harry Kloman was thirteen, he decided he wanted to read good books. "At that age Pulitzer Prizes sounded important to me. I preferred fiction to nonfiction, so I bought novels that had won Pulitzers, novels I considered classics, like *The Good Earth, Gone With the Wind,* and *The Grapes of Wrath,* at a bookstore near my home in Pittsburgh." Four years later, he joined the Book-of-the-Month Club. One of the first books he received was Gore Vidal's *Burr.* While waiting for *Burr*'s arrival, he bought *Julian* and *Washington, D.C.,* two earlier Vidal novels, because their jackets said they were by the author of *Burr,* "the way paperbacks do when an author has a new bestseller." He liked all three Vidal books. "This was during Nixon's presidency and I was looking for a writer who was as cynical about politics as Watergate had made me."

Kloman's father was a nightclub singer in the nineteen-thirties and then a clerk in a large wholesale drug company. His son remembers him as a grumpy old man who didn't read books—only the paper and some magazines that reaffirmed his own prejudices that the world was going downhill, and that he was right about everything.

Kloman speaks fondly of his mother. "She would have gone to college had she not been the seventh child of immigrant parents in the nineteen-thirties when she was of college age. She is largely responsible for my love of reading. She didn't even mind when I brought *Myra Breckinridge* home when I was in high school, although she knew it was the story of a double transsexual who, as a woman, rapes the All-American Boy."

Kloman describes himself as "the spoiled only child of Jewish parents." He was the first person in his family to go to college. He graduated from Allegheny College in Meadville, Pennsylvania, in 1979, worked for almost a year on a newspaper in Punxsutawney, Pennsylvania, then spent eight years as a reporter, editor, and movie critic for the Meadville *Tribune*. In 1988 he was delighted to return to Pittsburgh ("I rather hate small towns"), and he received a master of fine arts degree in nonfiction writing from the University of Pittsburgh in 1991. He currently reviews movies for *City Paper*, teaches journalism part-time at the University of Pittsburgh, and is the adviser to the daily student paper at Pitt.

Throughout the nineteen-eighties Kloman kept buying each new Vidal book after publication, usually waiting for a remaindered copy, but he would not have said, "My name is Harry, I am a Gore Vidal collector," as he has since 1993. That was a turning-point year. By then he had a hard-cover or paperback copy of all Vidal's collections of essays and most of the Vidal novels that were still in print. He was missing a first edition of Vidal's second novel, *In a Yellow Wood*, published in 1947 when Vidal was twenty-two, and out of print in the United States since that year; his third novel, *The City and the Pillar*, published in 1948 (he owned only the 1965 revised edition), and *Season of Comfort*, Vidal's fourth novel, published in 1949, and out of print in the United States since then.

Kloman realized that the only way to find these first editions would be to visit antiquarian booksellers. He found these three missing first editions. In the process of searching, he came upon first editions of books with dust jackets that he possessed only without dust jackets, and decided to obtain hardcovers with dust jackets of all of Vidal's books and leave it at that. In the process of upgrading his collection of first editions, he bought a few British editions of Vidal's books. "While I was visiting Ann Arbor with a friend in 1994, I bought a British edition of *Hollywood* and said 'This is fun, I'll look for more editions from the U.K.'" He found additional British editions.

Nineteen ninety-four was another significant Vidal-collecting year. "Bookselling discovered the Internet and I discovered the Internet. I love the Internet."

The Internet has made "rare" books much less rare and has expedited the collection process. Since 1994, Kloman has acquired scores of Vidal books and other items for his collection: videos of Vidal movies, playbills of his Broadway plays, magazines and journals with articles by or about Vidal, writings copied on two pilgrimages to the Vidal Archives in Madison, Wisconsin—including four collections of unpublished poetry from the nineteen-thirties and nineteen-forties and *Some Desperate Adventure,* an unpublished novel probably written in the fifties—and numerous books about Vidal. "I'm a book whore. There's almost nothing related to Vidal I won't buy." He bought a teleplay Vidal wrote in 1955 on amazon.com's auction site and a 1965 U.K. paperback on Yahoo! Auctions.

What has given Harry Kloman the greatest pleasure in the last half-dozen years is collecting foreign editions of Vidal, which would have been impossible without the Internet. "Internet dealers are usually quite lovely people. I once asked Misha, a dealer in Kiev, if a Russian book he had found for me had a dust jacket. He did not know that term, and so he replied, 'The book is not dusty, it is very clean.' When I explained what 'dust jacket' meant, he wrote, 'Let us both laugh together.'

"A book searcher in Germany has added books in Albanian, Estonian, and Slovene as well as German to my collection. I met a Danish fellow on the Net who found some books for me in Danish, Swedish, and Norwegian. He wanted some tea from a California company called the Republic of Tea, which doesn't ship overseas, so I sent it to him. When I get a book in a new language, I try to learn a little about the language. The Danish title for Vidal's novel *Messiah,* which is *Troldmandens Laerling,* translates as *The Sorcerer's Apprentice.*"

Kloman has tracked down Vidal's books in German on a German book site (http://www.zvab.com) and in Greek on Books-in-Greek.com. A man in Belgrade who was aware of Kloman's Web page (http://www.pitt.edu/~kloman/vidalframe.html), which is a catalog of his Gore Vidal collection, contacted him to ask if he wanted a copy of a new Serbo-Croatian edition of a small Vidal essay collection.

By the end of 1999 Kloman had acquired Vidal books in twenty-eight foreign languages. In December, he discovered an Iranian bookdealer in Baltimore, who ordered *Julian* and *Creation* for him from Iran. The prospect of adding a twenty-ninth language, Persian, and also a seventh alphabet to his collection pleased him.

At the turn of the millennium, Kloman was fretting about the arrival of these books. As he would later e-mail a friend, "Do you remember back in the nineteen-sixties when they sent Apollo spaceships to the Moon, and when the orbiter would go behind the Moon, they lost radio contact, and they wouldn't know if the spaceship was okay until it emerged from behind the dark of the Moon? Well, that's my metaphor for when I have books in the mail to me. When the book is still in the hands of the bookseller, it's orbiting the Moon. But when the bookseller places it in the mail, it's out of radio contact, and thus on the dark side of the Moon."

Kloman usually asks to have books sent to him by registered mail and rejoices to come home from movie screenings or from his "Introduction to Journalism" course to find the herald of the safe arrival of a Vidal purchase—a yellow postal pickup notice in his mailbox. The next morning he goes to the post office to claim it, one of his favorite book-collecting rituals. He was pleasantly surprised by the Iranian books. He had expected two paperbacks, and instead received four hardbacks: two volumes of *Julian* and two of *Creation*. "I like hardbacks best of all. I was walking on air. I conducted the sacred ritual of putting them in dust jacket protectors and then put them on my shelves." He admires the calligraphic quality of alphabets like Persian, with which he is unfamiliar, "and the books from Iran have very vivid covers."

Kloman rents a one-bedroom apartment in the Squirrel Hill section of Pittsburgh, near the university. His living room contains bookshelves that house his Pulitzer novels (he has copies of all seventy-five winners) and some of his Vidals. Most of his 740 Vidals are in his study/office on four bookshelves and three rectangular platforms mounted on walls. Paperbacks on some shelves are doubled up—a row of paperbacks is pushed to the back, a second row pulled to the front so the books are at the edge.

All U.S. first editions are in one bookcase, with others thrown in because he needs to make maximum use of space. All foreign languages are also in one bookcase, with a few scattered elsewhere in "a reasonable way." All U.K. editions are together on three shelves on one bookcase. All plays are together. All leather Franklin Mint and Easton editions are together. Miscellaneous items take up several shelves.

The books on each shelf run in order of height, from left to right. "The height thing is my major idiosyncrasy. Some friends think I should have every edition I own of each book together, but that's not necessary. I know where everything is. I pass by these books dozens of time a day and I've seen the collection grow one or two books at a time. When I get new books I do a slight adjustment. I make things fit. I have no room to do any rearranging. I do have a shelf and a half of books that I can't fit into the study/office or the living room in a large walk-in closet."

In 1994, Kloman was at the Gotham Book Mart in Manhattan. He already knew that Vidal had written three mysteries in the late nineteen-forties, under the pseudonym Edgar Box, when he needed more money than he was earning from the sale of his novels. Vidal acknowledged authorship of these books and Kloman owned them. At the Gotham Book Mart he saw two other books among the Vidals of Andreas Brown, the shop's owner. One was a paperback exclusive called *Thieves Fall Out,* written by Cameron Kay. The other was a paperback copy of *Cry Shame,* by Katherine Everard. Brown had asked Vidal, who often came to the shop to sign books, if he had written those books and Vidal had said yes. Kloman bought both paperbacks.

"I still *needed* the original Dutton Katherine Everard 1950 hardcover—with dust jacket, of course." It was called *A Star's Progress.* "Over the years I've found two booksellers who each once held a copy. Sold long ago. In California, at Vagabond Books, owner Patricia Graham has a signed copy of the Everard hardcover. She bought it from Vidal while rummaging through boxes of books in the basement of his home on Outpost Drive in Hollywood Hills. When she saw it, she remembered reading the book as a young girl in the early 1950s. It was salacious for its time, and so it stayed in her memory. She told Gore that she liked the book and wanted to buy a copy. He said, 'You have bad taste in literature' and sold her one (autographed).

"I visited Pat's shop in the summer of 1999 while in Los Angeles. She wouldn't sell the damned book to me! And she had it safely at home, not in her shop, so I had never even seen the book and its dust jacket. There's a copy in the L.A. public library but I didn't have time to go see it when I was there. Frankly, I didn't want to: it would only have upset me too much, and I might have just lunged for the door with the book in my hand, hoping to break through security and disappear into the mean streets of L.A.

"After years of searching, I thought that my only hope for finding a copy of the book was approaching Vidal himself. I had interviewed him in 1991 when he was in Pittsburgh playing a small part in a movie. In 1999 I sent him a letter in which I told him of my extensive collection and, after a few paragraphs of gentle flattery and a mention of some unusual foreign editions I'd rounded up, I dropped the question: Would he please please please consider selling me a copy of *A Star's Progress*—price no object.

"He wrote back to me, saying he didn't know that a copy of one of his novels was in Albanian and Estonian or that another had been published in Slovene—these editions were all unauthorized. He also wrote that he had only one copy of *A Star's Progress* and would leave it to me in his will."

Kloman knew Vidal was kidding but was pleased to have an engaging letter written to him by the author. He suspected that Vidal collectors with more resources had scoured the country and gobbled up every extant copy. He consoled himself with the fact that he had the paperback and had of course read it. "But of course, with book collecting, it's not just the words. It's the object, and this object has eluded me."

Kloman is up in the morning by seven o'clock—earlier if a book is on the dark side of the moon and has "murdered [his] sleep"—and clicks on to the Advanced Book Exchange site. On Saturday morning, May 13, 2000, Kloman clicked on to http://www.abe.com and under "author" typed in EVERARD. To his astonishment, Wonder Book and Video, in Frederick, Maryland, had a copy of Katherine Everard's *A Star's Progress* with a dust jacket for fifteen dollars. From the price he was sure no one there was aware of its real author. He e-mailed an order for the book and telephoned, but the store was closed on the weekend.

"It was a long weekend for me, worrying that another maniac Vidalophile out there had found it first." On Monday, the fifteenth, he learned that no one had beat him to it. He paid more than fifteen dollars to have it sent UPS overnight, but considering the fact he had expected to pay hundreds or even thousands of dollars for it, the cost was trivial. On the sixteenth the book was sitting on his desk, its dust jacket preserved in a Brodart cover that he had installed moments after opening the box. "The dust jacket is quite beautiful. I hope to scan it soon and put it on my Web pages."

He spotted differences between the two editions. The paperback had a three-page prologue that hadn't appeared in the hardcover original. "This prologue makes the narrative begin much more soberly, giving the reader a strong sense of impending doom, as if to proclaim at the start, 'The woman you will read about here *will* be punished for her scandalous life.' Back in the nineteen-forties, paperbacks were published for less 'sophisticated' audiences than hardbacks. Even the paperback title takes away the hardcover's sense of success—*A Star's Progress* (she's a star and she succeeds)—and replaces it with a scolding: *Cry Shame*. I'm searching for numerous other items for my collection and I'll be glad when I find them, but this is definitely the crown jewel."

Kloman put the jewel in the crown on a blue cantilevered platform shelf all by itself. It reclines against a clear plastic display piece, a gift from a salesperson at a nearby Barnes & Noble.

In the summer of 2000, Kloman found a 1989 paperback he hadn't known existed of *Kalki*, a novel that Vidal published in 1978 about a death cult and that Kloman considers to be "a very good read." He also bought the Hebrew edition of *Creation*—his thirtieth language and his eighth alphabet. Then a Latvian librarian found him a Latvian edition of *Washington, D.C.*—language number thirty-one. "I can follow enough Latvian to determine that they removed a mild sexually explicit passage from the book. I had suspected they would." He bought a "Vidal for Congress" button on eBay for $205 after a bidding war.

"I'd expected to pay at least a thousand dollars for the Katherine Everard, so I could sink my savings into that extravagance. I've been able to afford almost everything of Vidal's that I've wanted. I'm single. I drive a Honda Civic DX, no air conditioner, no sunroof. My apartment is simple. I've never cared much about the aesthetics of my surroundings.

"I buy every new edition of Vidal's books published in America and every foreign edition I come across. This is a pastime. It's one of the ways I happily pass the time. I don't want to complete the collection and I probably never will. I know of two foreign languages Vidal has been published in that I don't yet have—Lithuanian and Thai. Once I find them I'll go on to search for others. I'm willing to bet that many of Vidal's books will soon be published in China, if they haven't been already."

Nineteen

Judy Konnerth:
Two by Two

Step into a room in the home of Judy Konnerth—any room will do—
and you'll see examples, striking examples, of her passion on display. Judy
Konnerth and her husband, Jim, collect Noah's arks. There are over a hundred of them in their three-story house in northern Illinois.

Jim Konnerth, an antique-toy collector, was responsible for the purchase
of the first ark, a mass-produced contemporary model with resin animals
that he and his wife had seen together at a neighborhood decorative arts
store in 1987. Three months later he brought it home for her, saying, "This
is the good-wife-of-the-week award."

As a child, Judy Konnerth had enjoyed playing with dolls and doll-
houses. "I had a small tin kitchen, all one piece with cabinets, a sink, a dishwasher, and a refrigerator," she says. "This self-contained unit had little
plastic dishes, silverware, glasses, cups, food that went into the refrigerator,
and a broom that went into the broom closet. I still have that kitchen. I
guess the arks are similar to these toys that came with accessories, and there
is a similarity to 'playing house' and 'playing ark.' All those wonderful animals fit so neatly into the ark. I knew when I saw that ark in the neighborhood store I was smitten."

Several years later the Konnerths were at the Chicago Antique Toy Show,
which is held three times a year at the Kane County Fairgrounds in St.
Charles, Illinois. Judy Konnerth walked into the main building, spied an ark
sitting on the top shelf in a far-off booth, and headed toward it "like a hom-

ing pigeon." The booth was Marianne and Bob Schneider's. "They brought the ark down for me and let me unwrap all the animals and play with them," Konnerth says. "Then we asked the price and I almost started to cry because it was so much more than I felt we could pay for an ark. But they agreed to take time payments from a couple they had just met. The Schneiders are antique-toy dealers from Lancaster, Pennsylvania, and very special people. Marianne called me sometime the next week simply to see if I was having fun playing ark and animals." Konnerth remembers saying she wanted only one antique ark. "And I really meant it at the time."

In June 1992, while the wife of the week was visiting relatives in Ohio, Jim Konnerth went out to the Kane County Fairgrounds in his red Corvette convertible. He was walking the show and came to the Schneiders' booth. "I've got an anniversary coming up in August and I need an ark," he said. They didn't have one in the booth, but they had one in their van. A collector from Kansas had asked the Schneiders to bring it and had failed to show up.

Marianne Schneider took Jim Konnerth out to inspect the ark. It was big and beautiful, with a deep red hull, gray-blue sides, three windows on each side separated by Grecian columns, a wavy roof, and a paper applied frieze. It came with many animals as well as with the entire "Noah family"— Noah, his wife, their three sons Shem, Ham, and Japheth, and their wives. He bought it. The ark was too large for the Corvette. The Schneiders drove it to his house in their van. The ark was put in the basement.

When Judy Konnerth returned home, she was instructed to stay out of the basement. On August 23, the Konnerths' twenty-third wedding anniversary, she unveiled the ark. "I was speechless," she says. "That ark has incredible animals, sixty-nine pairs of them, including spiders and grasshoppers. I couldn't believe there would be spiders on an ark." Bob Schneider had already built a flat stand for the ark and a zigzag ramp leading up to it, to display the animals. "The anniversary ark," as it is still known, was made in the middle of the nineteenth century in the Erzgebirge region of southeastern Germany, also the first antique ark's place of origin. "The second ark made my arks a collection," Judy Konnerth says.

According to Genesis 6:19-22, when the animals entered the ark Noah built to escape the flood, they did so two by two. Arks entered the Konnerths' home at a faster clip. Jim Konnerth is a manufacturer's representative for lighting companies; Judy Konnerth and the Konnerths' married daughter also work in the business. The family likes to celebrate birthdays, Christmas, and other holidays.

In 1993, three arks were added to the Konnerths' collection. One was an

Ireland ark, patented by a man named George Ireland, an American toy-maker who is believed to have taken a German ark and put a scroll mechanism in it; as you turn it, the animals move in a procession. Another was a German ark with an unusual oval window design and an animal set that was exceptional for its carved anatomical details. The third was a small, plain, barge-style ark. On one side is a door, half the ark's length, that opens on canvas hinges. On the other side, painted above and between two windows are the words "This model of the house that Noah lived in 4172 years ago was given to little Ellen Charlotte Streatfeild by her Godpapa on the First of May 1829 Anno Domini." Konnerth assumed it was an English ark, because the child's name struck her as English and her godfather had addressed her in English.

"I remember opening up the three boxes and feeling my heart pound," Judy Konnerth says. "I couldn't believe them. They were fantastic. I had read an article about the Ireland ark, but it said there were only three known to exist in the world. I was sure I would never have one, and here I was holding one. The oval-windowed ark is great, but it's the animals that speak to me. Many of them even have ribs showing. And when I touch an ark that was given to a child in 1829, I feel I'm truly holding on to history. I've always called that ark 'the history ark.'"

Dealers are often instrumental in assembling collections. "Without a doubt, Bob and Marianne built ours," Konnerth says. "We didn't have the time to travel to Europe and the East Coast and they worked very hard to find us wonderful arks." In the past decade the Konnerths also bought arks from a few other dealers in New York and London, and, after they were invited to join the Antique Toy Collectors' Club, they bought from collectors they met at the club's biannual meetings. "Arks pass subtly from one collector to another," Bob Schneider says. "And Judy didn't collect, as many people do, for the sake of collecting. Through collecting, she has gained a great deal of knowledge about all the different arks that are out there."

In the spring of 1992, Konnerth came upon an article published the previous December in *Antiques Magazine,* written by Mary Audrey Apple, a dealer who specialized in German toys. Apple, a librarian by training, had spent time in the Erzgebirge region and had become an expert on the arks of this area. She wrote that by the early part of the eighteenth century, the region's mines were depleted. Its soil was poor. Residents turned to the forests for a livelihood. They made small wares, and they began to make toys for a good part of the rest of the world. Noah's arks were among the many wood and papier-mâché toys made in villages like Grunhainichen,

Seiffen, Olbernhau, Waldkirchen, and Hallbach. The method of producing ark animals was unique to the Erzgebirge. The villagers took trunks of pine trees, cut them into sections, hollowed them out, and mounted them on lathes to shape the contours of the particular animal being made. A ring of horses, cows, or lions was sliced like a cake, with each yielding about seventy-five animals. The sliced animals were then rounded by hand and sanded; ears and tails were glued on before the animals were passed to other villagers to be painted.

Apple studied the catalogs compiled by German wholesalers, which showed the diversity in size, style, and price of the arks offered by toy-makers. America was a major market, and Erzgebirge arks were sold to FAO Schwarz, Montgomery Ward, Sears Roebuck, and John Wanamaker until the depression that followed World War I in Germany. By then arks were being made in England and in America.

Konnerth kept buying examples of many styles and sizes of Erzgebirge arks. She found an old Seiffen ring, which is more difficult to obtain than most arks. "Until you see one, you don't understand the slice-and-carve animals," Konnerth says. "Arks and animals were often parted and it's almost impossible to be positive that a specific ark came with the specific animals currently with it, but after a while you get a sense of which animals belong with an ark and which don't."

Judy Konnerth also bought a Converse ark (made in Massachusetts), Bliss arks (made in Rhode Island) and arks made by Bumpa, an early division of the Milton Bradley Company. She bought a rare early twentieth-century German biscuit-tin ark (most biscuit arks are English), an American tin sand-pail ark, a nineteen-twenties ark with log-cabin sides, a German cardboard candy-container ark, an English ark with paperboard flat animals on wooden carts with wheels, a German double-decker ark, a German zoo ark featuring six animal cages, a German Tyrolean ark with a horsehead prow, a German tin litho ark with tin animals, a German ark with windows edged in cardboard, a German ark with paper litho animals, and a German "musical ark" with animals that scroll by when a little crank on the back side is wound. "It goes 'plunka, plunka,'" she says. "That ark is quite small, about eight inches, but I've never seen another and no one else I know has, either."

Another favorite is a small Erzgebirge ark decorated with colored straw. "It's the most pristine ark I've ever seen," Konnerth says. "It has a sliding panel on one side and a top that, when lifted off, shows a storage area inside. It's the most spectacularly colored ark of all I have. I'm amazed that an ark that's about one hundred twenty years old can be so brightly colored and in such fabulous condition. Arks make my heart sing."

In December 1996, the Brandywine River Museum in Chadds Ford, Pennsylvania, borrowed twenty arks from the Konnerths' collection for its Christmas exhibit. The lead piece was the German ark with the unusual oval window design and the animals with the exceptionally carved anatomical details, including cows with udders. Another ark that traveled to Brandywine was an ark with a God's eye on the prow. "This unusual ark has been painted to resemble a wood-sided barn with simulated water lapping at its base," the museum exhibit card read. "The roof is hinged and the interior is fitted with animal stalls, feed troughs, gates, and stairways between the floors. This ark would be considered an expensive model and is matched with an equally expensive, fine quality animal set."

The "history ark" was also shown at the Brandywine River Museum. Mary Audrey Apple, who had been consulted by the museum, telephoned Judy Konnerth and questioned her about the ark. Konnerth went to visit Apple in Atlanta, history ark in hand. "I remember Mary Audrey holding that ark and saying that it was indeed what she had thought it was when I described it to her over the phone," Konnerth says. "She told me that it was the oldest example of an ark she had ever seen pictured in a German toy catalog. That was a very humbling experience. I wondered how on earth I was chosen to be the protector of such a piece of history. And that is really how I feel. I am just the temporary keeper of all these pieces that must be preserved. I hope I'm a good caretaker for the next generation."

Not long after the twenty arks returned to the Konnerths' living room, family room, dining room, kitchen, sunroom, basement, and bedrooms, they bought, at an East Coast antique show, the ark Konnerth knows is the finest she will ever own. The ark itself, made in the Erzgebirge region around 1860, is handsome, with an unusual hand-painted frieze ("Most are paper," Konnerth says) and the Biblical dove with an olive branch in its beak—dispatched by Noah to see if the flood waters had receded—painted on its roof. But for Konnerth it was the quality and the quantity of the animals and birds—291 pairs—that made this ark particularly special. "I'm enthralled by them," she says. "Especially by the eight pairs of primates.

"Also the birds. Most arks have quite a few birds, and some are nicely painted, but normally the birds are not highly sought after. These birds are out of this world. On one of the pairs the male has this little hangy downy thing under its neck. The female peacock is, of course, quite plain, but the male is resplendent. Then there is some bird, who knows what kind, that is bright orange with separate wings applied after the bird was carved. I could go on and on about the birds. I've never seen anything like them. Plus there are flies on this ark. And crickets and grasshoppers and two different pairs of butterflies, all of which have antennae. The detail is phenomenal. There are two pairs of cats—a pair of calicoes and a pair of tabbies." The Konnerths have three cats, one named Noah.

The largest ark the Konnerths own—or are ever likely to own—is one the Schneiders saw on eBay in July 1999. "It was a display piece made for Harrods' toy department in London in December 1992," Judy Konnerth says. "A woman with a shop in South Dakota apparently begged Harrods to sell it after the store no longer needed it, and Harrods obliged her. Some years later, she realized she had no room for it, so she put it on eBay. The Schneiders called Jim and asked if he wanted it. He said yes. It was to be a surprise for our thirtieth anniversary, and it was a huge surprise."

The Harrods ark was supposed to go in the basement, but it was too big to make it down the Konnerths' stairs. It entered the house through the kitchen's double French doors. From the kitchen it was carried through another set of double French doors into the sunroom, where it has stayed. "With that ark, I no longer have a sunroom," Konnerth says. The sunroom has an eight-and-a-half-foot ceiling. The ark consists of a base (which is two and a half feet tall and five feet wide, and reminds Bob Schneider of a hot tub); a mountain that fits into the base (it, too, is two and a half feet tall); and an ark that is almost two feet tall. Glued to the mountain's ledges are numerous pairs of animals, most of them ranging in height from three to five inches. The five-and-a-half-inch giraffes are the tallest, the ladybugs on lilypads, the frogs on leaves, and the mice with chunks of cheese are among the smallest.

"Ark collectors tend to buy arks that look alike," Bob Schneider says. "Judy Konnerth's collection reflects her catholic outlook. She has the capacity to admire the early nineteenth-century 'history ark' and the glossy late twentieth-century Harrods ark. And while most collectors stop when they have, say, twenty-five arks, Judy's enthusiasm for acquiring additional arks is undiminished. It's no wonder she has the largest collection of arks in the country."

Konnerth can think of a dozen arks she would still like to buy. One is a Bliss ark with two dormer windows. "Once, early in our collecting years, the Schneiders offered us eight arks and we couldn't afford them all," she says. "I did find a Bliss ark with one dormer window, but I haven't seen another two-dormer Bliss ark, so I'm sorry that one got away." She longs to own two transformer arks, which she describes as "relatives of the Ireland ark"; a little toy penny-bank—a tin ark with a slit in the roof for the coin to be dropped in—which she has seen in a museum in London; an ark with tiny propellers (the Forbes Magazine Collection, better known for its

Fabergé eggs, has two of them); a whalebone ark, which is in the Museum of American Folk Art in New York City; and a few arks that are in the hands of private collectors of her acquaintance.

The most elusive ark she would like to have is one she has never seen. It is known as the peephole ark. "The only person I know who has seen it is Noel Barrett, one of the appraisers on *Antiques Road Show,*" Konnerth says. "Noel told me it has Noah and a diorama of animals in the hull of the ark, which can be seen through a hole in the hull. Knowing it only by his verbal description makes it especially enticing. Still, it would probably be better not to acquire every ark in existence. In life, it's always better to have something to look forward to, so I don't ever want to have them all."

Twenty

Steve Spreckelmeier: All Steamed Up

Here is how Steve Spreckelmeier happened to come into possession of a 168-ton, nonfunctioning, seventy-five-year-old locomotive that would have to be moved halfway across the country:

"A gentleman by the name of Henry Todaro, out in Texas, contacted a friend of mine, Edward Archer, in Lantana, here in Florida, asking if he knew anyone who wanted to buy a steam engine. The only thing Ed could think of was to call me."

Two things to point out: First, it wasn't just any old steam engine. No. 253 was one of twenty-nine engines ordered by the Florida East Coast Railway in 1923 and manufactured at the American Locomotive Company's Richmond, Virginia, plant. Along with two lookalikes, engines 251 and 252, No. 253 had been delivered in July 1924 and had run on the FEC for a dozen years, until a September 1935 hurricane destroyed the railroad's southern connection to Key West and finished off its already shaky finances.

Sold to the Louisiana & Arkansas Railroad as part of the FEC's bankruptcy proceedings, 251, 252, and 253 had continued in service for another two decades. Then, in 1956, 253's running mates had been scrapped, and 253 and its tender had been run out to the end of a spur line and placed on display at a fairgrounds in Texarkana, Texas, where they had sat for more than three decades as a monument to the Buchanan family, who had founded the Louisiana & Arkansas line and first brought trains to Texarkana.

By the time Steve Spreckelmeier got word of 253's existence, in 1998, an interstate had been built through the fairgrounds, and the engine had been moved to Texana Tank Car and Manufacturing, four miles outside of Texarkana in the small industrial enclave of Nash, Texas. Of all the twenty-nine engines ordered by the FEC seventy-five years earlier, No. 253 was the last survivor.

Just as important, Steve Spreckelmeier wasn't any old train enthusiast.

"I'd been involved with full-size steam engines for twenty-six years by then. When Ed called me, I contacted Mr. Todaro immediately. The Louisiana & Arkansas people had had the good measure to build a roof over the engine when they put it on display—a kind of pole barn. Once I found that out, I said, 'We've got a hot cookie here!'"

Thus began the "253 Project," named in honor of what was to become the object of Steve Spreckelmeier's affections: FEC Engine No. 253.

Steve Spreckelmeier was born and raised in Cincinnati, Ohio, a center of the rail industry since the late eighteen-thirties, when four steam-locomotive manufacturers were competing there for business. At least once a week, Spreckelmeier's grandfather would get his son, Larry, after school, and the two would head down to watch the steam engines come through the local stations. Larry Spreckelmeier would go on to become an industrial designer, but he never forgot those childhood expeditions. Twenty-six years before Steve set out to buy No. 253, his father had purchased his own steam engine: the Louisiana & Arkansas Railroad's No. 509. That was in 1972, when Steve was just eight years old, and where steam engines are concerned, it's been pretty much a nonstop love affair ever since.

Larry and Steve worked on No. 509 for eight years before they ever got her to steam. Along the way, Steve also started volunteering weekends at the Hocking Valley Scenic Railway in Ohio. While other teenagers were racing cars along the country roads outside Cincinnati, he was powering a restored steam-propelled train at full throttle along Ohio's country tracks. "When you're running a four-hundred-thirty-ton train at speeds of seventy miles an hour, it's quite a rush. The adrenaline gets moving. The tracks are pounding. You can't hear anything. Dirt and dust are flying everywhere."

After high school, Spreckelmeier enlisted in the navy, serving a two-year stint in the early eighties in San Diego. A construction job brought him back across the continent to Florida, where he met his wife and eventually found work with a powder-coating company that does high-quality paint jobs. But whatever he did during the day, Spreckelmeier was never far from steam engines in his off-hours. In the navy and afterwards, he got involved with the railroad museum in Campo, California, about an hour east of San

Diego on the Mexican border. There, he helped put back into operation a steam locomotive that had once run on the Feather River Railroad in the Sierra Nevadas. In Florida, Spreckelmeier signed on with other rail museums, helping out wherever he could. All along the way, he says, he was learning at the feet of people who knew steam from the inside out.

"I've been involved with these people all my life, and they pass on these little bits of information, these do's and don'ts. It's been invaluable."

Clearly, he has listened well.

A sign hangs over the workshop behind Steve Spreckelmeier's house in the southwest corner of Broward County, about twenty minutes from downtown Fort Lauderdale: LAKE PARK & WESTERN RAILWAY CO., framed inside a neat, black-and-red diamond pattern. The name and logo are of Spreckelmeier's invention—he started the shop when he was living in Lake Park, Florida, near Palm Beach, and he liked the sound of it all—but as he was to discover, the name is not original. The first Lake Park & Western was a narrow-gauge short line that ran a mile or two into the woods off the Florida East Coast Railway main line, to service a business that cut and creosoted railroad ties for the FEC.

Inside the Lake Park & Western shop sit milling machines, drill presses, three different welding machines, and a crane set on rails "so I don't have to be calling the neighbors every time I need to move something." Rare railroad manuals are shelved in a corner office. But it's what Spreckelmeier has built from scratch in the shop that catches the eye: the centerpiece of his railway, Engine No. 25. Modeled after an engine built in 1913 by Baldwin Locomotive Works for the two-foot-gauge Sandy River & Rangeley Lakes Railroad in Maine, No. 25 is a third the size of the original, weighs twenty-eight hundred pounds, burns coal, and is plenty large enough for the engineer (Engineer S. Spreckelmeier) to sit on.

Once Spreckelmeier throws open the doors to the back of his two-acre property, the grandeur of his vision is revealed. Inside the shop, his locomotive sits on a piece of elevated track. Beyond the shop doors, the elevated track leads to a raised ridge of land that Spreckelmeier created out of fill in the near-infinite flatness of southeast Florida. Suddenly, instead of cruising a mechanic's shop, you're in a private railroad world. A platform eventually will sit at the back of the shop. Beyond that, the track runs along the ridge, across a trestle bridge Spreckelmeier built over a culvert he dug and poured the concrete for. From there, his imagination is the only real limit.

Spreckelmeier is planning a railroad turntable, fourteen feet in diameter, near the trestle bridge. Once the train circles around the perimeter of the back and side yards, he intends for it to cross in front of his house on removable tracks. Further adornments are to be determined, but it's a near certainty that the train will sport a three-chime steam whistle that can announce its presence all through the neighborhood. Larry Spreckelmeier has a national-caliber collection of steam whistles, and that apple hasn't fallen far from the tree, either. The whole railroad is being built on 7 1/2-inch-gauge track, about seven and a half times narrower than the standard rail gauge of 56 1/2 inches, which, as Steve points out, is just a tad wider than the space occupied by two horses' backsides.

"It all goes back to chariots," he says. "Their wheels had to be spaced wider than the butts of the two horses that pulled them. Wagon wheels are fifty-six and a half inches, too, because they kept breaking axles when they got outside the old chariot ruts. When it came time to lay rails, they used the same gauge."

The 7 1/2-inch-gauge track only scratches at the surface of Spreckelmeier's ultimate ambitions. He's also restoring a two-foot-gauge steam locomotive built in 1972 by Crown Metal Products for a West Palm Beach amusement park known as Lion Country Safari. Taken out of commission after three years, the locomotive sat rusting for more than two decades before Spreckelmeier got his hands on it. Now, with the engine almost ready to run, he's thinking about trading in his two-acre property for five acres and laying two-foot track instead of the smaller gauge. Ever since Collis Huntington, Leland Stanford, Thomas "Doc" Durant, and the others who conquered nature and geology to build the transcontinental railroad, train men have thought big thoughts and dreamed big dreams.

When Engine No. 253 came silently chugging into Steve Spreckelmeier's life, he had the knowledge, the experience, the tools, and the lore. He even had the time, in a sense. Both Spreckelmeier and his wife were holding down full-time jobs—she as an executive in the insurance and finance industry—when they decided one of them needed to stay home and attend to their young daughter and infant son.

"My wife does quite well, and we're concerned parents. We love our kids, and we thought this would be in our best interests. The powder-coating company was expanding, and it was a stressful job. I'm a workaholic to begin with, and I saw people not much older than me dying of heart attacks. We thought, Let's hold off here. Our daughter was already in school, but we didn't want to just throw our son into day care."

Being a stay-at-home dad wouldn't lessen Spreckelmeier's workload, but it would give him the flexibility to take on the 253 Project and the shop time to work on it. First, though, he had to buy the engine and move all 168 very immobile tons of it.

Purchasing No. 253 would prove relatively easy. Shirley Brooks, the owner of the locomotive and of Texana Tank Car and Manufacturing, where it sat, was asking five thousand dollars, essentially the engine's scrap value. Spreckelmeier says, "I called Robert Bates, a longtime steam friend of mine. He was in his mid-fifties and mechanically a wizard. We hemmed and hawed, and after about a week and a half, we said, 'Let's buy a locomotive.'"

Moving their purchase would be the bigger challenge, as others had already learned. Back in 1988, just before the interstate came through the Texarkana fairgrounds where No. 253 had been on display, a group called the Yuma Valley Live Steamers from Arizona had bought the engine and its tender from the Louisiana & Arkansas Railroad, with the intent of hauling them back to Arizona.

"They moved it over to Texana Tank Car while they figured out how to get it to Yuma," Spreckelmeier says. "They had to move it by truck, but the Department of Transportation people said no. The bridges couldn't take all that weight. So they started to disassemble it. They spent thirty days at the tank car company, got exhausted, and ran out of money. They had spent almost ten thousand dollars and hadn't moved it an inch."

Another group of steam enthusiasts out of Kansas made a try at buying and moving the engine, also without much luck or progress. Meanwhile Shirley Brooks, who had been renting the siding space at his tank car company, took over ownership to fulfill back payments, and there No. 253 was sitting when the Spreckelmeier team bought it.

"It was so far away," Spreckelmeier says. "That had stopped everyone else, but I love challenges." And he had one clear advantage over the Yuma group: No. 253 could be brought all the way to Florida the same way it had gotten to Texarkana—by rail.

"It was nerve-racking dealing with the railroads, cranes, the insurance companies. It took me five months of preparation after the sale before we ever went out there. I made sixteen hundred hours of phone calls getting this organized. People move steam engines all the time. I've seen it. I knew what it took. But I didn't realize all the ulcer-making crap that goes along with it. I almost pulled out of it a couple times. I thought, This is crazy. I'm trying to move an iceberg. But it was a good experience for me because I could intermingle with all these top-end railroad people. And I thought this was going to be neat—to save an FEC locomotive and to bring it back home."

Happily, once Spreckelmeier started jawboning the railroads that would need to get involved, they thought it would be neat, too.

The Texas Northeastern Railroad was the first to get involved, hauling the flatcars that carried No. 253 and its tender over to Texarkana, where the Union Pacific was to pick the cars up and carry them on to New Orleans. There were problems almost from the first. Spreckelmeier says he had to wake up the Union Pacific president in the middle of the night to break a stalemate over transferring the flatcars, but the load got to New Orleans and the Union Pacific eventually decided to donate its services. CSX, the old Chessie system, took over in the Crescent City, carrying the load to Jacksonville, where it was transferred to the Florida East Coast Railroad for the run down to Hialeah. At Hialeah, CSX took over again, carrying No. 253 and its tender to their final destination, the Gold Coast Railroad Museum, near the Metrozoo at an abandoned naval air station in South Miami, about a half hour from Spreckelmeier's home.

The FEC donated all its services, and CSX turned back half its shipping costs to the museum. In all, a trip that should have cost about twenty thousand dollars had cost a fraction of that, and Steve Spreckelmeier—volunteer head of the mechanical division at the Gold Coast museum and volunteer chief of volunteers as well—finally had a full-size steam locomotive to work on, almost in his own backyard.

"Steam engines are always 'she' or 'her,'" Spreckelmeier explains. "You almost have to love them to work on them. They beat you up. The other day I was in the smoke box. When I got out, you couldn't tell what color my coveralls were."

Around his feet and knees as he speaks are No. 253's "appurtenances"—a lovely railroaders' term for the staggering complexity of parts in almost any piece of train equipment. In this case, the appurtenances include an injector feed line, an oil preheater, a smoke box petticoat pipe, a cross-compound air pump, and much more, all pulled off of Engine No. 253 and waiting for treatment. Spreckelmeier estimates that, counting every nut and bolt, the locomotive might be made up of 850,000 parts. He photographs his project section by section and has created a grid to keep track of every inch of the locomotive.

"Nothing goes unmarked," he says. "Otherwise, when we go to put it back together, we won't know what goes with what. The memory is good, but not that good."

The Louisiana & Arkansas line had done well by Old 253 when they took her out of service, and not only by putting a roof over her head to prevent rust and aging. "They pickled the thing down, and left all the valves open," Spreckelmeier says. "There wasn't a thing we couldn't open."

Still, enormous work remains. Some of it gets done on site, by Spreckelmeier and his team of volunteers, because part of the idea behind the 253 Project is to let museum visitors see a locomotive restoration in progress. "People are fascinated to watch you work on something that requires a forty-eight-inch crescent wrench. The wrench is as big as many of the kids who are asking questions."

Some of the work can be done thirty minutes up the road at the headquarters and sole outpost of the Lake Park & Western Railway. "There's probably two hundred valves in that locomotive that will have to be rebuilt in my shop," Spreckelmeier says. But other parts will need to be shipped out to other experts. Spreckelmeier and Bates took on two additional partners in the 253 Project once they got the locomotive to South Florida. One of those partners, Allen C. Harper, is president and CEO of American Heritage Railways, the parent company of the narrow-gauge Durango & Silverton Narrow Gauge Railroad in southern Colorado and the equally scenic Great Smoky Mountains Railroad. Harper's shop will be doing some of the most demanding restoration work.

In the meantime, No. 253 waits at the Gold Coast Railroad Museum in the company of some of the nation's most distinguished retired rolling stock, including a dome car built in 1949 for the Union Pacific's *Silver Crescent* passenger train and the *Ferdinand Magellan*, a 1928 Pullman sleeper that was refitted and heavily armored in 1942 for the use of President Franklin Delano Roosevelt.

Among such beauties, Engine No. 253 is something of a beast. Fifteen and a half feet high and thirty-eight feet long, she has a boiler large enough for a man to stand in. As locomotives get designated, No. 253 is a 0-8-0. That means she has neither the small lead wheels nor the trailer wheels that help guide an engine's main wheels as she speeds through turns. Engine No. 253 rolls on eight drivers only—fifty-one inches in diameter, with steel "tires" formed to cast-iron wheels. Her tender carries two thousand gallons of Bunker C oil—basically, crude oil—and fifty-five hundred gallons of water. (An oil-fired engine is less likely than a coal-fired one to spark fires in Florida's sometimes drought-plagued grasslands.) This is a locomotive built for hauling, not racing—it's a muscle engine—and hauling is just what Spreckelmeier and his partners intend her future to be, although of a more genteel kind than the locomotive once was used for.

If everything goes according to plan, Old 253 will come steaming up the

FEC tracks into downtown Fort Lauderdale on July 4, 2002. Christmas of 2002 might be a more realistic goal, Spreckelmeier concedes. Beyond that, he and his partners envision adding vintage coaches and running regularly scheduled service, most likely starting at the Gold Coast Railroad Museum and rolling to Homestead, Florida, the southernmost railhead in the United States ever since the FEC line to Key West got wiped out. There's talk of evening dinner trips and mystery train rides.

None of the partners is looking to turn a profit on No. 253, but the project has to earn its keep and maintain a safe reserve in the bank. "You don't want to get caught with your pants down," Spreckelmeier says. "A locomotive goes out of tube service"—the two hundred two-inch fire tubes without which there is no forward progress—"you're going to need sixty thousand dollars to repair it."

One of the partners, though, has every intention of being at the controls when Old 253 finally does get rolling. And he'd like nothing better than to pass the controls on to his son when the time comes for him to hang up his own engineer's cap. "I'm not going to make him do what doesn't want to do, but if he's a Spreckelmeier, steam is in his blood."

Twenty-one

Patricia Corrigan:
"Thar She Blows!"

Patricia Corrigan, the restaurant critic for the *St. Louis Post–Dispatch*, periodically goes around to schools to give talks. Not always about the metropolitan area's seventeen hundred places in which to dine out, but about the world's cetaceans, a biological order of mammals that includes seventy-seven species of whales, porpoises, and dolphins. Corrigan enjoys good food; she prefers watching whales. "I was born and raised in St. Louis and I don't remember learning much about the ocean, so I think it's important for land-locked midwestern children to learn about the ocean and its largest inhabitants," she says.

Corrigan traces her love of whales to a specific date. In July 1982, she read an article in the travel section of *The New York Times* about a whale-watching trip off Cape Cod. "The article was accompanied by a photograph of a whale breaching—jumping completely out of the water." She corrects herself. "Not really jumping. Whales don't have legs. But they come flying out of the water, they propel themselves out of the water, sometimes you can see sunlight between the whale and the water. The whale in the *Times* was a humpback whale and it was almost all the way out."

The article propelled Corrigan to Cape Cod. "On September 25, 1982, I was on a business trip to Washington," she says. "I flew to Hyannis, rented a car, drove to a motel in Falmouth, and then drove to Barnstable for a whale watch, and I've never been the same." As she would eventually write in *The Whale Watchers' Guide*, a where-to-watch-whales book first published in 1991:

The first whale I ever met was a finback, a creature just slightly smaller than the 80-foot, 76-ton boat on which I was a passenger. The whale came toward us, dived, swam under the boat, and was gone before we could comprehend what we had seen. Finback whales are the second-largest creatures ever to live on Earth, surpassed in size only by the mighty blue whales, and they are among the fastest swimmers in the sea, reaching speeds of 20 knots (30 miles per hour).

The boat Corrigan boarded in Barnstable Harbor on that September 1982 trip was called the *Mystery*. She got close enough to see the asymmetrical coloration of the finback's head and the ridges in the shape of a chevron on its back, and spent a good part of the day watching humpback whales feeding, "their huge open mouths rising up through the columns of bubbles they blow under water to trap krill and tiny fish. The humpbacks also waved their tails ('threw their flukes') over and over, and two swam and dived together in unison, as though their dance had been choreographed."

She wrote her book after eight years of going around the hemisphere to watch whales because, she says, "I figured I should share my knowledge. Seeing that first finback changed my life and I wanted to change other people's lives."

Since 1982, watching whales has been a priority for Corrigan. She has gone on every day trip and extended trip she could afford. "Day trips are inexpensive," she says. "Off the coast of Oregon there are a couple that cost fifteen dollars for two hours because the gray whales come in close to shore so the boats don't have to take you far out. You can almost make an appointment with some species of whales because their migration patterns are well known. If you're there, the whales will almost always be there." In close to twenty years of whale watching she has never had to ask for a "whale check"—a free trip at a later date if a whale has failed to show. Sometimes whales do appear unexpectedly. On June 22, 1987, Corrigan was celebrating her thirty-ninth birthday on the St. Lawrence Seaway. The pilot of the M.S. *Bermuda Star* announced it was too early in the season for blue whales, whereupon four blue whales came into view. She is captivated by these mammals that have chosen to live underwater. "Do you know how complicated our lives would be if we made that decision?" she says.

Corrigan's longest and farthest whale-watching expedition took her to Patagonia. Off the eastern coast of Argentina, she saw the southern right whale, one of the rarest large whales in the world. "The right whale got its name in the nineteenth century when commercial whaling was at its peak," she says. "The right whales were slow swimmers and their bodies floated when they were dead, so they were easy to catch. In the nineteenth century there were over three hundred thousand right whales in the seas. Today about two hundred and fifty spend the year off the coast of Argentina's Peninsula Valdés. That's more than are spotted anywhere else. The North Atlantic right whale is also close to extinction."

Corrigan, who has become friendly with some of the world's foremost whale scientists, has read that there are only about forty-five hundred right whales left in the northern and southern hemispheres, but she says that population estimates are, at best, "voodoo mathematics" because whales are hard to count. And as Roger Payne, author of *In the Company of Whales* who also wrote the introduction to Corrigan's book, has told her, "What we know about whales fits in a thimble because we can't live under-water with them."

Corrigan speaks fondly of each of her close encounters with her fellow mammals. "In Newfoundland I saw twenty-six humpbacks close to the boat," she says. "They were breaching, spouting, and lobtailing—that's when a whale sticks its tail out of the water and then slaps it down. It makes a thunderous clap. Those humpbacks were also flipper smacking—they have the longest flippers of any whale. They were doing something every minute. The tail of every humpback whale has a completely different under-side. In New England, the whale conservation agencies recognize each and every humpback. They have photo IDs of them."

In San Ignacio Lagoon, off Baja California, a gray whale swam with her calf for a while alongside the boat Corrigan was in, and let her and the others aboard pet the calf and rub its back. On another day off Baja, a grown female whale opened her mouth. Corrigan reached in and ran the fingers of her right hand across her baleen—the fibrous material in the animal's jaws that serves as a filter when the whale is feeding—and touched the whale's pink tongue. The whale gently closed her mouth on Corrigan's hand, then opened her mouth and squirted a little water on her. Corrigan leaned far out of the boat and kissed her, drew back, and saw the whale looking at her with a large blue eye. "That was an inconceivable experience," she says. "It's hard to wrap yourself around that fact. She turned the tables on me. The gray whales in the San Ignacio Lagoon are sometimes called 'the Friendlies.' Gray whales have twice recovered from near extinction but they're carefully protected in that part of Baja and I often get the feeling that while we're whale watching, the grays are people watching."

Corrigan has never put her hand in the mouth of a large whale with teeth. "Among the great whales, only the sperm whale and the orca have teeth and neither of those species approaches boats to be petted," she says. "Moby Dick was an albino sperm whale and illustrations of Herman Melville's Great White Whale are so well known that many people understandably believe that the sperm whale, with its rectangle-shaped head and long, narrow jaw, represents all whales," she says. "In fact, the sperm whale is unique among whales. No other whale's head accounts for one-third of its length and no other whale has such a large brain. Some people who see the much smaller beluga whales, the only true white whales, think they've seen a Moby Dick, but the sperm whale is fifty to sixty feet long and the beluga grows only to something like sixteen feet. I think of the belugas as sea canaries because they do a lot of vocalizing. They chirp and squeal."

In September 1995 Corrigan, who is divorced, with a grown son ("Joel recognizes whales by their spouts"), was diagnosed with breast cancer. The only other person she had known who had breast cancer had died. She worried how much of a future she would have and she knew she still had a great many species of whales left to see. After completing chemotherapy and radiation treatment in March 1996, she had little of her customary mental and physical energy—and little hair. In early April, when her hair had started growing back, she telephoned a friend in Los Angeles and said she wanted to come out for a few days and go to the beach. She bought "an airplane ticket to the ocean." She left her wig at home. "You can't have the quintessential nature experience with a wig on."

Corrigan and her friend, Hope, went to a beach near Malibu. They sat on a chilly beach and saw a gray whale and her calf nine feet off the shore heading back to Russia. "It was a personal visitation as far I was concerned," she says. "Here were these incredible creatures I thought I'd never see again. April is late for the gray whale migration back to the Bering Sea. There were a lot of people who didn't see those gray whales. Often in life you see what you focus on. I could have been focused on watching the kids playing volleyball on the sand.

"There are ocean people and mountain people and desert people. I'm an ocean person. I've always had a great passion for the ocean, but watching whales added a new dimension to my life. The wind, the salt, the spray, they're so invigorating. I'm an entirely different person on a boat. I thought for a long time I should move to a coast. I imagined myself spending most of my time going out on boats, but then I thought that living anywhere is about going to the grocery store or the dry cleaner or renting a movie. The reality is I have to earn a living, so I'll stay in St. Louis and leave as often as I can on whale-related trips."

PART 5

Motion Pictures

Twenty-two

Lisa Ball:
Snow Job

It's a winter's day—maybe in December 1997—and Lisa Ball and some friends stand on top of Ajax Peak, in Colorado's San Juan Mountains. "Basically, it's the end of a box canyon," Ball says. "There's a four-wheel-drive road that goes over the mountain next to Ajax, but once you hit the end of the valley, Ajax is right in your way. The road isn't plowed in winter. We hiked up it, then went up the back side of Ajax and dropped over the front side to ski it."

North, nearly thirteen thousand feet above sea level, is the Savage Creek Basin, and beyond that are the scant ruins of an abandoned mine with the evocative name of Tomboy. West, not far away at the other end of the canyon, lies the booming ski resort of Telluride, with more than a thousand skiable acres, sixty-six trails, a dozen lifts capable of transporting nearly fifteen thousand skiers an hour, and even eleven ski-in, ski-out restaurants. Sweeping down toward Telluride, though, is what this particular group has hiked far and hard on their skies to find and what most vacationers at Telluride will never see close up: a series of couloirs, or gullies, one known locally as "the Dream Stream," filled with the sort of virgin powder that backcountry skiers like Lisa Ball dream about.

"It has three main avalanche paths on top of it, and then it has these two-hundred-foot cliffs below it," Ball says. "We skied down one of the paths and then hiked back up, and we had so much fun that we decided to do it again. We skied the second path—the Dream Stream—then hiked up and skied back down the way we had come up. It's a pretty wild thing to ski down a cliff, knowing you'll have to climb back up it, and then to do it again!

"It's a very avalanche-prone area. For the safety of the hikers down below, a helicopter will go up and bomb Ajax if they think it's going to go. It's the kind of situation where if anything ever did avalanche and you were skiing up there, you'd be gone, so you have to be nearly a hundred percent sure that something isn't going to go. But we had a great snowpack there that year, after years and years of waiting, and we finally did it.

"It's a once-in-a-lifetime ski. If you get the chance, you have to do it."

Skiing the couloirs of the San Juan range amounts almost to a subspeciality for Ball. By her own count, she has skied Wilson Peak four times, Mt. Wilson five times, El Diente twice, Mt. Sneffels (whose name sounds alarmingly like "Mr. Sniffles") five times, San Miguel ten times, and San Joaquin five times. On all those mountains—and most of them crest at over fourteen thousand—and on many more, Ball has been either the first woman to ski the couloir or the first person of either sex to ski it in the free-heel setup that she favors. (In free-heel skis, unlike downhill or alpine skis with their hard, inflexible boots, the heel is unrestrained so that the skier has the range of motion to climb up the mountain—a necessity, since where Ball skis there are no lifts or T-bars or any other mechanical device to get you to the top.)

Ball also claims the first descent ever, for a person of either sex on any type of ski, of a gully which she has named "the Notch couloir"—since, as she explains, "Here, if you ski it first, you get to name it."

Couloirs, though, are only part of the story. Before the birth of her daughter, Kaelie, in 1994, Ball had skied seven days a week, for up to seven hours a day, from October through June. Even with Kaelie, who goes to school in the afternoons and soon will be starting grade school full-time, Ball is skiing three to four days a week, for most of the year. With a group of friends, she skies through aspen and fir forests, above the tree line when the snowpack is good and the chance of avalanches diminished, below the tree line when the snow is falling in buckets and everything up high is too unstable to risk, down gullies and along paths the avalanches have plowed through southwest Colorado's vast national forests, wherever the snow is and other people aren't.

To support her skiing and to allow herself the time to pursue it, Ball, who lives in the tiny town of Ophir, has been cleaning offices in the evening in nearby Telluride for a dozen years, "vacuuming, scrubbing, that kind of thing." Most of her friends are doing "some kind of work where they can have most of their days free to ski." The income isn't much, but for Lisa

Ball, time and place are money, too, and she doesn't need a lot of the real money in any event. While resort-based alpine skiing can be brutally expensive—lift tickets alone are a small fortune—backcountry skiing "is free once you have the gear."

Even the "real job" Ball's husband and fellow backcountry skier Grant Kennedy has recently taken leaves him three days a week free to ski. "We get our friends to watch Kaelie so that we can ski together at times. Other times, when the snowpack is more dangerous, we choose for just one of us to go." Sometimes, too, Ball will take Kaelie along. "She can climb little hills with me. We take a lot of breaks, but she gets there eventually."

Skiing, Ball says, "is definitely important. It's the most important thing in my life besides my family."

Lisa Ball and her sister were raised in Coal Creek Canyon, near Boulder on the front range of the Rockies, catercorner across the state from where she lives now. "That's where I started skiing, alpining, just basically going downhill with your heel locked in." After high school, she spent some time knocking around the University of Colorado and Fort Lewis College, in Durango. Then in 1988, when she was nineteen, Ball moved to Telluride.

"I really wanted to live in Telluride because I knew it was changing. I took a year off from college and moved there, and really never left. I wanted to get to Telluride before it was ruined, and I did. It's a lot different now, but I still love it. They can change the town, but they can't change these mountains, and that's why I'm here."

At Telluride, too, Ball's understanding of what skiing could be and where it could take you would undergo a dramatic shift. "I met a bunch of people here who would ski backcountry. There was a gate off the ski area that you were allowed to use to access all kinds of amazing terrain. This group of people free-heeled. They got me into it. I tried to follow them everywhere in my alpine gear, and I realized it was a lot of work. That's why I switched over, and I've been on free-heel ever since."

Two years after she arrived in Telluride, Ball moved to Ophir, and with that, the shape of her days achieved a kind of completion even though she was only twenty-one years old. Ophir is on the north-facing side of the mountain, where the snow is colder and fresher than it is on the sun-drenched south sides of mountains. There are no ski lifts in or around the town, which means the surrounding terrain is by definition backcountry for skiing. Nor are the areas Ball is skiing belabored, at least yet, by the big diesel-powered Sno-Cats that have turned backcountry skiing into package tours elsewhere in the West. As for the skiing itself, nature, climate, and eons upon eons of geological formation have taken care of that. For nearly three-quarters of the year, once her daughter is off to school, almost nothing stands between Lisa Ball and her heart's desire.

"I leave my door with my skis on," she says, "and my skins."

The "skins" she refers to are made of a synthetic fur somewhat like cat's hair—silky smooth when it's brushed in one direction, made to stand on end when pushed in the other. Along with the free-heel binding on the skis, the holding power of the skins allows backcountry skiers to go pretty much where they please.

"You can grip into the snow with the skins, and it just stands there. We climb really steep things; we can go straight up something that's thirty or thirty-five degrees. The skins are held to the bottom of your skis with a kind of glue that doesn't stick to the skis at all. You just rip the skins off when you get to the top, put them in your pack, and you're ready to go."

On a typical day in midwinter, Ball and her friends might spend two hours hiking up to the top of whatever spot they've picked out. Breaking the trail in virgin powder is always the hardest part, and it's not made any easier by the twenty-five-to-thirty-pound pack that skiers carry with them, loaded with everything from avalanche beacons, shovels, and probes to first-aid kits, extra warm gear, and food and water.

"We'll ski the upper pitches a few times. Then our last lap, we'll ski all the way out. We're usually out for six or seven hours a day. It's a lot of work, but if you do it all the time, it's fun work. I get a lot out of the hiking. I enjoy pushing myself to see how fast I can go. It feels really good to hike for a couple of hours, not stop, just go and think about whatever."

In spring, when the whole snowpack freezes together into a single unit at night (what's known as "corn") and the higher elevations are less avalanche prone, at least until the afternoon sun has loosened the bond, Ball is likely to hike up for three hours, something on the order of three thousand vertical feet, before she ever takes her first downhill run.

Even though they ski the backcountry, Ball and her friends use parallel turns—with the skies together, just as it's taught on the bunny slopes—rather than the flashy telemark turn, where the skier drops one knee behind. The free-heel skis give them the option of either, Ball says, but in the unmanicured terrain they ski on, anything could be lurking below the surface. "We're making turns in trees. You get your knee beneath the powder, and you don't know what's there."

Ball has pulled a hamstring by skiing into a covered pile of rock debris, and she once fractured a bone on the outside of her hand by whacking it on a rock, just at the end of a day of early-season skiing when she slipped on some rocks covered by a scant half-foot of snow.

Also in the interest of safety, Ball and her friends will give a slope a good testing before heading down it, especially if they're above the tree line and things seem right for drama. Avalanche paths make for great skiing because they strip the terrain clean, but it doesn't do to forget what made the paths in the first place or the often fragile nature of what they are skiing on. A typical winter pack is made up of all sort of different snows—powder, windswept, sugar, and others—none of which bond particularly well with the others and all of which can be rent by deep fractures.

"We have so much fun in what we do," Ball says, "but we take it very seriously. You have to. You don't want to mess around with it. A lot of people have died out there. We have to keep up on the snowpack. By being out there, we can feel it and know what it's doing. We take it seriously, and we take our partners seriously. I don't want to be out there with someone who doesn't know what they are doing. I want them to be able to save me if they have to.

"We'll really jump on a slope and try to get it to go if we can before we ski down. We never go out alone, and we ski silently. If something does happen to go, your friends can whistle or shout down at you to tell you the snow is sliding. If you're skiing and someone yells 'Yahoo!' you don't know if they're saying 'Yahoo!' or 'Oh, no!'"

Even when Lisa Ball does court danger—and she loves to launch herself into the air off accommodating rocks—she tries to weight the odds in her favor. "I take airs all the time. My favorite is about ten to fifteen feet, but I've done thirty-foot airs quite a few times and skied out of them. Anyone can throw herself off a rock. The challenge is to land and ski out of it. I did a back flip once, and I've actually been waiting for the perfect time to do a front one, when the conditions are just right. I've found the perfect rock. The last couple of times I skied that area, the conditions weren't right. It wasn't deep enough, but someday it will be."

Ball says she still enjoys the occasional trip to ski areas like Telluride because "You can ski fast. In the backcountry you've got to ski cautiously." But she also thinks that her preferred form of skiing—her way of life, really, since the two are all but inseparable—is on the edge of a trend, and for good reason.

"Backcountry skiing is growing. More people are starting to realize that they want to get away from other people. They don't want to be always riding a lift and skiing where it has already been skied. We're skiing untracked powder every day. There's nothing like it. It's a floating feeling, with snow all around you flying up in your face. It's a hard thing to explain, but it's heaven—the closest thing to heaven I know of."

Happily, too, in the rugged peaks and couloirs of the San Juan Mountains where Lisa Ball has chosen to make her home and raise her family and clean offices by night to help make it all work, there's so much heaven to be found.

Twenty-three

Steve Everett:
Blade Runner

One physical feature sets Steve Everett apart from the other patent attorneys in San Francisco. He has a scar across his chin that required twenty-seven stitches to close. Everett, fifty-one, got the cut when he tripped over a friend who had fallen in front of him while they and some other men, most of whom are about half Everett's age, were skating down the ramps of a parking garage. Everett goes in-line skating with his young buddies most Fridays in San Francisco and most Wednesdays in San Mateo.

"There is a six-story parking garage on the peninsula near San Mateo we call 'Haji's' after the assumed name of a security guard who at one time patrolled the garage," Everett says of the scene of his most serious Wednesday-night mishap. "We made our peace with Haji, since he seemed content to allow us to skate a run or two as long as we did not abuse the privilege. Now, however, due to funding cutbacks or whatever, Haji no longer patrols the garage. We have it all to ourselves.

"Unlike most of our skate venues, Haji's offers a free elevator ride to the top. But it's the wide, smooth, continuously descending ramps, not the free ride, that attract us to the place. We gather at the top floor of the building and enjoy the open sky and panoramic view. Then we get ready to race and someone yells out, 'Ready, Set, Go!' And we're off, sprinting to the first one-hundred-eighty-degree turn.

"Here is where tactics come into play. The idea is to get to the turn first, take the best line through the turn, accelerate out of the turn as soon as possible, guard against an inside pass, and set up for the next turn. If you take an inside line into the turn, your momentum will make you swing wide at the exit, creating an opening for others to pass on the inside. If you take an outside line into the turn, you can usually work your way toward the inside to pass coming out of the turn.

"Once through that turn we scramble for the next, taking quick crossover steps to accelerate and set up. If you take an outside-in line through one turn and hold an inside line between the turns and into the next turn, you will probably swing wide at the exit, opening up the inside for someone else to pass. We see a lot of passing and repassing for that reason.

"There are two one-hundred-eighty-degree turns per floor, about five seconds apart at race speeds. There are nine ramps and nine turns from top to bottom, plus a flat ground floor. Whoever is first through the last turn is the winner. Passing is very common. It is rare that anyone leads from start to finish. Visibility is good, so any vehicles that we might encounter can be spotted well in advance.

"Traction is another key. We coast through the apex of the turns with both skates on the ground to maximize cornering force. If your skates slide, best case is that you will lose some time relative to the other skaters and worst case is that you will go down and lose a lot of time. The transition from coasting through a turn to crossing over between turns is tricky because if you do it too soon you will lose cornering force, driving you wide, or your skates may slide out. If you do it too late, or you just coast the whole way, you will lose ground to the more aggressive skaters. Anyone with new wheels has a definite advantage at Haji's. New wheels are stickier than worn wheels and give you better traction. Plus, the new wheels are all the same size, so every wheel is doing an equal share of gripping the pavement.

"We are all very competitive racing down Haji's garage. No matter who leads through any given turn, we all sprint to the next and try to pass. Body contact happens a lot, especially in the turns. Sometimes when two skaters come together in a turn, the trailing skater may give the leading skater a forearm shove exiting the turn, causing the leading skater to swing wider than otherwise and allowing the trailing skater to pass on the inside. Sacrifices to the pavement gods are not uncommon.

"Once the race is over, we glide to the elevator and power-slide to stop. Everyone is grinning because skating at Haji's is just so damn much fun. High fives are usually in order. Then we jump back onto the elevator for another run.

"Sometimes we join up and skate down together as a train. The driver at the front of the train is very important, and not everyone can do it well, as we have painfully learned. The driver needs to be smooth and predictable so that everyone behind can follow. The caboose position is important, too, since that is the only skater who can kick freely without worrying about hitting another skater. We start off with everyone striding together and then we coast through the first turn. The driver usually crosses over coming out of the turn to move the head of the train around into position for the next turn. We continue the process down to the bottom. Lots of fun.

"One night Herb suggested that we do something a little different—divide up into two smaller trains and race each other. There were six of us skating that night, so we raced three against three. What a blast! You have the competition of racing, but also the difficulties of getting groups of skaters to coordinate. No one skater can dominate because each train is no faster than its slowest skater. Of course, passing is more difficult because of the length of the trains. Sometimes the head of a trailing train jams into the middle of the leading train, fighting to pass, and causing one or both trains to break apart. Positioning is critical, especially at the start. When I drive a train and we start on the outside of the other train, my strategy is to take the outside approach to turn one, then pass the other train on the inside when they swing wide coming out. Of course that sets us up for a repass on turn two, so we just need to be quicker through the turn.

"One time I was driving a four-man train with the four lightest skaters against a three-man train with the three heaviest skaters. We had the lead and everything was going well. We had the inside position through several turns but they had a little more speed. We forced the other train wide through one turn, but then they cut into the middle of our train, forcing us inside and causing my number-two skater to pull me inside. The next thing I knew, I got spun around backwards, lost my balance, and fell. Our train lost that run.

"Another time I was driving a three-man train against another three-man train. Bill, my number-two guy, thought he would use guerrilla tactics to beat the other guys, so he pulled out my water bottle and squirted water at them, hoping to make them crash. The only guy who crashed, however, was Charles, the number-three guy on *our* team. Then, on the next run, guess who crashed because of the water? Bill and I. Paybacks are a bitch.

"So that is Haji's, one reason why we skate."

Steve Everett has been skating avidly for only a few years. One evening in the summer of 1994, he and his wife, Judy, were in a Safeway in Half Moon Bay buying groceries for a weekend in Santa Cruz. They stopped at the supermarket's magazine section. There were hundreds of magazines on the racks—"one for every hobby you could think of," Everett observes, "but none of them was *my* hobby." The Everetts had owned Rollerblades since the late eighties and skated occasionally. After taking ice-skating lessons at a rink near his office for two winters "just to work out," Steve decided to try in-line skating again. Early in 1995, he bought a new pair of in-line skates, Aeroblades. He became a man with a hobby—in-line skating. He subscribes to a magazine for people like him, *Fitness and Speed Skating Times,* known as FASST.

"There was a lot of blood," Judy Everett says of her husband's first few months on the streets and garage ramps in and around San Francisco. "It was like Why wash the sheets? Since then he's learned a lot about padding. Both he and the padding have improved. For Father's Day, I bought him a one-piece skinsuit like the bikers wear. You can go faster in a suit like that. He still gets a fair number of bruises." Everett also owns a pair of solar-yellow speed skates, which he uses when he enters races. "I came in third in my age group in the twenty-four-mile Napa-to-Calistoga race," he says. "My prize was a bottle of Gallo wine."

About a hundred and fifty people go in-line skating in San Francisco most Fridays—a small fraction, compared to the thousands who go in-line skating on Fridays in Paris—and since 1996 Everett has been one of them. He and his friends, who include a Sheetrock installer, a locksmith, a cable installer, and a landscape architect, sometimes skate the Friday Night Skate loop around San Francisco with the other skaters and then stop for a while for drinks at the Beale Street Bar & Grill.

After sitting at the Beale Street Bar & Grill for a while, Everett and friends warm up their muscles before heading for "the Afterblade," as he calls the post-bar skate.

"We don't tackle Pine Street immediately," he says. "We take time to skate some of the smoothest marble, granite, and concrete in the financial district. Eventually we make our way up the stairs leading to the Bank of America headquarters building. I like to skate backward circles around the black heart of a banker sculpture that's embedded in the plaza, then roll down the stairs a few times, power-sliding to a stop. After catching our breath, we climb up California into Chinatown, then cut over on Grant Avenue to Pine Street.

"Pine Street is our Nob Hill gateway to the Afterblade. We work hard for a three-hundred-foot elevation gain, which we cash in on the downhills to follow. Some of my deadbeat pals 'skitch'—they hold on to cars to get up the hill the easy way—but I don't. From Grant the first block is a killer—

long and steep—and it sucks all the energy out of your legs. The next block is a bit flatter, but much too short for my legs to recover before tackling the steep third block. I concentrate on my form—big push sideways from the heels, quick recovery, knees together, rotate hips to shift weight, then another big push from the other skate. I focus on one stride at a time, each stride bringing me closer to the top. My lungs are on fire, my heart is pounding, my legs feel like lead, but I keep striding. The beer and tequila that we drank at the bar help the mind cope with the immediate pain. Just before the body gives out, I crest the top of the block and look ahead to the next block—flat—giving me a much needed recovery. I'm still three blocks away from the top, but as my lungs fill with air and my legs come back to life, the last few blocks are no problem.

"We stand at the crest of the slope looking at traffic, waiting for the right moment to dive in. It's well after midnight, so traffic is relatively light. The traffic lights are timed, and the street is one-way and three lanes wide. A pack of cars pass through our intersection and head for the next. When they clear the Hyde Street intersection, we are off—striding hard to pick up speed on that first downhill block. We hit the flat at Hyde Street at a good speed, avoiding the uneven pavement patch left by San Francisco's Department of Public Works. Then the speed kicks in as we hit the steepest block, sometimes passing laggard cars. I concentrate on keeping my weight back and evenly divided between my skates, and on hopping over manhole covers and rough pavement. We move in formation, semiconscious of where our buddies are and going with the flow of traffic. Sometimes we are close enough behind a car to get sucked along in its draft for an extra boost of speed. Our speed carries us quickly down to Polk, and then we slow down on the uphill block to Van Ness. Cheers and hoots from the cars and pedestrians are common, but we barely hear them over the rush we feel. Stopping at Van Ness, we are all smiles from this warm-up, the first of three hills in the Afterblade.

"Franklin Street is my favorite run of the night. The excitement of Franklin is what keeps me coming back week after week. Discovered by my buddy Kevin, this six-block run lasts for only half a minute or so, but it is definitely an E-ticket ride.

"We have to climb one more steep block to get to Franklin, but it's worth it. No question. From Pine, we skate a few blocks along Van Ness, then cross over and go up Sacramento to Franklin. I'm worn out at the top, so I take to the sidewalk to recover as a pack of cars pass by. After skating a few blocks and letting the cars pass, we're back out on the street—one-way, three lanes wide, and timed traffic lights. But best of all, the pavement is brand-new. The cars naturally group themselves into bunches at about a thirty-miles-per-hour pace, set by the timing of the lights. The packs are usually about six to twelve cars at this time of night, with a long empty gap stretching back to the next pack of cars, one traffic-light cycle back. Our strategy is to let a pack of cars get a few blocks ahead, then start skating just in front of the next pack but soon enough to catch the tail end of the light cycle.

"We wait for our light to turn yellow, then red, for the pack of cars behind us. I count aloud to eight, but Joe counts faster. We take off and sprint down the first block and clear the intersection as the light changes to red. Another block and we're really going fast, like Pine Street, but then we're at block three where the bottom falls out and we're screamin' down the hill, gaining so fast on the car pack ahead that we have to straddle the lanes to split the traffic. I head right, some of the others head left, and wham, we're through the pack at Union; we regroup in the left lane and lay on a hard left at the next block, then consciously breathe for the first time since we started, feeling, Wow, that was intense.

"We circle around back to Union Street and gather at the corner. Major smiles. Hand slaps in congratulations. 'Yeah! Wahhoo!' Bill says. 'See, that's what I really can't explain to people—how you feel after a run like that. And you can't just bring them here and show them. They'd need to skate a long time to be able to handle something like this.'

"Yeah, Franklin is my favorite.

"We skate along Franklin to get to Divisadero. Divis is the capper. We pick one guy to watch the four-way stop at Greenwich Street, while the rest of us climb up Filbert. Yeah, one more climb. We showboat down Fillmore through the Bermuda Triangle—as the bar area is called because some kids go there to drink and are allegedly never heard from again —then do a stylish turn for the Friday-night crowds and coast along for a while. Once past the bars it's so quiet now on this residential street in Pacific Heights. Time to reflect on what a great skate night it has been and to be thankful for one more downhill ride to come. We reach the top and look down: one very steep block, the steepest on the skate, then a flat transition at Greenwich where our buddy is watching, then a moderately downhill block to a traffic light at Lombard Street, two blocks away. We'll go when the traffic light is green, which stops cross traffic two blocks down. We rely on our buddy to stop any cross traffic one block down.

"When the time is right, off we go—a few strides and then tuck because we're screamin' already, get set for the transition then suck it up as your legs are driven upward, then down the next block and across Lombard, barely conscious of the bright lights, focusing on Chestnut Street coming up and, traffic willing—traffic is the wild card—a hard left and then relax and breathe. It's over so fast—three intense blocks in a flash.

"We skate leisurely back to our cars breathing deeply but easily, thinking about what a great skate we had and reliving the fast and fleeting moments just experienced. We shake hands and say our good-byes and promise to be here next time."

Twenty-four

Mike Gaines:
Hot into the Corner

If Mike Gaines were racing on NASCAR's premier Winston Cup circuit, he would need a big car—a Chevrolet Monte Carlo would be ideal, he says—and a minimum of $5 million a year to equip it and keep it in competition. Pit-crew chiefs alone can make upwards of $250,000 annually on the Winston circuit, and that's just for the boss. The rest of the crew needs to be hired and paid. Then there's transportation for the car and several backups for it, too, each of which represents an investment of roughly $500,000.

Most Winston Cup cars are, in Gaines's word, "moving billboards" for everything from Miller Lite beer to DeWALT tools, various automotive products, and the cigarette maker that sponsors the races for one very good reason: they have to be. Driving a car covered with decals round and round a track in front of tens of thousands of fans and millions more watching on television justifies the sponsorship agreements that help offset some staggering bills.

Gaines himself drives somewhere in the third tier of NASCAR competition: the Dash series sponsored by Goody's, the maker of headache powder and other pain relievers, and one of ten regional circuits sanctioned by the stock-car racing giant. Even here, endorsement agreements are not uncommon. "The top dozen Dash teams might have two hundred thousand to four hundred thousand dollars a year in sponsor money," Gaines says, but in the Goody's Dash circuit, as in none of the higher-level ones, there's room for the amateur. To race in what he calls NASCAR's "red-headed stepchild," Gaines needs nothing more than a pair of Pontiac Sunfires; an unpaid pit crew drawn mostly from in and around the B&D Quik Stop up in North Wilkesboro, North Carolina; and a desire to see some serious asphalt go flying by.

Like all NASCAR entries, Gaines's cars must meet rigorous specifications on size and power. The idea is to reward the skill of the driver and his team over the technology under the hood and along the drive train. But plenty of horses remain. Gaines's two Sunfires are outfitted with V-6 Chevy engines that burn superrich 110-octane gas. (Winston Cup cars use even more explosive 115-octane gas, nearly a third richer than standard service station blends.) Left to their own devices, Gaines says, his cars will top out at about 182 miles an hour. Even with the acceleration-restrictor plates that NASCAR insists all its cars use, Dash circuit cars are capable of speeds above 160 miles an hour.

Equality of opportunity to go fast, though, does not guarantee an equality of results. Mike Gaines has never won a Dash race, and he's not likely to. Nor does he have any sponsorship deals, or any real prospects of one. His fire-retardant racing suit reads "CMG Autosports," which could be the logo of a sponsorship arrangement except that "CMG" stands for Charles Michael Gaines and the "Autosports" are his own cars. Instead of product decals, Gaines's Sunbirds sport a large black sticker on the rear of either side that reads "Emory," for the prestigious Atlanta university two of his daughters have attended, and a smaller decal in the left rear window that reads, "Miss Porter's School," for the elegant Farmington, Connecticut, boarding school that has educated all three of Gaines's girls as well as his wife, Alice.

Yet if Gaines defies in many particulars the standard image of a stock car racer, he doesn't lack passion or intent. He got into the sport, he says, with one clear goal in mind: "My long-range vision was simply to get to Daytona"—as a driver, that is, not as a spectator—and that he has accomplished. On February 12, 1999, Mike Gaines roared off from the starting line in the Discount Auto Parts 200, part of the annual Florida Speedweek that culminates with the famous Daytona 500. Alice Gaines was in the stands that Friday to watch her husband race for the first time. A few days earlier, Gaines had qualified with an average lap speed of 159 miles an hour. He was sixty years old at the time.

"I had never driven a race car in my life until I was fifty-one," Gaines explains in the den of his center-hall colonial in the leafy suburbs of Greensboro, North Carolina. "But I have these three buddies I go to the Bahamas with every year and then to the Daytona 500, and I'd been talking with them about what fun it would be.

"I made appointments for the four of us to go to the Richard Petty Driving Experience in Charlotte. The other three didn't make it, so I decided I'd go myself. I told Alice that I was working and would have to spend the night on the road, but I went on to Charlotte. These were Winston Cup cars minus one hundred horsepower. They didn't want the weekend warriors getting in over our heads."

Even minus 100 horsepower, Mike Gaines was bitten. Soon, he found himself back in Charlotte, this time at Petty's advanced course, and from there it was on to the Buck Baker Racing School's course at the North Carolina Speedway, in Rockingham, near the South Carolina border.

"He's quite a disciplinarian," Gaines says of Baker. "He told me, 'You might like to get an old car and do some dirt racing.' I said, 'I don't know about that.'"

Instead—and perhaps in light of his late start in the sport—Gaines enthusiastically embraced a plan that would have had him pay an established driver to slip behind the wheel of his car during a qualifying run at Daytona.

"This guy said, 'For ten grand, I'll put you in my car.' We ran it by [veteran NASCAR official] Ed Cox, and he called and said, 'Mr. Gaines, there's no way you're going to get on this track unless you get a car and do some runs on the Dash circuit.' I said, 'Well, I figured I'd get a little practice in.' He said, 'That's not enough.'"

Happily, Mike Gaines already knew the B&D Quik Stop from his work traveling around North Carolina, selling paper products to the hosiery industry, and from his own tendency to favor such places. Even more happily, Wilkes County, home of the B&D, is also home to the legendary stock car racer and former moonshine runner Junior Johnson. Almost providentially, Benny Combs, who had once crewed for Johnson, was both a B&D regular and a very distant cousin of Dean Combs, who helped found the Goody's Dash series in 1975, right in North Wilkesboro.

Before long, Benny Combs had brokered a deal with Dean Combs to get Gaines on the Dash circuit. With the help of both Combses, Gaines came into possession of his Pontiac Sunbirds. Best of all, Benny Combs agreed to serve as his pit-crew chief in return for free lodging and steaks when the team has to go on the road. (At three hundred or so pounds, Benny has been known to eat some steaks.)

Along the way, Gaines also picked up some additional motivation to follow through on the realization of his dream to race at the Daytona International Speedway in Florida.

"One guy at the B&D said, 'Gaines, you're crazy as hell. They'll never let you drive down there.' One word led to another," Gaines recalls. "Then you let your mouth overload your tail, and you've got to back it up. . . .

"And so I just beat and banged around different tracks, not having much success. But finally it was enough so I got to go to Daytona."

"Beat" and "banged," in this instance, are not just metaphorical. Stock cars not only go faster than regular road cars, they go harder.

"When you watch them on TV, you don't realize it," Gaines says, "but they're awfully rough. The first time I was at Daytona, I was shocked. The car was shaking hard the whole time. It's hard on the lower back. And the sound is deafening. This year for the first time, I used the form-fitting earplugs."

There's also the heat to contend with, both from the racing surface and from the cars themselves.

"I worked in the oil fields in Louisiana growing up. I even laid out one year from school and worked in them to make money for college. I thought I was hot then, but last year at the Myrtle Beach Speedway [in South Carolina], it was a hundred five on the track and a hundred thirty in the car. The floorboard of the car got so hot, I had a spot on my right heel an inch long that was burned. The shoe heel itself didn't burn, but it convected the heat through to the heel.

"It smells like gasoline and asphalt, and then you've got burning rubber. These are smells a lot of the guys dearly love. I'm not as fond of the smells as they are, but I've gotten used to them—about as used as I intend to get."

From the stands, stock cars can look pretty much like regular cars covered with excessive decals. In reality, they are completely unsuited to the open road. Because they're modified to run counterclockwise on a banked track, stock cars are lop-eyed—raised up on the driver's side so they can lean more effectively into the curves. To translate engine power as effectively as possible into miles per hour, stock cars also use treadless tires: the rubber meets the road entirely. That's why races are delayed whenever even small amounts of rain begin to fall. It's also why oil slicks on the track are so dangerous. Without any tire tread to brake against, stock cars just slide and slide, until they meet another object, be it wall or fellow competitor.

To protect against such eventualities, NASCAR stock cars employ state-of-the-art safety equipment. The superrich fuel is kept in the trunk, in a separate cell that breaks away from the body of the car at almost any impact. Drivers also have fire extinguishers within easy reach—pull a knob, and the car fills with foam—and they ride so surrounded by roll bars that drivers have been known to walk away from wrecks in which nothing but the roll-bar cage remains. Within the cage, drivers wear helmets with built-in radios that keep them in constant contact with their spotters. (With almost no peripheral vision and without side mirrors—which are aerodynamically unsound—or the time to look in them, NASCAR drivers are completely dependent on spotters to tell them what's happening behind and beside them.) Drivers also are strapped down to within an inch of their lives, Gaines says.

"We have these long, heavy belts across the chest and lap and up through the crotch. You're in there so tight that you can't stick a hand between those belts and your chest. I'll get down in the seat and take a big breath. Then I'll exhale and give the belt a good hard pull. I can hardly breathe when I'm racing. You don't want to be comfortable in there. If you're comfortable, you're doing something wrong."

About the only thing that isn't protected in the event of a serious wreck is the connection between the driver's head and his body. Many of the worst broken necks in auto racing are by elongation: hit a wall hard enough, and the strapped-in body sometimes will stay in place while the unrestrained head shoots forward until there's no repairing things.

Protecting against the essential nature of those who pursue NASCAR racing may be harder than protecting against the mechanical and technical dangers the sport presents. Stock car driving is, by necessity, a continuous gut check, and in some ways, the later anyone comes to it, the more there is to be tested.

"I have a fear, a deep respect when I'm in that car going a hundred sixty miles an hour," Gaines says. "I don't think a lot of my competitors feel that. It's not part of their makeup. They were five and six years old when they started racing go-carts. If they're twenty-five now, they've been doing this for fifteen, twenty years."

Imagine a dozen cars heading into a banked curve at speeds double the Interstate limits—all of them arriving at the "corner," as curves get called in the sport, within a few seconds of one another—and you'll have some sense of just what there is to feel fear and respect for.

"Part of the challenge is saying, I can go into that corner deeper than you can. I'll drive the car in deeper and longer before I'll let off the gas, and I'll hit the gas harder when I come out."

Saying that, of course, is also a large part of the danger of the sport. In his scant few years on the Goody's Dash circuit, Mike Gaines has already hit the wall five times.

"Dean Combs says that you don't race into the corner, you race out of it. But I go into the corner so hot—that's part of my problem."

One of Gaines's crashes, this one decidedly not his fault, came in February 1999, in his long-sought appearance at Daytona with his wife in the stands. "At the first of the race, a guy cut down early and took eighteen of us out. One fellow bit the end of his tongue off; another guy broke his leg. For a melee like that, that's not too bad. We had a great week, and a poor finish."

Inevitably, crashes are part of the explanation for the popularity of NASCAR racing, Gaines says. "There's an overwhelming need for a lot of people to see cars go fast at close quarters. People are there to see real good racing. They're not there to see the crashes—there's no morbidity to it. But they know the crashes are going to happen, and they anticipate them."

But crashes are far from the whole explanation, Gaines contends.

"Racing is a teamwork thing, and it's amazing what a team can accomplish. You never hear a driver say, 'Well, I won it.' They say, 'We won it.' It also may be the only sport where you can hobnob with the stars. If you can get a pit pass, the drivers will come over and shake your hand. They really are good old boys although a lot of them now have college degrees."

The same might be said of Gaines. Even though his daughters prepped in New England and his wife is descended from a minor railroad magnate who helped open the upper Midwest to the iron horse, Gaines's own degree is from the Citadel, the no-nonsense military college in Charleston, South Carolina, and his roots run into the deep Deep South. "I come from a redneck background. My dad moved from Mississippi to coach football and teach high school at Olla, Louisiana. Later, he became postmaster and then got into insurance and finance."

It was in Olla, forty-eight miles due south of Monroe, that Mike Gaines got his first taste of what it felt like behind the wheel of a car hurtling down the road into the dark.

"When I was growing up in Olla," he says, "Highway 165 ran straight out of town. You could see this light seven miles down the road. We'd race down to the light to see who had the fastest car. My dad had a power-packed 1957 Chevrolet, with way too much motor for the car. The Olla marshal saw me one night racing. He didn't ticket me, but he went to my daddy and told him what I'd been doing. He sold the car the next week and got a considerably slower one. "I think that might be part of my racing today—never growing out of sixteen, or getting much beyond it."

Stock car racing is also a sport where a man nearing retirement—a man who has never won a race, a man without a single sponsorship decal to his name—can find himself confronted by starry-eyed strangers less than a quarter his age who want to grow up to be what he is and do what he does.

"There have been a couple of kids," Gaines allows, "who walked up to me and said, 'Do you drive this car?' And I'll say, 'Yes, I do.' And they'll say, 'Can we have your autograph?' I'll say, 'You don't know who I am, do you?' And they'll say, 'No, but if you drive this car, that's good enough for us.'"

Both of Mike Gaines's Pontiac Sunbirds are in the garage as he talks. The one he drove into the wall at Daytona still needs repairing. So does the one he drove into the wall at Myrtle Beach, the day he burned the inch-long scar into his heel. (At a little over half a mile in circumference, the Myrtle Beach Speedway oval is one of the tightest on the NASCAR circuit.) Gaines had promised his wife that all he wanted to do was get to Daytona and drive on the track there. Now, having actually raced at the legendary speedway, if only for two laps—"four if you count the parade laps"—Gaines is not so sure. "I know that I don't need to be out there. I don't have a lot to prove. I've had about all the fun I can stand."

Still, he says, he's not quite ready to sell the cars and hang up his racing suit. The Charlotte 500 is coming up, and Mike Gaines would like to be there—on the track, shaking so hard his back hurts, smelling that gasoline and asphalt, going hot and deep into every corner.

Twenty-five

Jim Murphy:
Call of the Wild

Eleven months of the year, Jim Murphy works for a living, but his close friends know that he lives for the twelfth month—July—when he goes canoeing in Canada's vast barren tundra. He knows it, too.

"When you've grown up where I have, maybe it's a less unusual pursuit than it would be for most people," Murphy says. "I've spent most of my life in the small twin cities of Moorhead, Minnesota, and Fargo, North Dakota. I think the North Dakota landscape with its open spaces, limitless horizons, and subzero winters makes me feel comfortable at latitudes of seventy-one degrees north." The Arctic Circle is at sixty-six degrees thirty-two minutes north.

"I grew up on the banks of the Red River of the North," Murphy says. "It is one of the few rivers in the lower forty-eight that flows north to Canada and the Arctic." Kathie Murphy and her late husband, Vince, bought a cabin on Floyd Lake, in Minnesota, fifty miles from Moorhead, in 1955, the year Jim Murphy was born, and Jim spent his early summers there.

Now, during the summer, when he isn't paddling in the trackless northern wilderness, he commutes between his office in Fargo (where he and his brother, Tim, a published poet, sell life insurance and raise equity for small start-up companies) and the cabin on Floyd Lake. According to Murphy's "Canoe-ulum Vitae," he received his Boy Scout canoeing merit badge in 1968 and a B.A.—in philosophy—from Kenyon College in 1978. His first long trip in Canada was right after graduation, when he and three young friends went canoeing there. It is a trip he views, in retrospect, as a cautionary tale.

"In 1978, on my first long northern canoe trip, I wiped out in a potentially deadly rapid on the North Seal River in Manitoba," Murphy says. "My partner was flushed downstream out of sight and I spent forty-five minutes standing on the overturned canoe in the middle of the rapid contemplating what I thought was his probable death and my impending one. I finally mustered enough courage, or fear, to cut the packs loose, push the canoe upright, and swim for it. I was lucky that day. We had done everything wrong, yet we both were fine, recovered our gear and the canoe, and continued all the way to Hudson Bay. Perhaps because my mishap didn't end in tragedy, it was a life-affirming experience that I have carried with me ever since. The sense of elation, serenity, and hope has never left me and I truly feel lucky every day, especially when I am paddling."

In 1987, while on a canoe trip, Murphy met a Canadian named Ivan Robertson, at the time a bush pilot flying float planes that took fishermen and native trappers in and out of Stony Rapids, Saskatchewan. Robertson is now an airplane mechanic; he repairs aerial water-bombers the Canadian government uses to try to extinguish forest fires. Robertson and his wife and children reside in La Ronge, Saskatchewan, five hundred miles north of the border between Montana and Canada.

"Meeting Ivan was a great stroke of good luck," Murphy says. "We're closely matched in age, ability, interests, and temperament. He couldn't be a better partner."

Since 1989 the two men have gone canoeing virtually every summer, on rivers like the Fond du Lac, the Waterfound, the Cree, and the MacFarlane in Saskatchewan, and the Kazan, the Nowleye, the Kunwak, the Back, the upper Dubawnt, the Finnie, the Thelon, the Lockhart, the Baillie, the Ellice, and the Kuujjua, in the Northwest Territories. (On April 1, 1999, about two million square kilometers were peeled off from the Northwest Territories by the Canadian government and the new territory of Nunavut was created. Of its twenty-seven-thousand inhabitants, 85 percent are Inuit. Most of the rivers Murphy had canoed are now part of this native self-ruled territory.) These rivers are little traveled and are ice-free for just a few brief weeks. And then not always.

"The greatest variable in our canoe trips is the weather," Murphy says. "You don't know what kind you're going to get. Nineteen ninety-two was extremely cold. That was probably our most difficult trip. We had to drag the canoe over ice on every single lake. On Tulemalu Lake we had solid ice for thirty miles and had to sneak through open leads—little openings in the ice—near the shore. I doubt the ice went off that summer. At one point the Kunwak River just disappeared under a vast field of ice. We had no choice but to portage. Portaging is such slow and hard work you do it only when forced to by some obstacle such as an ice jam, or rapids, or when traversing between watersheds. Generally we have to carry three loads of ninety to one hundred pounds each. So to portage everything one mile you have to walk five miles, three across with a heavy load and two back. I enjoyed the trip, but it was intimidating. It was like glacial travel. I'd prefer to have had nicer conditions, but you take what comes."

Wind is another hazard. "Sometimes it's too windy to paddle or even to portage the canoe, so we drag it, often for miles," Murphy says. "Sometimes it slides pretty well, sometimes it doesn't. Wind can delay us as much as ice. We waited out a wind-and-sand storm on the Back River for three days in 1994. It was in the low forties with a fifty-miles-an-hour wind, so we stayed in our tent, ate, slept, and read bad books. Patience is an important virtue if you're windbound. It's not one of my great strengths, but I know that if the wind makes the waves too high we'll swamp if we try to paddle in it, so I read. *The Portable Shakespeare* has been on a few canoe trips." Robertson teases Murphy when he reads "chick books," like *The Bean Trees* and *Pigs in Heaven*, by Barbara Kingsolver. "I was amazed at how much Ivan liked [John] Ciardi's translation of Dante's *Inferno*," Murphy says. "Perhaps it was because he recently converted to Catholicism at his wife's request and he enjoyed the irony of popes in hell. Often we paddle at night because that's when the wind usually subsides and it never gets fully dark because we're so far north."

Sometimes it's too dry to paddle. There's no water in the rivers. "We are always looking for interesting and out-of-the-way routes," Murphy says. "A well-rounded canoeist goes upstream as well as down. Tracing unnamed streams is part of the fun. In 1996, we really wanted to do the Finnie River, which is in a very remote part of the Thelon Game Preserve. We were attempting to go nearly seven hundred miles over five heights of land in thirty days. The problem was when we got to the Finnie we were way behind schedule and there wasn't any water in it. We dragged the canoe down the riverbed for fifteen miles until a tributary added enough flow to float it. It was a beautiful valley, but literally 'a drag.' When we got to the Thelon River we were able to make up time and averaged over forty miles per day. We got back home to work on time. Sometimes you just have to tough it out."

For most people, brutal portages, howling winds, driving rain, hailstones, merciless sun, swarms of mosquitoes and horrendous blackflies, sore arms, backs, and shoulders, soggy feet, and fatigue—these are just a few of the phrases used in Murphy's accounts of canoe trips—would not be amusing. "I'm not an ascetic," Murphy says. "The nice days make up for the occasional discomfort."

Nor would most people be in proper shape to undertake these voyages. Murphy is five nine, weighs 145 pounds, and is fit. He swims, bikes, and skis. He has been running between forty and fifty miles a week for twenty years. Since turning forty, Murphy has run nine marathons, including Boston twice. His fastest time was 3:05:48 in the 1999 Twin Cities Marathon. "Luckily time fades memories of discomfort," he says, "otherwise no one would run in more than one marathon." In the past decade, he has consciously and conscientiously worked at staying fit. "For long-distance canoeing without any kind of resupply by float plane, it's best to be in shape," he says. "You don't go out on trips like these to get in shape. You need to be in shape before you go. And resupplying is very expensive."

Murphy generally keeps the cost of his trips down by driving as far north as he can—two thousand miles from Fargo to Yellowknife, in the Northwest Territories. He and Robertson then charter a single-engine float plane to take them, their canoe, and supplies to the starting point of that year's trip. When they set off, they agree on a time and a place where they will be met by boat or float plane.

"On a thirty-five- or forty-two-day trip I spend between two and three thousand dollars," he says. "As I own all the equipment, airfare is the most costly part of a trip. The primary expense is time. Most salaried people can't afford to take six weeks off from work or family obligations. A high preponderance of canoeists are self-employed. I've been very lucky to have a wife and a brother who are tolerant. I have often pushed those tolerance levels further than I should. My wife, Meg, would be happier if I spent more time traveling with her, to France and Italy. She was an art history major. We married in 1994 and I made it abundantly clear as a condition of our marriage that I was not going to give up canoeing."

When Robertson and Murphy embark on a trip of eight hundred and fifty miles through an area with no roads, no towns, and no people, and have no intention of being resupplied, they carefully consider what they are going to take, keeping weight to a minimum because of portages. They take a very tough plastic seventeen-foot Old Town Tripper canoe, specially rigged for wilderness travel. The bow and stern lines are attached through the hull for pulling the canoe up and down rapids. A portage yoke is attached to the center so one person can carry it. The seats have been moved to allow for extra gear, so the two men can kneel when shooting rapids. Everything is tied into the canoe and then covered with a waterproof-fabric spray cover, which cinches around their waists, enabling them to handle very rough water that would swamp an open canoe. Their marathon racing paddles, made of carbon fiber, are extremely light and tough.

"When you take thousands of paddle strokes each day, even a few ounces of extra weight in the paddle add up to hundreds of pounds of unnecessary weight lifted," Murphy says. Their tent, sleeping bags, pads, extra clothing, and medical kit are all lightweight. They use small Coleman gas stoves for cooking, because the tundra yields little or no wood for fires. Everything must be useful, or it stays home. "Our only extravagances are our personal journals, a few books, and our camera equipment," Murphy says.

"In 1978, I didn't keep a diary and all I have left of that trip are some photographs and my probably changed memories. We also carry an Emergency Locator transmitter, which weighs just a couple of pounds. We would only turn it on in dire circumstances and, because rescue could take up to a week if the weather was bad, you really need to rely on yourself and be careful."

Murphy and Robertson pack about 350 pounds of food. Murphy says most store-bought camping meals are "way too expensive" and calls the portions "meager," so he uses a large dehydrator to prepare most of the food for the voyage. Breakfast is usually cereal and coffee. Lunch consists of crackers, peanut butter and jam, dried fruit, nuts, cheese, and tea—or perhaps there will be a freshly caught trout or grayling. The catch-of-the-day may be boiled, blackened, or fried. A typical evening meal is rehydrated beef-and-barley stew, fresh-baked corn bread, and tea. "All our food is carefully packed in waterproof packs and then organized into meals so all we have to do is grab it," Murphy says. "I went hungry on one of my first trips, so we always carry seven to ten days of extra provisions in case we get delayed."

For Murphy, the hardships of tundra travel are outweighed by such pleasures as getting close to birds and animals that have never seen humans and are unafraid. He has admired soaring peregrine falcons and terns, arctic and yellow-billed loons and mergansers, sandhill cranes, whiskey jacks, blue-winged teals, swans and songbirds, eagles, and geese. A peregrine sliced two long rips in the hood of Robertson's raincoat ("scary") and an arctic tern pecked Murphy on the head ("not scary"). He has seen wolves frolicking, musk-ox ("strange woolly beasts") sunbathing, and hundreds of caribou taking a few steps and nibbling, taking another few steps and nibbling.

"In 1992 on the lower Kazan River, we encountered one of the three major herds of barren-land caribou," he says. "For several days—from Thirty Mile Lake down to Baker Lake—we were surrounded by thousands and thousands of them. Obviously the term 'barren lands' for the tundra is a misnomer [used] by whites who felt intimidated by the lack of trees and shrubs. The profusion of flora and fauna is amazing. In 1998, on the Ellice River, Ivan took his cup of coffee up to the top of a hill to look around. He does that most mornings. As he was walking back, I noticed he was being closely shadowed by a large gray wolf. Intensely curious, it stopped on a rise a few feet away and stared at us for a long moment. I think there is great value in getting close to truly wild animals."

Murphy realizes why canoeing is so important to him. "For me, being out in the wilderness is a profound experience," he says. "After you have been out for a number of weeks in one of the last really wild places on the planet, you start to feel a deep sense of solitude that few people have a chance to experience. You aren't distracted by modern life with its buildings, vehicles, television sets, and clocks, and the endless back-and-forth of human argument and conversation. It is a chance to get in touch with your own thoughts and practice quieting the mind. Sometimes we paddle in silence for hours, listening to the wind and waves and birds. At times your movement over the water is so smooth and rhythmical it is almost trance-like. You begin to feel as if you are motionless and the horizon is rolling up to meet you. At those times you can let your mind wander and reflect and relax, and all seems well. So while paddling is intensely physical, it can also be meditative. There is something so basic, so joyful about moving silently in a canoe across a vast wild landscape that it's not easily described. I get a similar feeling from running and cross-country skiing, and perhaps it is better left unsaid."

Murphy considers Robertson one of his best friends. The two men exchange frequent e-mails and plan upcoming journeys months ahead of time. "The possibilities are limitless," Murphy says. "I hope I'm going to be canoeing for a long time unless I suffer some unforeseen malady. I've done as arduous and difficult trips as anyone I know, but I realize I won't get to all the rivers in Nunavut or the Northwest Territories. You could canoe every summer of your life and not cover all the rivers. I'm not trying to rack up miles or to see every river. I've been on the Kazan River twice. I may go back again because it's so beautiful.

"Meg has asked me a number of times why returning to the same area doesn't bore me. I canoed the Fond du Lac River in 1990 and again in 1999. The most famous aphorism of Heraclitus, a pre-Socratic Greek philosopher, is 'One cannot step twice into the same river.' On one level Heraclitus was talking about a river running. A river is never at rest, therefore one can't step into it twice. Like most good bits of philosophy, that can be interpreted on a number of different levels. The river hasn't changed in geologic time. What has changed in the intervening nine years is me. In 1999, I was older, I was more experienced, I felt more relaxed. Some things looked familiar, some didn't. We shot some of the rapids we had previously portaged.

"On the second trip, I had a copy of David Thompson's *Narrative of His Explorations in Western America, 1784–1812* with me, and I didn't have it on the earlier trip. It's a superb historical narrative. We sat around the campfire and read Thompson's account of a terrible accident he and his two Native American guides had had. They had lost most of their possessions and nearly died and here we were in the same place over two hundred years later. That added a dimension to what had already been a wonderful trip. At Thompson Rapids so much less had changed than in the rest of the world. In our increasingly crowded world it's amazing that you can find a place like that.

"When I was younger, I was trying to see in what sense Heraclitus was right. As I grow older and try stepping back into the river, there is some sense of longing for my past, but the experience is so different each time that it's pleasurable in the present as well, so canoeing becomes a continuum for me. It's a connection with where I've been, and where I'm going to go."

PART 6

Callings

Twenty-six

Jerry Traufler: Masterwork

I'm an average man and an average carver, but I took on a job that isn't average.

—Jerry Traufler, who spent seven years carving a life-size sculpture of Christ and the Twelve Apostles inspired by Leonardo da Vinci's mural *The Last Supper* in the Church of Santa Maria delle Grazie in Milan.

In 1975, Jerry Traufler, a postal worker in Le Mars, Iowa, and his wife, Arlene, drove to the Ozarks. At Silver Dollar City, outside Branson, Missouri, he watched some craftsmen carving figures. One of the men asked Traufler if he'd had any carving experience. Traufler said no, but the man handed him his tools and told him to continue his carving of a farmer while he took a break for dinner. By the time the man returned, Traufler had completed the farmer's face. "I thought you said you couldn't carve," the man said. "You've got the touch. I wish you luck."

When Traufler returned home, he asked a friend for a piece of wood. The friend gave him a tree limb. Traufler put the tree limb in a vise and sharpened a screwdriver. He chose a shoe as his project. He stayed up late that night, went to work at the post office the next morning, and resumed carving as soon as he got home, staying up until midnight. "I was really excited," he says. "It was my first foray into carving and my shoe looked exactly like a shoe." His friend tossed him a catalog and told him, "If you can do this with a screwdriver, buy some tools." Traufler followed the advice.

The next year, Traufler made thirteen carvings, took them to Waterloo, Iowa, site of the state wood-carving show, and won eight ribbons—firsts in "realistic animals," "human figures," and "fish," and seconds and thirds in other categories.

Between 1976 and 1986 he submitted carvings to shows in Alaska and California as well as in Iowa and won many ribbons: "About half my carvings won prizes." He discovered he had more aptitude for realistic human figures than for, say, birds. In 1986, Traufler won first place in the "human realistic bust" category at the International Woodcarvers' Show in Davenport, Iowa, with a carving of his wife.

Several years earlier, he and Arlene had driven to Spooner, Wisconsin, to see a rough-hewn carving of *The Last Supper*. His reaction to it: "I can do that." They had subsequently driven to Kansas City, Missouri, to see another Last Supper, which was stylistically "more refined." Traufler stopped entering competitions in 1986 and made a decision to carve his own Last Supper, to be displayed in Iowa. His rendition would be less rough than the one in Spooner, but less refined than the one in Kansas City, which had been done by a professional carver.

Traufler first read a number of books about the lives of the apostles and studied photographs of Leonardo da Vinci's mural. He is a devout man who currently works as a distribution clerk in the post office from five to nine in the morning, then attends Mass with Arlene, eats an early lunch, and returns to work from ten until two in the afternoon.

In 1986, after work and on his days off, Traufler started carving Bartholomew, the apostle who stands to the far left of Christ in Leonardo's painting. He borrowed pants and a shirt from his brother-in-law, who is somewhat larger, stuffed them with newspaper, and wrapped heavy number 9 wire around to create a standing mannequin. He used pine two-by-fours, gluing the boards together, employing Sheetrock screws—"which was all I had in my little shop"—to hold the boards tight until the glue adhered. The task took him three months. "I kind of took Bartholomew's face off da Vinci but it's no one in particular," he says.

After making what he calls "a bad decision" to carve James the Lesser and Andrew, the two apostles to the right of Bartholomew, out of a single block of wood (the block weighed six hundred pounds and was hard to move around the shop), he made a couple of "good" decisions. He bought bar clamps to hold the wood together, which speeded up the gluing process, and later switched to a hydraulic clamp, which cut the gluing time to two and a half weeks.

And when his brother, Dick Traufler, a feed dealer, came by and asked if he was going to use models in his carving, Dick became his model for James the Lesser. "If I hadn't used models, Christ and the twelve apostles would have looked too much alike," he says. "Carvers tend to duplicate faces. I didn't want to have thirteen men who resembled each other." Andrew was the only other apostle Traufler carved using a combination of Leonardo and his imagination. His model for Judas was a fellow postal distribution clerk, Bill Fitzpatrick, who was "reluctant at first to pose for the betrayer, but he's a nice man and he agreed."

A priest from Traufler's parish gave him an alb, the long white linen robe with tapered sleeves worn by a priest during Mass. Traufler draped it over each model. He posed the models in a few different ways and photographed them from the front, back, and both sides. Later, as he carved, he studied the photographs. Ken Plueger, a concrete contractor, who is bald, asked Traufler if he could use a bald model. He became Peter. Both Leonardo and Traufler depict Peter with not too much hair. One night during a blizzard, Traufler asked Arlene to be John.

Traufler had chosen the model for Jesus, the central figure, first, but carved him last. "I wanted all the experience I could get before carving Christ," he says. Bruce Lahrs, a meter reader with Iowa Public Service, was the sculptor's choice for Jesus.

James the Greater was modeled on Dick Kellen, a farmer; Thomas on Tom Reuter, Arlene's sister's husband, a contractor; Philip on Dolores Paulson, a housewife who is one of Arlene's customers ("Philip was painted by da Vinci in profile and Dolores had the perfect profile for Philip"); Thaddeus on Emmet Freking, a retired farmer; Matthew on Tom Walsh, a letter carrier; and Simon on Rich Helmer, a retired highway patrolman who was working for the sheriff's office in Le Mars.

"Most of the apostles have retired by now but they're all still running around Le Mars," Traufler says. "Bruce Lahrs is still reading our gas and electric meters."

Traufler didn't put facial hair on the apostles the two women posed for. "That worked out fine; I wanted some with beards and some without," he says. "And while I didn't copy da Vinci, I just let him inspire me—da Vinci's John and Philip don't have beards, either. I did what I felt like doing at the time." He added beards to most of the others. Traufler, who was born in Le Mars in 1938, went into the National Guard after graduating from high school, and worked as a barber from 1959 to 1970, before going to work for the post office.

Traufler's shop and garage became crowded as he carved, with some apostles stored in each. A few years into his work, he added a fifteen-by-twenty-two-foot room onto the side of the shop so that he could assemble the group. He carved a table that is covered with a tasseled tablecloth and rests on four carved sawhorses. He placed carved goblets, bread, bowls, and other vessels on the table. He switched from pine to basswood ("I couldn't find a supply of it when I started") for the table, for the last four apostles to the right of Jesus, and for Jesus.

Jerry Traufler completed his Last Supper in 1993. He had originally hoped it would remain in Le Mars, "the ice-cream capital of the world," where more ice cream is produced by one company—Blue Bunny—than is produced anywhere else. The City Council had no suitable building in which to display it, however, and no inclination to build one. Traufler could easily have sold his carving for a significant sum of money, but he did not want any money. He decided that the best place for his Last Supper was at the Queen of Peace Shrine in Sioux City, Iowa, about twenty-five miles from his home. An octagonal room was constructed there to house the carving and a meditation chapel. The Last Supper was moved there in 1995. No admission is charged to see the twenty-two-foot-long sculpture and no changes can be made to it in Traufler's lifetime without his consent. For the past several years attendance has been about eighty thousand. "It's where it belongs," he says.

"At first I kept track of the time I spent on the Last Supper but I stopped because after a while I didn't want to know," he goes on. "Some days I probably worked only a few minutes because I wasn't getting what I wanted to achieve. Before undertaking the Last Supper, I played golf seven days a week. I gave up golf and bowling to finish it. I golf once or twice a year now. I don't even miss golf. That seems weird. I think the Last Supper is one of the best things I've ever done—to have made it and to have given it away. It lasts longer than a ribbon or a post office career. I put my carving ribbons in boxes years ago. I threw out the bowling and the trap-shooting trophies I'd won."

Since 1989 Traufler has been carving Rosa Mystica statues—renditions of Mary that stand about twenty-eight inches tall. Each takes about a hundred hours to carve and paint. He donates the Rosa Mystica statues to poor churches, usually in distant lands, upon the request of priests and bishops and missionaries who serve in countries like India, Peru, and Papua New Guinea: "I only want to give my work to people who cannot afford it."

Traufler delivers some of the statues personally and also takes other trips abroad for pleasure. "Cisco stock has taken us to South America once and to Europe about half a dozen times in the past ten or twelve years," he says. "I made a Rosa Mystica for a convent in Italy, met the Holy Father, and had a statue I carved blessed in Rome. We've also been to Ireland, Yugoslavia, Switzerland, Portugal, France, and Luxembourg, where my grandfather came from. My favorite trip was to the Holy Land. We went to the Sea of Galilee, to Jerusalem, to the Dead Sea. We walked in the footsteps of Christ.

"There is no point in buying stock and never selling it. I could have retired from the post office years ago, but I'm not ready to quit. I'll know when it's time. We keep our lives purposely quiet, so I have plenty of time for the Rosa Mystica. We don't belong to anything, except a small Sunday evening prayer group at our church."

Twenty-seven

Walter Pforzheimer:
I, Spy

"Mata Hari, which is Javanese for Eye-of-the-Morning, is dead," Henry G. Wales wrote from Paris on October 18, 1917, for the International News Service. "She was shot as a spy by a firing squad of Zouaves at the Vincennes Barracks. She died facing death literally, for she refused to be blindfolded.

"Gertrude Margarete Zelle, for that was the real name of the beautiful Dutch-Javanese dancer, did appeal to President Poincaré for a reprieve, but he refused to intervene."

That the French president should have turned a deaf ear to the alleged German spy is hardly surprising. Mata Hari had already petitioned Raymond Poincaré's government for the return of her passport. Without a passport, Gertrude Margarete Zelle couldn't leave the country, and without leaving the country, she was, by October 1917, doomed.

Walter Pforzheimer owns Mata Hari's last visa application, the one that had gotten her into France. He also owns Hermann Göring's self-annotated wartime telephone directory—Pforzheimer rescued it from the German Air Ministry at the end of World War II—and he has a rare transcript, in shorthand, of the 1777 trial of "John the Painter" Aitkein, the only American convicted of espionage on English soil during the Revolutionary War. Aitkein set a fire on the Portsmouth dock in December 1776 that destroyed a significant portion of the Royal Navy's rope supply. He was hanged the following March.

Maybe most impressive, Pforzheimer has a letter written during the Revolutionary War in George Washington's own hand. The letter, addressed to
Colonel Elias Dayton, is dated July 26, 1777, and reads, in part: "The
necessity for procuring good intelligence is apparent & need not be further
urged. All that remains for me to add is, that you keep the whole matter as
secret as possible. For upon secrecy, success depends in most Enterprizes of
the kind, and for want of it, they are generally defeated."

"I was lucky," Pforzheimer says of his ability to purchase the letter. "It
wasn't cheap, but it wasn't life-threatening, and it's a very great letter that
brings tears to people's eyes. The director of the CIA almost wept one day
as he took the letter to the Hill.

"George Washington, I would say, is the first and greatest of the American intelligence officers. Here was a tremendous figure. He knew he had to
do it, and he understood it. I have no fear in saying that he was the greatest
intelligence officer we ever had."

High praise, indeed, from a man who can reasonably be said to have
known every major American intelligence figure since the creation of the
Central Intelligence Agency. Walter Pforzheimer is one of the "Old Boys."
Along with James Angleton, Richard Helms, Lawrence Houston, Ray
Cline, and a handful of others, Pforzheimer was there at the beginning, in
1946, when the CIA was formed as the Central Intelligence Group, to
carry on in peacetime the work that General "Wild Bill" Donovan's Office
of Strategic Services had undertaken so effectively during World War II. At
the dawn of the new century, Pforzheimer was very nearly the last of them
all, along with Helms, and by common consent the Agency's institutional
memory.

Beginning in the nineteen-seventies, press accounts routinely referred to
Pforzheimer as the CIA's unofficial historian, but he might also be thought
of as both historian for and librarian to not just the Agency but also the
peculiar business he has spent his adult lifetime in service to. Mata Hari's
application for her passport, Göring's phone directory, the transcript of the
trial of "John the Painter," and George Washington's letter on the necessity
of espionage are part of a collection of spycraft documents and other intelligence mementos that has grown to include some ten thousand books.
Almost certainly, Pforzheimer's collection is the largest such assemblage in
private hands in the world, although those who amass such things tend, by
nature, toward the secretive.

Appropriately—and ironically—Pforzheimer stores most of these items
behind a locked steel gate on the second floor of one of two apartments he
owns at the site of the most famously botched espionage caper in American

history: the Watergate, home to a "third-rate burglary" that toppled a presidency.

Like many collectors, Walter Pforzheimer seems to have been genetically programmed for the chase. His father, Walter Senior, and his uncle Carl H. Pforzheimer had both played a role early in the twentieth century in forming the New York Curb Market Association, which later became the American Stock Exchange. Both made handsome livings in finance, and both occupied mansions in Purchase, New York, in suburban Westchester County. In 1922, though, the brothers had a falling-out that drew a fault line through the entire family. Walter Pforzheimer was not to see his uncle again until after his father's death in 1955, only two years before Carl Pforzheimer's own death. But whatever drove the brothers apart, they remained linked throughout life by a singular devotion to the gathering of books and literary memorabilia.

Carl Pforzheimer's was the greater fortune—he was a pioneer in trading Standard Oil shares after the company was broken up in 1911—and the more famous library. "He collected Shakespeare and the Elizabethans and everything up to 1800," Walter Pforzheimer says. "Then he had a separate collection after 1800. Uncle's collection [largely the material before 1800] has now been purchased for the University of Texas library by a local sponsor named Perot. I think it cost him nineteen million dollars." (The actual sale price for what is known as the Pforzheimer Collection of Early English Literature was $15 million. Billionaire and later presidential contender H. Ross Perot fronted the money for the purchase in 1986.) Without Perot's assistance, the Texas library also bought a Gutenberg Bible from Carl Pforzheimer's estate, for $2.4 million. Pforzheimer had paid less than $60,000 for the Bible in 1923. Carl Pforzheimer was also a benefactor of the New York Public Library, whose Pforzheimer Collection of Shelley and His Circle—some twenty-five thousand books, manuscripts, letters, and other objects—remains one of the world's leading repositories for the study of English Romanticism.

The holdings amassed by Walter Pforzheimer's father tend to pale before those of his uncle, yet the senior Walter Pforzheimer still managed to build three significant libraries: one that his son calls "probably the best private collection of Molière in the country, though it is by no means final"; a second collection devoted to royal French book bindings; and the "definitive collection" of the nineteenth-century writer Frank R. Stockton, now largely forgotten but once among the most popular of American authors and humorists.

"The Stockton family, which came out of Philadelphia, had gotten tired of carting the stuff around," Pforzheimer recalls. "They were bored to tears with Uncle Frank's letters, and they weren't terribly bright at any rate, so they decided to sell it all in Newark, New Jersey, on 'x' date. Unfortunately, they had to change the date by a day or two. Father and his bookseller went on the appropriate day and were able to beat out those who didn't have the change of date.

"That's how you build a collection. You stumble over the right place at the right time and hope the others don't get there. You have a pair of fast hands, and you have luck coming out of your pants."

Pforzheimer keeps all three of his father's collections with his own books and other memorabilia, locked behind the steel gate in a space designed neither for collecting nor curating. Shelves are lined up in halls and where beds were meant to be. Even the bathroom has been pressed into use for storage.

"I have the original drawings by A. B. Frost for the Stockton books—a hundred or more of them are up there in my bathtub," Pforzheimer says. "It better not start dripping." Better not, indeed. Arthur Burdett Frost, who lived from 1851 to 1928, is still prized for his book and magazine illustrations and for his sporting art, especially the hunting prints.

A lifelong bachelor, Pforzheimer has lived in a single-floor, one-bedroom apartment elsewhere in the Watergate complex since 1966. It was the last one-bedroom to be sold in the initial offering of the residences, six years before G. Gordon Liddy, Chuck Colson, Richard Nixon, and others managed to turn "Watergate" into a household word. The two-story apartment has always been for the books, the letters, the things that matter.

"I slept there and dressed there," Pforzheimer says of his smaller apartment, "but I came up here when I got home from work."

Over the years, Pforzheimer has added marginally to both the Molière and royal French binding collections, filling holes and shoring up weaknesses as he discovered them. He also has served as a custodian for the Stockton collection, carrying on correspondence with other repositories of the writer's papers, books, and wood engravings, Stockton's first calling. Mostly, though, Pforzheimer's curatorial attentions have been devoted to his own books and artifacts. And that, he says, has had much less to do with avocation than vocation. For Walter Pforzheimer, spying seems to have begotten spy collecting, of necessity.

Ever since he suffered a stroke in February 1998, Walter Pforzheimer has had to make do with a motorized wheelchair. Unable to knot a regular necktie, he favors string ties held in place with a specially designed black-on-white bolo. One side of the bolo reads "CIA"; the other, "Y35," for his university and year of graduation—Yale, class of 1935.

"Those are really the big points of my life," he says. "There aren't many things so great in life that you want to remember. I put them on there so I would remember them."

Students of the espionage literature Walter Pforzheimer has so thoroughly amassed will immediately note the linkage between the two sides of Pforzheimer's tie bolo: Yale was heavily represented in Donovan's Office of Strategic Services, and the links between the university and the intelligence community linger still. Drive along the George Washington Parkway, on the south bank of the Potomac River, looking for the Central Intelligence Agency, and you will be directed by road signs instead to the George Bush Center for Intelligence: a headquarters building named for a former spy chief and the forty-first president of the United States, Yale class of 1948, just off a tree-lined parkway named for America's first and greatest spy.

Pforzheimer already had graduated from Yale Law School and was practicing law somewhat unhappily with a New York City firm when a brief encounter turned his life upside down.

"A guy smacked me on the shoulder and said, 'Would you like to be in intelligence?' I'd never seen him before. I've never seen him since. I thought for thirty seconds and said, 'Yeah, I think I would.' I went into the intelligence business on 8 December 1942, and I've been in it every day since, without fail."

Pforzheimer spent the war with the Senior Air Intelligence Staff, first in London, finally in Paris. Among his colleagues was Lewis Franklin Powell Jr., later a justice of the Supreme Court. After the war, Pforzheimer helped write the enabling legislation that created the CIA and defined its early boundaries. He served a dozen years as the Agency's legislative counsel and later as its general counsel and the founder and custodian of its historical intelligence collections. Along the way, Pforzheimer says, he had to give himself an education on espionage and intelligence gathering—and do so on the fly.

"In 1946, when I joined the Central Intelligence Group, there were all these guys, and I needed to know what they were talking about. Jim was reading this book on spies. Joe was reading that one. I began to pick up a book here and there because I wanted to find out what I was getting into, and suddenly I discovered that the collection was getting quite large."

Large, and continually growing. In 1994, after the CIA's Aldrich Ames was arrested and accused of spying for the Soviets, Ames's sister sold part of his library to a used-book dealer in suburban Virginia. Naturally, Pforzheimer had to have the volumes.

"I never expected to build a spy collection, but I think it's the best grouping of intelligence books that's in existence. . . . It's a helluva collection. That's a terrible thing to say, but it's true."

Inevitably, Pforzheimer has found his favorites among his books over the years. *The Agency: The Rise and Decline of the CIA* by the British writer John Ranelagh was "the first really comprehensive book on the CIA"—it takes the reader up to 1987 in the trade paperback edition—"and is still probably the best single book" on the subject, he says. (Pforzheimer himself, it should be noted, was interviewed for Ranelagh's book and appears in it in a relatively minor role.)

Pforzheimer disdains spy fiction: "None of us want to collect it. We don't believe in it. But look," he adds, waving his hand at two long, jam-packed shelves of paperback spy novels above his desk. The best of them, he says, is Compton MacKenzie's *Water on the Brain*. "It's a novel about his intelligence experiences in Greece in World War Two. The British immediately suppressed it, but it's *the* book on comics in the intelligence business."

The first floor of Walter Pforzheimer's two-story apartment is something of a museum to his work and his associations. A CIA flag stands by his desk. There's a stained-glass medallion with the seal of the Agency hanging from the curtain rod, in front of the sliding glass doors, and a bumper sticker tacked to the bookshelves that reads: THE WORLD IS AT PEACE 'CAUSE THE CIA IS AT WAR.

Signed photos dot the walls: from General Donovan and Allen Dulles, who directed the Agency through the early years of the Cold War while his brother John Foster Dulles was running Dwight Eisenhower's state department. In another photo, former CIA head Richard Helms is shown presenting Pforzheimer with a special commemorative book, *In the Name of Intelligence: Essays in Honor of Walter Pforzheimer,* assembled for his eightieth birthday in August 1994. The same event brought personal letters from George Bush ("self-typed," the letter notes) and Ronald Reagan, who had named Pforzheimer to be one of three ex-CIA officers on his 1981 transition team for the Agency. The Reagan letter begins, "A little birdie told me that today is an important occasion in your life." Both are framed and hang on the crowded walls, along with a letter from George II to Prime Minister Robert Walpole, a map tracing the round-the-world tour by the British code breakers "Sir Edward Travis & Rear Admiral [Edmund] Rushbrooke & Staffs, 14th March–27th April 1945," and a representation of another famous spy, Nathan Hale, about to be hanged by British troops during the American Revolution.

Also hanging on the wall are two silk screens, one in color and one in black and white, done by the Soviet spy Colonel Rudolf Abel while he was serving time in the federal penitentiary in Atlanta. Posing as a commercial artist and photographer named Emil Golfus, Abel had run a spy ring in the United States for nine years before his arrest in 1957. Sentenced to thirty years in prison, he was released in 1962 and traded to the Soviets for the downed American U-2 pilot Francis Gary Powers.

On a tabletop a small statue of Bill Donovan sits cheek by jowl with a figurine of the dancing Dutch-Javanese Mata Hari; a Royal Canadian Mountie on horseback; and a bust of Felix Dzerzhinsky, "a very good intelligence officer" who abandoned his background—he had been born to wealthy Polish landowners—to become the first head of the Cheka, the ancestor of the Soviet KGB. The objects on the tabletop and hanging on the walls, Pforzheimer says, "are just things you add when you're in the game."

Beside and around him as he talks are small stacks of books, on the floor and on his desktop. "I never fixed this room up after the stroke," he says. "I had enough problems fixing me up. Meanwhile, I keep adding books. Look at them. They all have to go upstairs to be shelved."

And there's the problem: Pforzheimer's apartment has no elevator. When we talked, it had been more than a year since several visitors carried him in his motorized wheelchair up the narrow staircase so he could once again unlock the steel gate and browse among his belongings. Otherwise, he's downstairs, and the collection he has spent his life amassing—"the best grouping of intelligence books that's in existence"—is upstairs, effectively locked away from him like some final secret of life.

"It's been fun collecting it," Pforzheimer says. "I wish I could get up there and see it. But, hell, who expects to get to be eighty-five?"

Twenty-eight

Claire Miller:
Family Ties

In November 1987 Claire Miller's mother died at the age of sixty-seven in Des Moines, Iowa. Miller, forty-one, who was living in Florida with her husband, David Kerben, and their son Joel, three, flew to Iowa for the funeral. "At my mother's house was this weekender-size suitcase full of documents, photographs, lists, and rudimentary genealogy charts," she says. "My older brother asked me, 'How should we divide this up?' I told him I didn't think we should. I asked him to let me take the suitcase home for a couple of months so I could sort through it. My brother didn't care—he's much more interested in Corvettes."

When Miller took the suitcase, she thought that genealogy would be a temporary pursuit. At night, she spread the photographs out on her dining table, which, when all its leaves are deployed, is 110 inches long. Fourteen years later, she is more passionate about genealogy than she is about anything except her husband and son. A whole room in her home in Santa Rosa, California, is filled with electronic equipment, file drawers, boxes, and over sixty linear feet of bookshelves devoted to family history.

"I was probably more interested in my family than most people are because my mother, Hazel Irene Normandin, had twelve first cousins and my father, Jasper Chris Miller, had sixteen," she says. "I grew up in Des Moines and all my parents' siblings and three of my four grandparents lived in Iowa. The fourth, my paternal grandfather, Odes Bert Miller, died in 1943, three years before I was born. After my mother's death, when I sat down to make a pedigree chart, I soon had the dates of birth of most of my ancestors back to the early eighteen-hundreds. I just happen to descend from people with list-maker genes and people who didn't divorce much."

When she first examined the photographs of her ancestors, spread out on the table, she saw a young woman as she looked at twelve, as she looked as a bride, and as she looked when she was older and had started losing her teeth. This woman and others seemed to be inviting Miller to uncover their life stories; she accepted the invitation. She started making lists of ancestors and their descendants, along with any vital statistics (birth, marriage, and death) she had for each one. "That was part of the sorting process," she says. "And some of the photographs had names or soon would. One of my earliest genealogical memories is of my mother and my great-aunt Edna studying an old photograph. Edna was attempting to identify the ancestors while my mother wrote their names on the photograph's cardboard backing."

To Claire Miller, certain photographs in the suitcase were particularly compelling. In one, a three-year-old boy appears as a blur. "Obviously he couldn't stay still for twenty seconds," she says. "Everyone else in the photograph is sitting or standing quietly. I figured out when the photograph had been taken by knowing the date of birth of that restless three-year-old. I also surmised that the photograph was taken before another son in the family went off to the Civil War, because that handsome young man, James Monroe Potter, didn't come home from the war."

When Miller was in Washington in the summer of 1999 to attend the Institute on Genealogical Research at the National Archives, she decided to do some research on James Potter at the Archives. She learned that he had enlisted in Company C of the 112th Regiment, New York Infantry, on August 4, 1862. He stood five feet six and a quarter inches tall and had a light complexion, light hair, and hazel eyes. He was promoted to corporal before the end of 1862. He was killed on June 1, 1864, at Cold Harbor, Virginia, in one of the bloodier battles of the Civil War.

On one page in the packet she was given—the compiled service records for Union troops from northern states have not yet been microfilmed—the heading was "Inventory of the effects of James Monroe Potter." On that page she read that all of his effects had been lost on the battlefield. "I wonder if they were looted, or taken by a friend for safekeeping," she says. "A genealogist does a lot of wondering." Miller learned exactly where Potter took the bullet and how long it took him to die. "The company history is written in flowery prose by the company chaplain," she says. "It makes his death sound so high-minded. It leaves out all the blood and pain."

By 1999, Miller knew a great deal about the Potters. James Potter's parents, Abram and Abigail, had lost a daughter before she reached her first birthday. Abram Mattison Potter was a prosperous farmer in western New York. The Potters moved to Iowa a year after James Potter's death. Grief followed them: another daughter died from typhus in October 1865 at the age of twenty-three. It troubled Miller when she spoke of James Monroe Potter to an acquaintance that her reaction was, "Oh well, he's not an ancestor, he's just an uncle." She thought of how much her twelve uncles had enriched her life and she felt sorry for all the nieces and nephews who never knew their uncle Jim.

In 1987, one of the first things Miller did after dropping the French classes and the nonfiction writing classes she had been taking to pursue her ancestors was to read a couple of how-to books, such as Jeane Eddy Westin's *Finding Your Roots* and Ralph Crandall's *Shaking Your Family Tree*. The books taught her some basic skills, among them how to fill in a pedigree chart, a fundamental record-keeping form.

"You start with yourself as number one," she says. "Your father is number two, your mother is number three. The males are always the even numbers, the females are always the odd numbers. It's a convention, just like a bridge convention. The father of one person will be that person doubled, so the father of ancestor number six will always be number twelve. I can send this chart anywhere in the world and people will understand it." On Miller's pedigree chart, Milton Augustus Potter, one of James Monroe Potter's brothers, is number twenty-six and his wife, Sarah Amelia Webb, is number twenty-seven. They are her maternal great-great-grandparents.

For each couple on a pedigree chart, you show only one child—"the child of interest"—the child that continues to lead down to number one on the chart. You need another form, a family group sheet, for every couple on the pedigree chart, "to show all of their children and to flesh out the bare bones with a little more information." For the husband and wife on a family group sheet, typical information might include dates and places of birth, marriage, death, and burial; occupation; military service; religious affiliation; appearances in the U.S. census; names of their parents; and names of other spouses, if any. For each of the children, the goal is to include birth, marriage, and death data, plus the name of the spouse. Miller has attempted to find her ancestors in every census year in which they could conceivably have been listed.

After the beginning genealogist has gone through his or her attic, interviewed elderly relatives, and sent away for vital records, the next step is to

search census microfilms. "In 1790, the United States became the first country in the world to take a national census," she says. "A census has been
taken every ten years since then. Prior to 1850, only the name of the head-
of-household was listed. Everyone else was represented by little tick marks
under sex and age columns. It can be infuriating when you're trying to figure out which Jones family in Clermont County, Ohio, is *your* Jones family.
Beginning with the 1850 census, every member of the family was named. If
you have reasonably stable families and not very common names, it's not
much of a trick to trace back to 1850. In the time period before 1850, you
can't rely on the census alone, and so you have to turn to other types of documents." Genealogists tend to believe there is a special place in hell for the
men who designed the pre-1850 censuses.

"People tend not to realize that the keeping of vital records is a fairly
recent phenomenon in the United States," Miller says. "Marriage licenses
were instituted first—in order to prove legitimacy for inheritance reasons.
Birth and death certificates were issued much later, and compliance was
spotty. In Iowa, for example, birth certificates were mandated by law in
1880. However, my mother was born on an Iowa farm in 1920, and she
didn't have a birth certificate until she applied for one in 1943.

"Church records, divorce decrees, cemetery records, military records,
land records, ships' passenger lists, naturalization records, wills and pro-
bate records, court records, and employment records may all be useful.
There are potentially a hundred different sources to look at for each ancestor, and these sources change, depending on the time, the place, and the
biographical circumstances. For example, for the middle to late eighteen-
hundreds, I would look at passenger lists and naturalization records for my
German and Irish ancestors, but my English and Scots-Irish ancestors all
arrived before the Revolutionary War, so naturalization records would not
pertain, and very few passenger lists prior to 1820 have survived. Tracing
your ancestors is slow going. In genealogy circles we sometimes say, 'How
do you get your genealogy done quickly for you? You run for president.'"

Invariably people will ask a genealogist, "How far back can you go?"
The answer is, it depends on how far back record keeping was, in a given
area. "My husband is a Polish Jew and I know that it's tough to go back in
Poland before the early eighteen-hundreds," Miller says. "That's when
births and deaths became officially recorded there under the Napoleonic
Code. Two of my German ancestors come from an island where the parish
registers were begun in 1650. I have ancestors from France, where the registers in some areas started as early as the mid-fifteen-hundreds. In England the church registers started in 1538. I traced some English ancestors

back beyond that 1538 barrier by finding them on wills. I also found ancestors listed on guild records predating 1538. Of course, finding a noble line can quickly take you back to medieval times. I haven't found a royal line yet, but I expect to, because I'm about fifty percent English, and nobility intermarried with commoners in England more than in any country in Europe."

When Miller started delving into her ancestry, she wanted to know everything about every one of her ancestors. Experts told her she needed to focus, or else she would have so many names and papers that she would become hopelessly confused. When she began her quest, her earliest known ancestor was Benjamin Nickerson, born in 1796 in Kent County, Delaware, or Queen Annes County, Maryland. It didn't take long before she discovered the Nickerson Family Association. "So I wrote a letter asking if they had heard of Benjamin and his wife, Maria Jane (Williams) Nickerson. Within a week I received a response, taking my line back to the immigrants, William and Ann (Busby) Nickerson, who arrived in Salem, Massachusetts Bay Colony, in 1637. What a thrill to push back so quickly to the earliest days in New England!"

Miller started working with the descendants of Benjamin Nickerson (number thirty-six) and Maria Jane Williams (number thirty-seven). Shortly after their marriage in 1817, Benjamin and Maria, along with Maria's father and several other family members, left the Delaware-Maryland border for Warren County, Ohio. They may have made part of the journey by floating down the Ohio River on a flatboat. About 1836, the family moved to St. Joseph County, Indiana, which had just been opened up to white settlers—the Native Americans had been removed to points farther west. "Maria gave birth to her first child when she was eighteen years old, and to her tenth child when she was fifty-one years old," Miller says. "Two sons died in infancy, and one daughter died at age seventeen. I feel like such a wimp when I think about such ancestors. They left behind their childhood homes. They settled the frontier. They survived the grief of losing young children. Despite the hard work and hardship—or perhaps because of it—Benjamin and Maria lived very long lives. Maria was seventy-eight when she died, Benjamin was eighty-five at the time of his death."

After two years spent researching the Nickersons, Miller went off on another tangent. She discovered a cousin, George Hessler, who was living in Seattle in a retirement home. "In 1991, George invited me to his ninetieth birthday party. At the party I met a score of cousins I didn't know I had. The genealogical highlight was copying George's extensive address book and birthday-anniversary book—by hand, because the retirement home's copy machine was broken. George and I are both descended from Peter Gruenwald (number twenty-two) and Margarethe Hansen (number twenty-three), who came from Fehmarn Insel, Schleswig-Holstein, a small island where you catch the ferry to go to Copenhagen. The catalog of the Family History Library in Salt Lake City has two reels of census microfilm for Fehmarn Insel, and another sixty reels of microfilmed parish registers going back to 1650. Here's a perfect example of how the genealogist starts out thinking, 'I'll never find anything,' and ends up thinking, 'I'll never get off this goddamn island.' "

Miller says that these great-great-grandparents are of exceptional interest to her. "In 1857, at age twenty, Peter Gruenwald borrowed the fare to immigrate to the United States," she says. "Part of his reason for immigrating was because, as an ethnic German, he wanted to avoid serving in the Danish army. At that time Schleswig-Holstein belonged to Denmark. As luck would have it, four years after arriving in Iowa, Peter was drafted into the Union army. He borrowed nine hundred dollars at nine percent interest—usurious back then—to hire a substitute, a perfectly legal practice during the Civil War. He managed to pay back these debts, buy three farms, raise a large family, and leave each of his children enough money to buy a business or a farm when he died in 1913.

"Margarethe gave birth to eleven children. Three didn't survive early childhood. The story that has come down through the family is that she grew increasingly depressed. I don't know the specific reason she committed suicide in 1886, I know only that Peter's behavior was quite tyrannical, and she seemed to lose hope that life would ever improve. It's possible she discovered she was pregnant again. Her death came on a summer evening. She was just forty-five when she wandered away from a dance, fell from a bridge into the stream below, and drowned. Some genealogists are embarrassed to discover ancestors who have been convicted of crimes or who have committed suicide. I refuse to be embarrassed by anything that happened in 1886."

One of the Gruenwalds' children, Minnie Margaret Gruenwald, who married Christian W. Neumeier, was Claire Miller's paternal great-grandmother. The Neumeiers' daughter, Amanda Fredericka (number five), the wife of Odes Bert Miller (number four), was her grandmother.

Since 1987, Claire Miller has taken courses in genealogy and has spent a lot of time visiting well-known genealogical collections, such as the Newberry Library in Chicago, the Boston Public Library, and the Rhode Island Historical Society. She has spent a week at the Allen County Public Library in Fort Wayne, Indiana—the second-largest genealogical collection in the world—and has made six one-week trips to the Family History Library in Salt Lake City, the largest.

"Members of the Church of Jesus Christ of Latter-day Saints—Mormons—believe that families are united in eternity," she says. "While on the earthly plane, members are expected to complete their own genealogical research back four generations. The LDS genealogical collection began as an effort to help church members conduct their required research and extend that research further, if desired. With time, the vision grew and it became the goal of the collection to include as much genealogical material as possible. At any given moment, there are one hundred and fifty LDS microfilm crews spread around the world, microfilming parish records, vital records, land records, military records, and just about all types of documents imaginable that have genealogical value.

"The Family History Library in Salt Lake City truly is Mecca for genealogists. But you don't have to go to Salt Lake City. Hundreds of LDS churches have family history centers, where you can rent microfilms. And you don't have to be a Mormon to use the LDS resources."

When Miller first began to pursue genealogy, she felt sorry for people who could not trace their families very far back in time—her husband, for example, who was born in the Warsaw Ghetto on May 14, 1932. Dave Kerben's family arrived in New York in April 1938. On the ship passenger-arrival list, the surname is spelled "Kerszenblat," which is the Polish spelling of the German name Kirschenblatt, meaning "cherry leaf." The name was simplified by Kerben's Uncle Harry, who had shortened his own surname from Eisenstarr to Starr. "You can't go around with a name like Kerszenblat," Uncle Harry said. "No one can pronounce it, much less spell it." Unless Polish Jews come from families with lengthy rabbinical traditions, Miller adds, "it's difficult for them to trace their ancestry back past 1800. She now feels they are fortunate. "Polish Jews have some hope of completing their family trees," Miller says. "I don't. When I started down this road in 1988, I was only forty-one and figured I'd be able to trace all my ancestors back to the sixteenth or seventeenth century because the records are so good for their nationalities."

She has had her mind changed by running into some geneaological brick walls. The people she is currently pursuing went from Virginia to Kentucky during and immediately after the American Revolution. Frontier folk had no time for paperwork. But more to the point, Miller's ancestors often arrived in a place before it was under any sort of jurisdiction. "The only records they left were the ashes from their campfires," Miller says. "One ancestor has a common name—James Montgomery. There may have been eight or more James Montgomerys of roughly the same age living in central Kentucky between 1780 and 1800."

Miller believes she now knows which James Montgomery is *her* James Montgomery, but she has yet to document to her satisfaction the names of James's parents. "I think I know who they were but I will probably have to research all the James Montgomerys in central Kentucky and prove my James's parentage by process of elimination—by proving that all the other Jameses had different parents, and so the only possibilities are the ones I believe them to be."

Miller is content even though she is unlikely ever to complete filling out pedigree charts and family-group sheets. "The process is what's most important," she says. "I'm a generalist and I consider it the perfect hobby for the generalist because as you go back and research your family you learn about religion, diet, dress, politics, geography, language, transportation, migrations, economics, architecture, and the arts. Genealogy is history made personal. One of my gripes is that history is focused on generals, kings, martyrs, and crazy people. I'd rather read books like Beatrice Gottlieb's *The Family in the Western World: From the Black Death to the Industrial Age*. Gottlieb describes the life of ordinary people. If you just have a long list of hatching, matching, and dispatching, that's very dry. Long before I became interested in genealogy I wanted to know people's life stories because I wanted to know why they made the decisions they made. Why did they go from Denmark to the United States in 1857 or from Poland to America in 1938? I know people whose goal is to get a line back to the Sons or Daughters of the American Revolution, but I'm not one of them. I'm like the great majority of genealogists I know. I'm happy with whatever I find because I'm enriched by whatever I find."

At the outset, Miller didn't expect to become obsessed with genealogy. "It just happened," she says. "The more I got into it, the more exciting it became. It's difficult for me to understand why people watch soap operas on daytime or evening television when there are more exciting characters and probably just as many shotgun marriages and other untoward events in their own families as in the made-up ones on a screen. I'm slightly put off by friends who ask me what purpose I'm serving. Here I've increased my knowledge about history, our country's western expansion, and places in Europe and the United States where I've traveled just to get an idea of where my ancestors lived, as well as the cemeteries in which they were buried. Isn't that enough?"

With the Internet, genealogical research is becoming much faster and easier. "The Internet is loaded with mailing lists for surnames, localities, ethnic groups, religious denominations, and specific topics, such as geneal-ogy software programs," Miller says. "The place to go to find a mailing list is http://www.rootsweb.com. My first big Internet discovery came from the Malott mailing list on RootsWeb. I posted a query about my earliest-known Malott ancestor, Emily Malott, born in Ohio in 1837, who married Joseph Jones. In two weeks, I heard from a researcher who gave me my line back to the immigrant ancestor, a French Huguenot, who arrived in New Amster-dam in 1662. I've met dozens of cyber-cousins on the Internet. We share information and, in some cases, develop warm friendships through e-mail correspondence. Lots of research can be done on the Internet. Many libraries have placed their catalogs online. Untold numbers of Web sites have hundreds of useful databases and indices. The most exciting develop-ment is the appearance of actual document images on the Internet. Cur-rently, there's a race among various Web sites to see which will be the first to provide images of every page of every United States Census ever taken. Still, I don't think the genealogist will ever be able to research completely online. There will always be a place for paper and pencils and trips to libraries and courthouses. I know I'll never run out of questions to research about my ancestors. I plan to be a genealogist all my life."

Twenty-nine

Ted Furey:
For God and Man and Old Ireland

If the name Patrick Charles Keely rings a bell—and it would be most appropriate if it was a church bell—Ted Furey is likely the reason why.

Keely was born on August 11, 1816, in Thurles, County Tipperary, Ireland, the son of a sawyer. In the early eighteen-forties, he joined the Irish outpouring to America, settling in the burgeoning immigrant community in the Williamsburg section of Brooklyn. Apparently trained as a carpenter—there is no record of his early years—Keely was soon called upon to create a carved altar and reredos, or partition screen, for the Church of St. James. The commission must have been a success because not long thereafter, on May 30, 1847, on the east side of Wythe Avenue, not far from the East River in Brooklyn, Roman Catholic Archbishop John Hughes laid the cornerstone for the first church Patrick Charles Keely was to design—Saints Peter and Paul.

With no formal training that anyone has ever been able to document, Keely would go on to design more than seven hundred cathedrals, churches, and other buildings for Roman Catholic parishes and religious orders, mostly in New England and the Middle Atlantic states but scattered widely across the rest of America, too, and even into the Maritime Provinces of Canada.

Keely's first cathedral church, St. Mary's, was begun in 1850, half a continent away from Brooklyn in Natchez, Mississippi. Over the next forty years, he would design cathedrals for Fall River and Springfield, Massachusetts; Albany, Brooklyn, and Buffalo, New York; Manchester, New Hampshire; Burlington, Vermont; Cleveland and Toledo, Ohio; Newark and Paterson, New Jersey; Chicago; and more. Another St. Mary's, this one the cathedral church for Halifax, Nova Scotia, was begun in 1872. The next year, Keely began work on what is often said to be his greatest design, St. Joseph's, the Hartford, Connecticut, cathedral that burned practically to the ground in 1956. (St. Joseph's, it would seem, was star-crossed from the beginning: Keely's son, Charles, who followed him into the business, contracted pneumonia while helping supervise its construction and died in the rectory there on Christmas Day, 1889.)

Keely's most monumental design, and one still standing, is the eleven-story Cathedral of the Holy Cross, on Washington Street in Boston's South End, begun in 1866, just as the architect was turning fifty. He was in his sixties when he designed the St. Francis Xavier College and Church in New York City and the St. John's Hospital Chapel in Lowell, Massachusetts. In his seventies, he conceived and oversaw the construction of two cathedrals—for Providence, Rhode Island, and Charleston, South Carolina—as well as parish churches in Baltimore and elsewhere. Keely was nearly eighty by the time work got under way on Sacred Heart in Malden, Massachusetts, widely thought to be his last church design.

That such a prolific shaper of the urban ecclesiastical landscape should be largely forgotten today says something about both the fleeting nature of fame—you'll search in vain for Patrick Charles Keely's name in *The Encyclopedia Britannica*—and the changing nature of the urban landscapes he adorned. That Keely should be remembered at all more than a century after his death says something about the quiet determination of Ted Furey.

Ted Furey grew up in and around one of Keely's parish churches: the brownstone St. Patrick's, in Enfield, Connecticut, whose cornerstone was laid in 1888. Along with other parishioners, Furey's two grandfathers had helped dig the foundation for the church—a cost-saving measure common among the Irish immigrant communities Keely worked with. His family also helped adorn the new church when it was completed in 1904, eight years after Keely's death.

"It was their pride and joy," Furey says. "My mother's father and grandfather got together and donated a window. The honorarium for the window was five hundred dollars. The most educated person in the family at the time was my aunt, a schoolteacher. Her salary for the whole year was three hundred seventy-four dollars when she started—the same year the family pledged the five hundred dollars. You just don't get that kind of commitment today, but they saw their opportunities in America as unlimited."

Furey was a fifth grader in January 1949, attending a parochial grade school behind the rectory, across from St. Patrick's, when the church caught fire and was gutted in a spectacular blaze.

"The church was always kept up nicely," Furey remembers. "Before the Christmas holidays that year, they had varnished the wainscoting, and they had these candles, maybe four inches high, that you could buy and stick in a holder to light. Underneath was sand. They think one of those candles fell over onto the floor, melted, caught the linoleum floor on fire, and spread from there to the new varnish and the wainscoting. No one saw it until it was too late.

"We've had a friend, a priest in Rhode Island, who said that Keely made the walls look thicker by putting partitions in them. It wasn't a flaw—it was a common practice to leave room inside the wall for air to circulate. But the fire got into the partition, and the firemen didn't understand how gasses accumulate. The church was totally kaput.

"After the fire, my grandfather told me two things: I won't be buried from St. Patrick's because it burned, and just a few weeks before I'd been sitting there thinking, Well, it won't be long before I'm pushed down the aisle."

A lifelong bachelor, Ted Furey lives today in the house he grew up in, on the south side of Enfield. Nearby, well within walking distance, is the Catholic elementary school where he has worked as an art teacher, a library director, and earlier a sixth grade teacher, since 1965. About a quarter mile north of his house, St. Patrick's—it reopened a year and a half after it burned, in time for Furey's grandfather's funeral service—stands in almost splendid isolation in one of those old downtown areas that seem to be receding like a hairline. Across the street the shop of a small electrical contractor sits beside another building that houses a printer and a driving school. A tattoo parlor and a hair salon are just around the corner. Nothing nearby even approaches the church in mass, much less grandeur.

Furey's house dates from 1904, the same year St. Patrick's was finished. The wide front porch is filled with heavy wicker furniture. The living room that runs across the front of the house is crammed with family pieces. Jammed into the kitchen are six crèche figures that Furey hopes to find time to repair. (More crèche figures are elsewhere in the house.) Also backed against the kitchen wall is a commanding plaster angel executed by J. Sibbel, a New York City craftsman whom Keely used for much of his finest plaster and marble work. Furey rescued the angel from Keely's cathedral in Lowell, Massachusetts, before it was torn down.

Part family museum and preservation workshop, Furey's home is also an archive. Upstairs and scattered about are some seventy white three-ring binders that Furey uses to document the work of Patrick Charles Keely, along with as many as 150 enlarged photos of his churches. And the binders and photos, in turn, get Ted Furey back to how he came to focus all these interests—in family, church, and preservation—on one Irish-American architect.

"I was always interested in churches. Whenever I saw these historical societies that specialized in churches, I joined them. I'd write to them about things I wanted to know about—the stained glass in the Hartford cathedral, things like that. But I didn't know how to pinpoint what I was most interested in."

Early in the nineteen-nineties, Furey says, his attention began to become concentrated on Keely. Part of the impetus was the Lowell cathedral. Built for nine thousand parishioners, it had dwindled to four hundred before being put on the block for one dollar. There it would sit, vacant and unpurchased, for a decade, until it was razed in 1996.

"Everyone thought the government would step in," Furey says. "[Former Massachusetts Senator] Paul Tsongas was involved for a time, but he was sick with cancer. It ended up being an awful tragedy."

For Furey, the Lowell cathedral and, as he would soon learn, the other threatened Keely churches were part of a growing culture of disposability within the church. "All of sudden all these treasures became throw-away items. I've had friends tell me they got a call from their priest who said, 'We know your family gave this marble pulpit, but we don't use marble pulpits anymore. Do you want it?'

"Some of the ends of the pews crafted by Keely were of solid cherry. The pews were of oak. There's not enough solid cherry in the world to do that anymore, yet in the nineteen-seventies some of these pews were torn out and sent to the dump."

At the same time Furey's concern over the preservation of Keely's work was mounting, he got to know the man who was to become one of his strongest allies: the Reverend Frederick Murphy of the Keely-designed Holy Cross Cathedral in Boston.

"In nineteen ninety-one or ninety-two, I went over there and met Father Murphy. He was both rector of the cathedral and administrator of another

Keely church. He was very gracious. Often they'll tell you the church is closed, but he put on the lights and told me to stay all I wanted. That was in February. I sent him a thank-you note afterward along with some candy and said, 'Let me know if you ever need an extra hand.' He wrote back and said, 'We can always use helping hands on Holy Saturday.' So I went back over there the day before Easter, and that's how the friendship began."

Before long, Furey was traveling the East, documenting Keely's churches and helping to authenticate his work, by records where possible, by an increasingly educated feel when no records existed.

"There's something about a Keely church you can pinpoint," he says. "The design flows from the pillars to the capital and up through the arches and into the sanctuary appointments. I've never seen a church in which the plasterwork is anywhere near the same. Very few of his churches were ever finished. They'd get to the point of building the steeple but never build it. But there's something very pleasing about Keely's designs. They're cohesive. I go into other churches, and I can tell right away that they aren't Keely's."

The research led to acquaintances—even close friends, as in the case of Father Murphy—and the acquaintances began to create a community. In 1996, the year the Lowell cathedral was knocked down, Furey founded the Keely Society. Four years later, on May 20, 2000, the society held its first congress, appropriately enough at the Cathedral of the Holy Cross in Boston. By then, Furey had established connections with the Pugin Society, dedicated to the work of Augustus Welby Northmore Pugin, the English architect, author, and designer who had been instrumental in the Gothic and Roman Catholic revivals of the first half of the nineteenth century. Furey suspects Keely would have been familiar with and influenced by the master's work—Pugin died in 1852, the year Keely's first cathedral was completed—although, as he admitted in an article for the Pugin Society's newsletter, "What Keely saw of Pugin's work . . . we can only surmise."

One of the thirty or so attendees at the first Keely Congress submitted a blurb on the event to an organ magazine. An organist in Philadelphia who saw the notice sent word to Furey through a Brooklyn priest that one of Keely's great-granddaughters, Theresa Roberts, was living in Portland, New York.

"I got on the Internet and found her number," Furey says. "I called and said, 'Would you by any chance be related to the prolific Catholic architect Patrick Charles Keely?' She said, 'You're talking to her.' We talked for forty-five minutes."

"This whole thing," he says, "is so encompassing. It hits so many facets."

*   *   *

Like Ted Furey—like all of us, really—the churches of Patrick Charles Keely exist in a balance between past, present, and future.

They are, first of all, almost perfect expressions of the world in which they were constructed. Keely worked where the Irish came to America—driven out of their homeland by the potato famine, poverty, and English persecution—and his churches plot their progress as they moved through the New World: out of Boston and the Williamsburg section of Brooklyn, up through the mill towns of the Connecticut River Valley, and across and through the country.

Keely's churches also plot the varying fortunes of the immigrant communities he worked in.

"He adapted to what his clients wanted and what they could afford, and that's why he survived so long," Furey says. "Some had money—he'd do dormers. Some didn't. St. Mary's in Windsor Locks [between Enfield and Hartford, Connecticut] is a very simple brick church. They were canal builders. They didn't have much. St. Mary's in Yonkers is the same—a simple red-brick church. They put plain glass in, the building was secure, but they had no more money to do anything. They made plain pews. The altar looks like a wallpaper table.

"Lowell needed a huge church because they had nine thousand parishioners. They needed triforium galleries for overflow crowds. The people didn't get a great view of Mass, but for those who had been denied the chance to practice their religion, they were just glad to get inside a church. The parishioners weren't rich, but if everyone gave a dime, that was a lot of money in those days.

"In Hartford, he put the very best in the cathedral. It was a growing Irish population that gave readily to the construction."

Keely's churches also plot his own growing web of associations among Catholic priests and bishops. Wherever Keely's high-ranking ecclesiastical acquaintances would settle down, it seemed, they sent for him to begin building churches for their new Irish flocks. Flocks, though, move on in search of greener pastures; churches and cathedrals are less portable. Today, many of Keely's surviving churches are in inner-city areas that the Irish have long moved out of. And therein lies the challenge for Ted Furey: not convincing Irish Americans of the need to preserve and restore their architectural heritage but convincing Hispanic and African American parishioners, and in some cases the gentrifiers who are succeeding them, that the effort is worthwhile.

"It's not the Irish communities anymore," Furey says. "It's the Spanish communities, the black communities. And it's happening. There's a Keely church in Brooklyn—Our Lady of Victory. It's a totally black parish, and it's in magnificent condition.

"These churches are treasures that belong to their neighborhoods. They belong to the poor of these areas, and that's who built these structures. The Irish couldn't have grandiose for themselves, so they built it in the church. It's the same with the San Salvadorans and Jamaicans coming in today, and the others. They're taking these churches that were built for the Irish, had Italian parishes, and then nothing, and they're making them their own. It's remarkable."

In between past, present, and future—in between the old world of Irish Americans and the new realities of the inner city—stands the architect himself, and for Ted Furey that may be the greatest challenge of all: figuring out exactly who and what this genius of church design was.

Patrick Charles Keely left almost nothing behind: no building plans, no photos, virtually no mementos.

"His architectural drawings were done on linen," Furey explains. "The nuns figured that once a building was done, that was it. They'd take the drawings and bleach them for altar cloths. These weren't twenty-four by thirty-six inches, they were huge things. Also one of his daughters, Isabella, had a horror her father's things would end up in antique stores, so she burned them—the photos, the papers, everything."

That leaves the structures themselves. Increasingly, Furey says, he finds himself trying to read in their arches and windows the biography of a man who, with his wife Sarah, had seventeen children, only to see too many of them die in infancy or young adulthood.

"I began to look at the windows of Holy Cross Cathedral. There's an overabundance of children up there. There's a window of St. Cecilia. She has this very long braided hair, and there are four angels with her. Keely's wife and four girls were all dead at the time. Why didn't he have three angels in that window? No angels? A choir? There's a preponderance of boys in another window that has nothing to do with children. It's very rare you see a mass scene in stained glass and there are kids in it. Did he put his kids in them? Was he drawing around the dining room table, and the children said 'Dada,' as they called him, 'where am I?' and he said, 'There you are.'

"You wonder about his life. Nothing is written down. When you go to his house in Brooklyn and stand in front of 257 Clermont Avenue, it's like Keely still lived here. There are these eight-foot-high windows, but all of them have wooden shutters inside. How did they survive? Then you look at the street in back—these are imposing homes, what you'd call mansions. Why didn't Keely have an imposing home like that? Well, his fees were modest, and he had lots of mouths to feed.

"Maybe he was like [Christopher] Wren. If you're looking for a memorial, don't look at where I lived. Look at my churches. Now, that's supposition, too."

What we do know for certain about Patrick Charles Keely are the words spoken at his funeral Mass in September 1896 by his friend Father Sylvester Malone:

"He had genius, inspiration and the stimulus of Catholic principles, and of the Catholic Faith deep down in his soul. His was a great missionary work, and we would be unworthy of the Celtic race, unworthy of benediction, were we to allow the memory of such a man to perish."

Ted Furey, let it be known, does not intend to let that happen.

Thirty

Rose Kramer:
Spinning Yarns

Sometimes a gift can change a life. In December 1979, the third
Christmas after they were married, Jim Kramer gave his wife, Rose, a spinning wheel he had bought in an antique store. She had never done any spinning, but he knew that she had yearned to spin from the time she was a girl.
Rose Davidick had been raised in the eastern Pennsylvania coal-belt community of West Hazleton, where, she says, "no one spun, well, certainly no
one in the family or anyone I knew."

Rose and Jim had gone to college together at Pennsylvania State University's Hazleton branch. After graduating in 1977—Rose with an associate
degree in chemical engineering technology, Jim with one in mechanical engineering technology—they soon moved to Montgomery County, an hour
north of Philadelphia, which Rose Kramer describes as "Pennsyvlania German." When Jim gave her the spinning wheel, Rose didn't know if it was
usable, nor did she know anyone to teach her how to spin. She looked at it
longingly.

Sometimes a person can also change a life by showing the use to which a
gift can be put. In 1981, Rose went to the Goschenhoppen Folk Festival,
held each August in East Greenville, to see local crafts of the eighteenth and
nineteenth centuries demonstrated. There she met a seventy-five-year-old
woman named Alma Campbell, who was dressed in a top (the term for a
short gown), a petticoat (a long skirt), an apron, a cap, and a neckerchief.
Campbell was demonstrating colonial wool spinning. Kramer stayed after

the other spectators had moved on along a dirt lane to see how sausage was made in an eighteenth-century kitchen.

"Do you know how to spin?" Campbell asked Kramer.

"No."

"Do you have a spinning wheel?"

"Yes."

"You have a spinning wheel and you don't know how to spin? Well, dearie, you come to Red Men's Hall in the Goschenhoppen Museum on Sunday with your spinning wheel and I'll have a look at it." Campbell was a volunteer guide there.

Rose worked full-time but her Sundays were free. That Sunday she carried her wheel up the museum's three steep flights of steps.

Campbell inspected the hundred-and-twenty-five-year-old wool wheel. "This will work," she said. "The odds against finding a wheel that old without a single broken part are very high," Kramer says. "If a critical piece like a flyer had been missing the wheel would have been ornamental but unusable. One woman told me she'd had her spinning wheel made into a floor lamp."

Minutes after Campbell showed her how to spin, Kramer was spinning away. "When I picked up the fleece and twisted it between my fingers, it began to twist into a wonderful single yarn," she says.

"Are you sure you've never spun before?" Campbell asked.

"Alma chuckled that I must have spun sometime in another life. When most beginners attempt to spin, they get lumps. I had no lumps. I just spun from the beginning as I do now. Alma would introduce me to people as her student by saying that she had never seen anyone spin beautifully from the first twist. We would always say that I was 'an old soul.' It was our little joke."

In 1983 the Kramers bought a small 1870 farmhouse and eight acres in Harleysville. Their son Ian was born in 1986, their daughter, Abigail, in May 1989. Rose was still working full-time and spinning whenever she could. When Abbey was four months old, Rose quit her research-and-development job with a consumer products division of Johnson & Johnson.

A neighbor told the Kramers there had once been a barn on their property. In 1990 the couple built a new one on part of its foundation. The Kramers' son Will was born in 1991. A few months later, Jim gave Rose a fence for her birthday ("Hey, some women get diamonds, I got fence") and the following month the Kramers bought two sheep. Alma Campbell had been providing Rose Kramer with wool, but it was scratchy. Kramer wanted softer wool. In spring, a local shearer comes to shear the sheep.

Sheep can change a life as well. The first two sheep were Lily (who was white) and Heidi (who was black), both Finns. "The Finnish Landrace breed of sheep is in the Nordic short-tailed family and the sheep we call Finns in the United States are related to it," Kramer says. "Finns have soft wool and they look like cartoon characters. Their fleeces are heavy, their faces have no hair, and their legs are spindly."

Heidi died of coccidiosis three years later. Lily appeared lonely, and the Kramers acquired Penny, then Clover, and then Blossom. "Penny's a really tall white Finn and Clover is a white Rambouillet," Kramer says. "She's all crimp. Blossom is a black neutered ram, a baby doll—a miniature sheep.

"People say sheep are stupid. Granted, they're not the world's most intelligent animals, but when you raise them as pets they do have personalities. Lily just goes with the flow. She doesn't stir up trouble but she stands her ground with Penny. Penny is truly the piggy sheep. She is a bottomless pit and the most aggressive. When I got Clover, I would take grain out to them and separate it into bowls, never paying attention to who was eating what. Well, I discovered that Penny was using her size to intimidate the others. Penny was eating most of Clover's food and Clover was losing weight. I didn't see that Clover was close to starvation because of her thick fleece. I had to have the vet come out. By the time Clover was back in shape the vet bills were over two hundred dollars. Blossom is great and I think that's because he has horns. All four are very domestic and follow me wherever I go. They just hang out with me."

Rose Kramer has been spinning and knitting for some twenty years now and can tell which garment came from which sheep. "This scarf is my Lily," she says. "We dyed her fleece pink. Look at this bag of Lily's fleece. See her curls. These socks I'm wearing are from Penny. This cap is Heidi. This other cap is Lily and Heidi and some gray wool I had from a shawl. It looks like a nighttime forest."

The Kramers also own two rabbits, Patrick and André, whose angora fur has been spun into yarn and is being worn as a hat and a headband. "I've also spun a bit of dog," Kramer says. "A friend bought me a bag of malamute fur. Collies are fantastic. And if you wash dog fur right away, it doesn't have a doggy odor. If you're a spinner, whenever you see a long-haired animal you'll never look at it the same way. You'll check it out to see if it has hair and you'll ask yourself what can be made from it." Fred, the Kramers' cat, is the only animal they have that is exempt from spinning: his hair is too short.

Kramer's first spinning wheel, the Canadian Wool wheel from Jim, is in the living room. A two-hundred-year-old great wheel, which Alma Campbell gave Rose some years before her death in 1997, is in the family room. "Alma didn't want to have anything to do with modern spinning, but I did," Kramer says. "The old wheels don't ply well and they're slow. You spun thin and made cloth with them. I heard of someone who was selling a modern Schacht wheel and I was able to buy it at a deep discount." The Schacht is in the dining room. Kramer took a night course in modern spinning at Souderton High School. "I had to learn how to spin thick and how to clean wool with Dawn dishwashing liquid rather than homemade soap, which is what Alma did. I make sweaters with funky yarns on it." She met a number of other women who did modern spinning and helped form a fiber guild a few years ago. It is called Morning Fibre and meets on Wednesday mornings. Sometimes only four of the dozen members show up. A few have taken up other crafts.

"I ask myself, how can they do that?" Kramer says. "Some of the others dabble in spinning. For them it's a hobby. Alma made it my destiny. When I quit my job, many people said I had wasted my education. I don't see it that way. I wasn't interested in chemical engineering, I was emotionally and spiritually drawn to spinning. To me it's Shangri-la to have a sheep and spin it. When I'm doing something else, I feel I should be spinning. I don't get in a bad mood when I'm working with wool. I feel one with things. Spinning is both spiritual and intoxicating."

Rose Kramer gives demonstrations of colonial spinning at the Goschenhoppen festival each August, as Alma Campbell once did, dressed in colonial garb. She takes her great wheel into the schools attended by her children and to other nearby schools to demonstrate colonial spinning. She also takes her modern wheel into schools; she wants youngsters to know that their jeans don't just originate at a Sears or a Wal-Mart, and that natural fibers still have to be spun, even if they're now mass-produced on huge computerized machines in textile factories.

Kramer has no trouble combining her pastime with the twenty-first century. She and her husband and children—the five Kramers are tall and thin—are adept with computers. She drives a minivan. The kids have skateboards and bikes and boogie boards. She is a multitasker. When Ian is playing baseball, or Abbey and Will are playing soccer, she watches their games while knitting or spinning with a small drop-spindle made from a compact disk. "It's a wonderful craft, very portable," she says. "I love doing something so ancient on something as modern as a CD."

Once, when Kramer needed raspberry-colored fleece, she poured water and a couple of splashes of vinegar and Kool-Aid into a casserole dish, added the fleece to it, and put the casserole dish in the back of the oven. She put a meat loaf to bake in another casserole in the front of the oven, and turned the oven on. The family ate, she turned the oven off, the Kramers went to a baseball game. When they returned home the fleece was a glorious hue.

Rose Kramer's days are long. Jim Kramer, who spent six years going to school at night when the children were small to turn his associate degree into a full bachelor of science degree in mechanical engineering, often gets up at 4:00 A.M. and prepares for work; he is an engineer with Exelon Corporation. She kisses him good-bye and he flies out the door so fast that by the time she comes downstairs his pickup is usually out of the driveway and Ezekiel, the family's black-and-white rooster, is crowing. She spins from 4:45 to 5:45 A.M., when she wakes Ian, makes his breakfast, and wakes Abbey at 6:15. Ian leaves at 6:45. Abbey leaves at 7:20, Will at 8:15 A.M. The children attend three different schools.

"I'll spin during the day, but I volunteer at the schools in the textile classes, the computer room, field trips, anything else I can do for the teachers, and I go to three sets of parent meetings every month," Kramer says. "Then there are the kids' doctor, dentist, and orthodontist appointments. I volunteer every other Wednesday at Peter Wentz Farmstead, a historic site in our county. Some weeks I give lectures on spinning for home-schooling groups, day centers, or church groups."

Sometimes a passion gives one ideas about the afterlife. Several years ago, Kramer read a book by Elizabeth Wayland Barber called *The Mummies of Urumchi*. The book presented a detailed account of ancient mummies, some dating back four thousand years, that had been discovered in the Uighur region of western China. They had been wrapped in colorful woolens that were beautifully preserved. A short while after completing the Barber book, she went to the family doctor with a badly running nose. She told the doctor about *The Mummies of Urumchi*.

"Do you think when I die I could be mummified in wool?" Kramer asked him.

"Let's get you over this sinus infection first," the doctor replied.

PART 7

The Sporting Life

Thirty-one

Tom Blake:
Tiger! Tiger!
Burning Bright

On the face of it, what Tom Blake sets off to do three times a week on the James River, just southeast of downtown Richmond, Virginia, would seem to defy the laws of both balance and endurance. Seated only seven inches or so off the river, halfway down a shell twenty-seven feet long and all of eleven inches wide at the water level—think of a bean pod, impossibly long and thin—Blake pushes off from a dock at the Virginia Boat Club and begins striking the water with oars that are ten feet long themselves.

Coiled forward on a sliding seat with his feet set in stationary "shoes" in front of him, his knees bent into his chest, and his arms outstretched, Blake drops the oars straight down into the river to "catch" the water. Using first his legs and then his arms, he pulls the blades through the water until he has reversed his body position: now his legs are outstretched and his hands in close to his chest, and he looks for a moment as if he were lying back in a lounge chair. When the stroke is finished, Blake presses down slightly on the oar handles to lift the blades from the water, "feathers" the blades so they are horizontal to the river surface for recovery, reaches his hands forward and pulls his knees back into his chest as he resets the blades for the next "catch," and begins the whole process again. And again. And again.

In a typical workout, Blake might scull six and a half miles downstream, turn around, and come six and a half miles back up the river, often against the prevailing westerly winds. In all, his usual workout amounts to somewhere over 2,100 strokes, about an hour and a half of rowing. The only scheduled break comes at the halfway point, just long enough to bring about the "single," as such one-person sculling boats are known.

Seen from above—from a bridge, say—the adept single-sculler is one of the most graceful sights in sports. A single barely seems to touch the water. The metronomic regularity of the stroke makes the movement seem almost effortless, while the oars, extended to either side, give the tableau a cruciform quality that lends metaphorical support to rowing's status as perhaps the purest of amateur sports.

Even when rowing was a professional sport—and it flourished as such in the years after the American Civil War, until scandal brought it low—Thomas Eakins could make sculling seem innocently pastoral in his paintings, with their rich interplay of light and reflection glinting off the waters of Philadelphia's Schuylkill River. (Eakins himself is sculling in the background in his first rowing masterpiece, *Max Schmitt in a Single Scull*, completed in 1871.)

All that, though, is from above or captured for posterity on canvas. At water level, midships in this exquisitely slender craft, the experience is radically different, Tom Blake says.

"Singles are extraordinarily temperamental. They're very easy to flip. You can feel every little tiny reverberation of a ripple from a wave that passed through five minutes ago. You can feel the currents, the eddies. It's like being on a tightrope. The oars are your balancing stick. If you lose one, smack it on recovery, or it hits a buoy or is knocked out of your hand by a competitor, you're flipped."

The better the equipment, too, the more perilous in some ways the ride. Wood gives slightly with each force that acts upon the boat, but the only singles and oars made of wood anymore are those for beginners and sentimentalists. Blake's state-of-the-art shell—it cost seven thousand dollars—is made of carbon fiber, as are his oars. The weight is nearly negligible: twenty-seven pounds, or a pound for every foot in length. Bend is almost nonexistent with such equipment.

"You have all this force you want to get into the water. Everywhere the boat bends a little, you lose force. If you can have everything as light and as stiff as possible, you conserve more energy for the water."

The better the equipment and the sculler, the less likely the ride is to be anything like a Sunday outing on the water. Dedicated single-scullers don't just use the water, they attack it, Blake says.

"In rowing, if you're really doing it as hard as you can, it's a violent thing. You're hammering away in an almost angry way, but you have to come up to this edge and not go over it. The question is: How can we do this? How can we go up to this line of being out of control without going over the line?"

The kinetics of propelling a boat with oars also dictate that scullers sit with their backs to where they are going. On a reservoir built for rowing, that's fine, but the most intense sculling in the United States is done on East Coast rivers below the fall line, at sea level, and such rivers are, by definition, heavily used. Not far downstream from where Blake sets off on his training missions—just about where the Union naval blockade effectively turned Richmond into a landlocked renegade capital during the Civil War—is a large dock where barges load up with gravel from a cement quarry. Before he started wearing a little rearview mirror clamped onto the bill of his cap, Blake came uncomfortably close to rowing straight under the barges on more than one occasion.

Amazingly, given the litany of dangers rowers face on a crowded river like the James and the inherent instability of their craft, Blake hadn't been flipped out of his own single in four years when we talked. But his earlier experience, he says, was a memorable one. The time was early spring; the James was running high with melt-off from the snows near its source in the mountains of western Virginia; and when Blake, who is a doctor of family medicine, hit a log and tumbled into the river, his first thought was understandably medical: hypothermia. "It made me realize how foolish I was to scull through the winter."

Since then, Blake uses an ergometer—a rowing machine, or "erg," to rowers—to log his virtual river miles three times a week once the real water becomes too icy to brave. Another two days a week, summer and winter, he lifts weights. The schedule "isn't based on smart physiology. It's just my sense of it, and my effort to find an equilibrium with my family. I have to find what works with my wife, my children, and my job."

Rowing isn't necessarily how Tom Blake had intended to spend his forties. He had run track and cross-country in high school and showed up for Princeton his freshman year, in 1971, thinking he might do the same. Blake, though, fit a profile that crew coaches love: focused, already experienced in an aerobic sport, tall enough at six feet to take a long stroke, and light in relation to his strength. What's more, his father had rowed in the early nineteen-forties at MIT. Very soon after arriving on campus, Blake found himself recruited for the lightweight eights—sixty-five-foot-long shells, with eight rowers, each manning one oar, and a coxswain to direct them. And very soon after that began an on-again, off-again, love-hate relationship with the sport that would last nearly three years.

"I didn't row the whole time. A lot of people are part-time—it's such a huge time commitment. You start rowing the first day you get to campus, and the first race isn't until March."

In his junior year, just as spring was arriving, Blake quit the sport for a second and what seemed final time.

"I'd raced for seven months and quit about two weeks before the season began. I had tendinitis. The academic work was hard. My rowing status was slipping because of my physical status. It was reaching a crisis. So I quit. My coach was angry. When I quit on him that second time, I knew he hated me."

Through medical school at the University of Virginia and his residency in Philadelphia—indeed, through all the usual building blocks of a medical career, until he arrived in Richmond in the late eighties and a colleague introduced him to the Virginia Boat Club—Tom Blake was true to his intentions. Along the way, though, there were signs that what had appeared to be a valedictory was more in the nature of a moratorium.

For one thing, there was Blake's wife, a former captain of the women's crew team at the University of Virginia. There also was his chosen form of exercise in those desert years away from the river: a home rowing machine, not much different from the ones he had loved to hate at Princeton.

"The ergometers were the worst part of rowing in college," he says. "The coach could be right on top of you. If I ever had fantasized about anything then, about having any object from that time in my house, it never would have been an erg."

By the time he got back to rowing, Blake says, he had developed the kind of mind-set that rowing rewards, or maybe he had the mind-set all along and was waiting to rediscover a form of endeavor that fit it so well.

"There are a lot of doctors in rowing. Doctors tend to be obsessive people, and rowing is obsessive. There's not a lot of variation about it. You're trying very hard to perfect one motion. It's a complicated motion, but it's not free-wheeling like basketball. Even sloppy basketball is fun, but rowing is only good when you get to a certain level. There are a lot of creative people who can do amazing things, but this is about stick-to-itiveness—doing it over and over for years."

There was also the memory of that Princeton crew coach and Blake's unhappy departure from the sport.

"It's sort of like I had this bookmark in the back of my head," he says. "Freud talks about the unresolved conflicts of infancy and so on. When I first went back to rowing, I thought I had this unresolved thing, these unresolved feelings about why I had originally quit."

There was an unfulfilled ambition, as well. Physically, Blake had been part of a team machine at Princeton—one cog among the eight oarsmen that powered the boat. Mentally, he sometimes found himself on the Charles River in Boston, rowing on his own.

"I fantasized about sculling, particularly on the Head of the Charles. It's the largest regatta in the world. I'd find myself thinking: Wouldn't it be cool to learn to scull. And wouldn't it be cool to do that on the Head of the Charles."

The differences between crew or team rowing and single sculling are both marginal and profound. Both are premier aerobic activities. (Rowing ranks just behind cross-country skiing in the amount of oxygen consumed.) Both require enormous dedication. (There's an old joke among oarsmen that sex is sublimated rowing.) Crew members and scullers alike tend to use versions of the verb "to strive" when they talk about their sport. The two halves of competitive rowing almost always share common facilities, as well, and at least in the United States, single-scullers are mostly former "eights" themselves. But with rowing, surface similarities tend to give way to deeper differences, Blake says.

"Sculling is a very different thing in terms of muscles and training. Each stroke is harder because the momentum dissipates after each one. With an eight, you get the big thing moving, and it goes on its own.

"People say that eights, sweep rowing, any of the team boats is the ultimate in team sports. Everybody has to meld into one person. With any crew boat that wins, you have no way of knowing who did best because it all has to work together. In a big boat, if you're in the center, you're staring at the guy in front of you, at his shoulders. You're not supposed to let your eyes out of the boat. You have to infer everything by what you see of him. You're trying to get into his skin, be exactly what he is. You can't think strategy. All that is the coxswain's problem.

"There's this incredible camaraderie in an eight. When everybody does everything right, the boat has 'swing.' It's a palpable thing. The boat is much greater than the sum of the eight parts. It's a giddy feeling: My God, we're taking off! In a single, everything is up to you—the course, the strategy. You have to know where the other boats are. If you tune those things out, you're wrecked."

Singles practice, too, is different, Blake says: the sheer, gorgeous solitude of it, for one thing, and the sense of being entirely in command, for at least a brief period, of one's own fate.

"Just to be perched up on this thing—you can go much faster in your car, but there's a feeling of speed that is much greater because you're right on the water. At dusk or daybreak, there's the reflection, and you pick up things going by in the water out of the corner of your eye. And it's all your own effort.

"We row right across from a treatment plant," he says of the Virginia Boat Club, which takes up the bottom two floors of an abandoned power plant once used by a Richmond trolley company. "It's interesting to me that some of the really nasty smells no longer bother me because they're so related in my mind to rowing.

"The rest of my family is very musical. My brother and sister and mother all play the piano. I often thought I could have learned to do that, but to me, this is like music. It has rhythm. I sometimes think that a scull is like playing the violin. Just like there are no frets on a violin, a scull is so wide open. And the boats are so damn beautiful."

Blake also came to sculling at a different time in his life than he came to crew, and therein, he says, may lie the greatest difference of all: "I love it now, and I don't think I loved it then. It was something to do, a chance to be on an intercollegiate team. I can't even remember that person or time, but it wasn't anywhere near so important to me then as it is now.

"I've got enough infirmities that I can see not being able to row, but it's really important to me. When something hits, when I'm weight lifting and one more thing goes bad with my shoulder, it worries me. What's going to take this away from me? It went from something that was nice and evoked memories of college to something that I need. A lot of my identity is invested in this.

"It seems frivolous to say that rowing would mean as much to me as my career, but in a certain part of my head, it is that important. Anyplace I go now, I size up things differently. If I'm driving by a pond, I think, Well, only four strokes there, but what a great four strokes!"

The happiest memory Tom Blake will have to look back on if his rowing career is cut short by injury is the realization of his undergraduate fantasy:

sculling on the Head of the Charles. The Henley Royal, held on the Thames near London, is the world's most famous regatta, dating back to 1839, but the Head of the Charles is the grandest. Upwards of 250,000 people turn out every October to cheer on thousands of rowers competing in twenty different events, ranging from senior veterans singles races (whose winners tend to be in their seventies) to youth fours, club eights (with more than 150 entries alone, in the men's and women's divisions), and the closing championship singles, doubles, fours, and eights races that attract some of the top rowers in the world.

So tight is the schedule that boats leave the starting line every ten seconds to cover a three-mile course that snakes under six bridges, some of them so narrow that a sculler might have less than a ten-foot horizontal clearance on either side. And so great is the demand to compete in the regatta that most rowers are chosen by lottery, except for those relatively few who have met specific qualifying times in the previous year's race. In 1993, 1995, and 1998, Blake got in by lottery. In 1999, he was invited back because of his 1998 time.

"It's where rowing is important. On a daily basis, I don't care that nobody knows I'm doing this. But there are a quarter-million people there. Some of them just want to drink, but most of them care about it.

"I frequently finish races angry. There's so much that can go wrong. It's a beautiful day. I should feel lucky to be there, and I'm swearing. The last few times I came off the Charles, I was completely satisfied. I had done everything I could. I would have to have different genetics or make different choices about my life to do better."

Maybe, too, sculling and racing on the Head of the Charles have given Tom Blake a chance to resolve those unresolved conflicts from years gone back. Blake's single—the one that has consumed so many hours of his adult life—is a bright orange trimmed in black: Princeton colors. Its name, *Tiger Tiger*, evokes both the mascot of his alma mater and lines written more than two centuries ago by another Blake, in a poem strangely evocative of both the beauty of rowing and the violence of its competition, even when it's only yourself you are competing against.

"Tiger! Tiger! burning bright / In the forests of the night," William Blake wrote in his *Songs of Experience*. "What immortal hand or eye / Could frame thy fearful symmetry?"

Thirty-two

Robert Strupp: Good Deals

Milwaukee is a city celebrated for bratwurst, beer, gemütlichkeit, and Sheepshead, a card game brought over by Germans who settled there in the eighteen-hundreds. Robert Strupp, a.k.a. "Sheepshead Bob," is the man who has literally written the book—more accurately, the forty-six-page booklet—on the game. The title is "How to Play 'Winning' 5 Handed SHEEPSHEAD," and Strupp first had it photocopied in 1978. Since then, it has gone through five editions and ten printings. Over thirty-two thousand copies have been sold, mainly to Milwaukee residents or displaced Milwaukeeans. The booklet now sports a semiprofessional look—glossy cover, smooth paper, illustrations by Strupp's niece, Lucy—and an amateur air—Strupp reminds the reader that chapter 2 was written in 1970 and chapter 1 only in 1980.

According to Strupp, Sheepshead was originally called Schafskopf, and was played in the mountain ranges of Bavaria by shepherds early in the nineteenth century. They drew a line in the dirt for each hand they won until one shepherd had drawn a sufficient number of lines to form a sheep's head, thereby winning the game. Strupp, whose maternal and paternal grandparents immigrated from Germany, was born in Milwaukee in 1925. His parents, Thomas and Emily, opened a bakery in 1919, and the family lived above the store on North Thirty-third and Clarke Streets.

His older brother, Howard, taught him how to play Sheepshead. He and a few other boys—"Three of us were named Bob"—played the game when

e played, no matter which suit is led. There seem to be half-a-
d other rules like the "called ace" requirement.

point value of the cards is 120. Queens count as 3 points apiece,
, aces 11, tens 10, and kings 4. The sevens, eights, and nines have no
alue. The picking team must take in 61 (or more) points on every
) win. If they get a minimum of 61 points, they collect one chip from
the three opponents, picker getting two and partner one. If the pick-
m doesn't get 61 points, each of the opposition gets one chip, picker
two and partner one. The opposition needs only 60 points to win. If
position doesn't get 30 points, the picking team "schneiders" the
:ion and wins two chips from each of the opponents, picker getting
d partner two. If the picking team doesn't get 31 points, the opposi-
;chneidered" them, and each opponent receives two chips; picker
vo players, partner pays one. If the picking team gets 120 points—if
; all six tricks in a hand or game—they no-tricked ("schwarzed") the
:ion, with lucrative rewards: picker gets six chips and partner three.
re are additional rules and German words. *Forget them for now.*

Strupp and his wife, Carol, a retired nurse, moved to a small house
:th Ninety-third Street in Milwaukee after raising five children. Upon
ting from high school in 1943, Strupp went into the family baking
ss, and he still bakes bread, hard rolls, coffee cake ("things that need
I, and pies in an oven in the rec room; but he had never wanted to be
·ssional baker. He subsequently worked for the post office and a CPA
vent into business for himself doing bookkeeping and income tax
;, and played accordion in a polka band for fun until his retirement in
Before and after his retirement, Sheepshead provided him with the
un.

) in the rec room is a good-sized table where Strupp is content to
Sheepshead to a novice on a wintry dark gray December afternoon.
hree hours, the novice can play Sheepshead slowly, or enjoys the illu-
: being able to play it, by referring often to the booklet.

I an illusion it is. In the real Sheepshead world—for example, at the
ιg Place Pub in Menomonee Falls, on the outskirts of Milwaukee,
Strupp plays cards in Skippy's Sheepshead League with 125 other
nd women he describes as "fanatics" on Wednesday evenings from
) 9:15 P.M.—the novice is completely overwhelmed. Five people sit at
: according to the table number they have drawn on that particular
g. The cards are dealt and then plucked out of hands and tossed on
ble with alarming speed. German-sounding words fill the air: "All

they were fourteen-year-old ninth graders at Me
school. On days before school they played until ten
no school, they played later. Bob "Burky" Burkard
bach had been taught to play Sheepshead by the
some of the others, like Claude 'C. J.' Nuedling—th
his money for the first few years," Robert "Struppy
players had to pay their dues, but we only played fo

At first glance, a little knowledge of a more comm
such as bridge, would appear to help one unders
games share the concept of "trump." But in She
trump, whereas in bridge, whatever the final contract
bridge. There are more differences than similarities b

Bridge is played with fifty-two cards, Sheepshea
consisting of thirty-two cards, sevens through aces. T
must be discarded, because no manufacturer produce
fifty-two cards. There are two categories of cards in S
"trump" (fourteen cards), the other called "fail" (eigh
teen trump cards can take any fail trick. The four q
cards, followed by the four jacks and all the diamond
queen of clubs (the highest), to the queen of spades, the
the queen of diamonds, down through the jacks in the
of diamonds, followed by the ten, nine, eight, and seve
fusing as this may seem to a novice, the ten is higher th
ing to Strupp, Bavarian shepherds were disgruntled wit
them a lower rank in Sheepshead. Shepherds wished
made diamonds trump.

While Sheepshead can be played two-, three-, four-,
handed, five-handed is the most popular version. Each
dealt six cards. Two cards are left in the "blind." The p
dealer's left has the first chance to pick the blind, and is
picker. If he passes, the player to his left has the opportun
someone picks. If no one picks, the hand becomes a
leaster, at least for now.

Usually one player picks up the two cards in the b
("buries") two cards from his hand. By calling an ace he
partner for that hand. If he calls the ace of spades, whoe
spades becomes his partner. He must have a fail spade in l
keep it. The picker must play a card from the suit he calle
led, and the partner must play his ace. These two cards ma
on any other trick. The one exception is the final trick, wh

must
hund

Th
jacks
poin
hand
each
ing t
payi
the
opp
four
tion
pay
it t
opp

on
gr
bu
ye
a
fir
re
1
m

t
A
s

right, who's the mauerer?" a player asks. "When in doubt, schmeer," says another. Fifty hands must be played on league nights. A hand takes about 2.7 minutes to play. The novice should observe in silence, ponder the fact that a player's partner in one game is apt to be his opponent in the next, and enjoy a Miller High Life beer, which can be purchased for $2.25 a bottle. *Forget the beer.* The novice should sip a soft drink ($2.00 a glass) and commit some of the rules in Strupp's book to memory before being delusional enough to play Sheepshead: he will be out of his league in Skippy's League.

Rule 10. Always yell louder than the next guy, so they think you know what you are doing. Don't let anyone intimidate you. Yell right back, you'll gain respect.

Rule 16. Never, never admit the blind is good. Always bitch and complain, as it is no one's business what is in the blind. This is why it is called a BLIND. If they want to see the blind, let them pay as you probably will after picking such a lousy, miserable, stinking blind.

Rule 18. When in doubt, pick. (This rule is only 50 percent correct.)

Rule 19. When in doubt, schmeer. (This rule is 60 percent correct.)

Rule 35. Most important, count trump and remember which trump cards were played. Count points, too, if you can. If you can do this, you have the game completely under your control and can play every hand to its maximum.

The novice should also learn a few additional German-sounding terms. The "mauerer" is a player who refuses to pick the blind, no matter how good his hand is. "Schmeer" means putting points on a trick. And memorize a few principles: Queens and jacks are the power; aces, kings, and tens are the points. "Leasters" are played to punish the mauerers, with everyone playing alone. *Forget about trying to keep score*—the fanatics do it too quickly. The game is played for a dime a point. "At a table you'll win or lose just a couple of bucks per Wednesday," Strupp says.

"Sheepshead is a working-class game," Strupp continues with working-man's pride. It costs six dollars a night to play at the Trysting Place Pub. That includes pizza at the end of each evening, a banquet at the end of the season, and prizes. The player in first place wins a trophy and something over a hundred dollars. A player who comes in somewhere in the middle may win fifty dollars. "Last place gets a copy of my book and ten or twelve dollars," Strupp says. "If you want to make money, get a job. If you want to have fun, play Sheepshead for nickels or dimes, or, allowing for inflation, quarters."

Bob Strupp currently plays Sheepshead one Tuesday a month with his fishing buddies. He plays every Wednesday in Skippy's League, for four months in the fall and four months in the spring. On Friday he sometimes goes to Sheepshead parties—"They used to be called smokers"—at different churches in the city, but not when a grandchild has a band concert or is performing in a play. One Saturday a month, he and Carol play Sheepshead with five other couples. Sundays, Strupp may go to a Sheepshead festival at whichever church is having one. "The churches usually schedule the festivals around [Green Bay] Packers games," he says.

In 1983, in recognition of the city's proud German heritage, the "noble card game of Sheepshead" was declared Milwaukee's Official Card Game by the city's Common Council. It was further resolved that a "copy of this resolution be presented to Mr. Robert Strupp, who authored a comprehensive guide to the game of Sheepshead." A photograph in the booklet shows Strupp accepting the document. Since 1987, Sheepshead has been played at Milwaukee's annual German Fest in July. "My brother Howard—he died a few years ago—and I ran the first Sheepshead games at German Fest," Strupp says. "It costs two dollars to play twenty hands for an hour. You can rest your feet, you may win a T-shirt or a mug, and you can listen to some nice music. I've had a fuller life because of Sheepshead."

Strupp's book is dedicated to his very first Sheepshead group: Bob "Burky" Burkard, George "Georgie" Dreckman, Bob "Limpy" Limbach, Claude "C. J." Nuedling, Roger "Pete" Peters, and Leo F. "Moses" Staudacher. Some started first grade together at St. Ann's. Some attended Messmer High.

Robert Strupp is a soft-spoken man. His voice cracks when he says that all the members of his original Sheepshead group have died—but not before they had played over forty thousand hands of Sheepshead together. "The game kept us out of trouble as kids and kept us together as adults. We married after high school and played as couples. I gave the eulogies at the funerals for Moses, Limpy, and Burky."

Limpy Limbach served in the air force, was an enthusiastic duck hunter, a devout Catholic, and a dedicated Sheepshead player. Before his death, he designed his gravestone. Strupp says: "There's an American flag on Limpy's gravestone, a couple of ducks, a cross, and, in the right-hand bottom corner, a perfect hand of Sheepshead"—four queens, one club jack, and one spade jack. Strupp was once dealt one himself, on September 30, 1986, at the Trysting Place Pub. Laminated and framed, it hangs on his rec-room wall. "I clip the grass away from Limpy's hand at Holy Cross cemetery," he says. "I make the rounds of the graves of all my old friends." *Never forget the friends of your youth.*

Thirty-three

Kim Eisler:
Odds-on Favorite

"I frequently dream about being a jockey," Kim Eisler says. "I have these very vivid dreams of riding a horse. It's almost like I'm there. I've won quite a few Kentucky Derbies in my day."

What's unusual about this dream is that Eisler is a journalist and author, not an equestrian. He's ridden a full-grown horse only once in his life—very carefully, along a trail near Tampa, Florida. Nor is he likely to be asked to climb up on a racehorse even if he were a more experienced rider. About six feet tall and given to a bit of a potbelly, Kim Eisler is neither jockey-shaped nor thoroughbred user-friendly.

Eisler, though, can be excused for dreams of Derby glory because for more than a quarter of a century he has been following thoroughbreds with the diligence of a research scientist and betting on them just as ardently. Indeed, he is the inventor of the Eisler Empirical System for handicapping horse races, and if you haven't heard of that yet, you almost certainly will. Maybe.

"I did my first horse race in February 1976 at Hot Springs, Arkansas," Eisler explains. At the time he was a reporter for the Greenville, Mississippi, *Delta Democrat Times*. "I would slip across the border into Arkansas and make the short three-and-a-half-hour drive from Greenville every day and the short three-and-a-half-hour drive back that night so I could do my work. Fortunately, city council met only once a week."

In those days, Eisler relied on others to tell him how to place his bets.

"I read Andy Beyer's book *Picking Winners,* the seminal description of handicapping. It's based on the ultimately flawed concept that a horse's performance could be judged by its final time. This is flawed because (a) horses don't necessarily run back to the same race every time—just because they ran an eighty last time doesn't mean they're not going to run a sixty-two the next time—and (b) because a lot of racing is horses taking it easy and getting ready for one big effort. The bread-and-butter horses in this country may win only two or three races a year. They're going to win only a certain number of times because there's only so much gas in the tank. It can happen anytime, and you've got to figure out when the spot is right.

"The other seminal handicapping work back then was Tom Ainslie's book, *Ainslie's Complete Guide to Thoroughbred Racing,* which dealt with pace, not final time: the concept that a horse's future performance could be judged on the basis of whether a race had been run at a fast or slow pace. Any horse in a field of closers could go out in the lead and win a race, but if that horse were in with a bunch of speeders, it would burn out."

The Beyer book, especially, became Eisler's bible.

"I'd spent many years calculating these Beyer numbers, punching in spread sheets, doing all that sort of stuff, and then came my realization, which led to my great discovery, that horses are herd animals who instinctively run to the head of the pack. One of the great contradictions that a lot of people don't understand is that good trainers aren't trying to make their horses go faster, they're trying to slow them down so they can go a certain distance around."

Armed with this fundamental notion about the nature of racehorses—and not getting any richer from his betting efforts—Eisler began to rethink his whole approach to handicapping. And as that happened, other revelations began to fall neatly in place.

"At some point I concluded that people are creatures of habit and tend to do the same things over and over again in certain situations. If you're a poker player"—and Eisler decidedly is—"you need to realize that most people will respond the same way in the same circumstances. Even humans, who have a conscience, have trouble varying their patterns, and horses are horses: they're animals!

"Pursuing this theory that horses are animals, I began to keep complete result charts of all the races run at a particular track, assuming that in a circumstance and an environment where everything was the same, you could accurately predict the results of a horse race by comparing it to another race. Beyer had claimed that through speed handicapping, you could compare the performance of a horse that ran at Aqueduct with one that ran at

Laurel. The seminal leap I took was to realize that you can only compare horses running at the same track, in the same conditions."

Thus was born the Eisler Empirical System.

"Let's take Gulfstream Park," the inventor explains. "I began to enter the *Daily Racing Form* result-charts information into my Fox Pro database, starting in the early nineties: the last finish, odds he went off at, post position, the jockey who rode him last time, the trainer, the size of the field, the distance of the race, whether the horse was a filly or a colt, whether the track was wet or dry, whether it was a race for maidens [horses that have never won a race] or nonmaidens, whether it was a race for three-year-olds or for older horses.

"I put all this raw information into my database, and now if I go out to Gulfstream in January, and the first race is eight furlongs for maiden fillies in an eight-horse field, I can begin to segment out all these criteria. I can get the results for every maiden race eight furlongs for fillies run within the last eight years. I can then look at the results, and I can find out, for example, the following: that ninety percent of that type of race are won by horses going off at odds of less than three to one, that ninety percent are won by horses from the number-five post position inside, that a particular jockey has a knack for winning at that distance with that type of horse. And from that information, it's only a short leap to being able to say who's the three-to-one shot starting from inside the five hole and being ridden by a jockey with a good past history at that type of race.

"I'm able to isolate that horse, take all the money I have, bet it on that particular horse in that particular race, and live the life of Riley!"

It's worth remembering, of course, that even Riley didn't live the life of Riley in the old television and radio shows by that name. For one thing, the Eisler Empirical System just eats up time.

"I would say that entering the data, punching in the information from the *Daily Racing Form* chart, would take one and a half hours every night. And that's just to punch in the data, not pull it out. When you're handicapping—pulling the data out—you can start at eight at night and not be done until two in the morning.

"This is an important point: You wake up in the morning, and you get your breakfast, and you take your *Racing Form* to the coffee shop and lay it out on the table and look at the entries for the day. You go out to the racetrack, and you're there, say, at twelve, and you're going to be there until five. On the way out the door of the track, you buy the *Racing Form* for the next day. Then you have to get some dinner and unwind because it's been a draining experience—a lot of almosts, a lot of things have screwed you over that shouldn't have happened. You did everything perfectly, but there was a lot of buffoonery, something you missed, some disaster that befell you, so you have to decompress.

"Quite frequently, you'll leave the track and say, I'm not ever going to bet again. But then you have dinner, and usually by eight-thirty or nine you're ready to go again, so you're probably punching in the results from that day, the new information in the *Racing Form* for the result charts, and so you're not ready to handicap until ten at night, and that takes you up to two or three in the morning. It can get pretty grueling. You really need to skip a day every now and then. Otherwise, you get so far behind."

Add in familial obligations—Eisler is a husband and the devoted father of an elementary-school-age daughter with an uncanny feel for odds—and his duties as a journalist, and all this would seem to be an impossible situation of burning the candle at both ends. What eases the pain is this: the Eisler Empirical System has begun to show its worth.

"I look at all those years I lost before I found the System, all those years I walked around in the desert. I figure it's like a college education. People think nothing of spending $120,000 for a college education so that they can do better later on. Well, I figure I've lost about $120,000 on the races, but it was all for my education. Now, I try to zero in on races where the Empirical System is most effective, and I've started to make a big dent into that $120,000. I figure one of these days I'll hit the Pick Four at Santa Anita and make it all back. It's not a question of if that will happen. It's only a question of when."

Fortunately, too, Eisler says that there's a kind of timeless quality to the track that cannot be measured solely in bets won or lost.

"No matter where you go—Florida, New York, Arkansas, California—horseplayers have the same face. You walk around the track, and you feel you know all these guys. There's something about them—the glasses with one lens missing, the grizzled look. The great thing about the track is the egalitarian nature of it. You have the down-and-out punters on the rail mixing it up with the bluebloods who own the horses or who are just coming out there for a day of sport. The rich people are hardly even betting, and then there are the people like me, living from paycheck to paycheck and betting everything they have. It's really interesting."

Not, of course, that a sportsman has to go the track to bet. Once, off-track betting was limited to bookies. Nowadays, thanks to simulcasting and a more favorable legal climate for gambling generally, horseplayers not only can wager remotely, they also can watch races from more than a dozen tracks at the same time from the comfort of a betting salon or even their own home. Eisler's two favorite betting venues are the clubhouse at Laurel Raceway, halfway between his home in suburban Washington, D.C., and Baltimore, and the Cracked Claw, a sprawling bar and restaurant complex south of Frederick, Maryland.

"I'm sort of a romanticist. If there is live racing, I like to go out and look at the horses running on the track, especially if it's a nice day. There's nothing wrong with fresh air. But if I'm betting the horses in Florida, I'm watching them on the TV right up here in Maryland."

As for the racehorses, Eisler says his two favorites over his quarter-century of devoted attention to the track have been Alysheba, who took the Kentucky Derby in 1987, and Silver Charm.

"I have a special feeling for Alysheba because I saw him in the Pacific Classic against Ferdinand, who had won the Derby the year before, and he completed a huge Pick Three for me. I fell in love with Silver Charm in 1997 when he went to the Kentucky Derby as the four-to-one shot and won. Then he won the Preakness, and I won on both of them. I took everything I had and bet on him to win the Triple Crown, and in a valiant effort he was run down in the Belmont by Touch Gold. But I had the exacta boxed, so I didn't get hurt too badly."

Boxing the exacta—betting on all the possible combinations by which a given number of horses might finish one-two in a race—and other forms of easing the pain inflicted by fickle animals failing to run to expectation would seem to offer one final piece of proof that Kim Eisler and history are on a pleasant collision course. Just as the Eisler Empirical System is rounding into form, there are so many more ways to employ it: "When I first started betting at Oaklawn Park in 1976, you had the daily double and win, place, and show betting. That was it. Even as late as 1983, when I was living near Santa Anita in Los Angeles, exactas were not offered on every race, and a trifecta was usually offered only on the last race of the day. Now, because of the influence of the lotteries on the gambling psyche, people no longer want to grind out winning at the track. Everyone wants to win a lot of money at once. In California they have the Pick Six where you can pick six winners in a row and win $200 million."

Over all, Eisler sees this proliferation of opportunity as a healthy trend.

"The idea of racing is to bet a little and win a lot. I try to remember that. The other thing I was taught by this old gambler in Tallahassee was: 'Never bet the farm to win half a farm.' That's what's so nice about all these trifectas and superfectas—you can bet a little money and win a lot. This is a concept I find appealing."

Thirty-four

Larry Kahn:
Tiddly Wonks

*My most significant accomplishment to date is winning more national
and world tiddlywinks championships than any winker in history.*

—Larry Kahn

After Larry Kahn was accepted by the Massachusetts Institute of
Technology in the spring of 1971, the college sent him its freshman handbook. He looked through it at his home in Miami and decided he would
join the Tiddlywinks Club. "I was seventeen, it looked like a real fun game
to play, and I wanted to change from being a nerd into being a person," he
says.

Kahn was familiar with the children's version of tiddlywinks, a simple
one in which players flip small discs into a cup by pressing on them with a
larger disc. The children's game was patented in England in 1888.

The far more difficult game to which Kahn was introduced during his
first year at MIT was tournament tiddlywinks. This game was started at
Cambridge University in 1954 by two unathletic undergraduates, William
Steen and R. C. Martin, who thought it would be beneficial to be able to
claim on future résumés that they had played a varsity sport. As Bill Steen
would later recall, "The idea of starting a new sport was the simplest way
in, but what sport? Surf bathing was too complicated to organise; tree
felling had its complications in the fen land; camel racing had an attraction,
particularly if the course was from London to Brighton, but the zoo does

not like letting its camels out for this sort of thing. Then like a thunderbolt both Martin and I realised it must be tiddlywinks, a game we had both enjoyed greatly in our early life."

In 1958 the English Tiddlywinks Association (ETwA) was formed, and the game caught on at Oxford as well as at Cambridge. The Oxbridge students developed the game into one of skill and strategy. The key difference between the new game and the nursery game was the addition of the concept of "squopping"—shooting one's discs onto opponents' winks so as to immobilize them. Once a disc was squopped, it remained immobilized until it was freed.

The game crossed the pond in the early sixties. In 1962, Oxford defeated Harvard in a challenge match. The game became more popular in the United States when NATwA (the North American Tiddlywinks Association) was founded in 1966, and teams were started at MIT, Harvard, and Cornell, and other colleges. During Kahn's years at MIT—he received a bachelor of science degree in ocean engineering in 1975 and an M.S. in ocean engineering in 1976—the game of winks was near its peak of popularity in the United States, with Cambridge, Massachusetts, one of the centers. The center did not hold. The best MIT players moved away—Larry Kahn; Dave Lockwood, '75; and Rick Tucker, '76, to Washington, and "Sunshine" (a pony-tailed man who chooses to go by one name), '69, to Philadelphia. The two places in the United States where the winking is alive, if not as well as Kahn wishes, are Washington, D.C., and Ithaca, New York. Severin Drix, Cornell '69, teaches an advanced placement class in mathematics at Ithaca High School and tries to recruit his students as players. "We've been called tiddly wonks," Kahn says. "Most people who play the game well are into math or science."

A few aspects of the tournament game are easy for liberal arts types to understand. Each player has six winks—four slightly smaller than a dime, two slightly larger—in either blue, green, red, or yellow. Tournament-quality winks are imported from Italy. "The commercial sets made here are cruddy," Kahn says. In a pairs game, which Kahn considers much more fun than a singles game ("It's neat to play with people, help each other, have your games mesh—singles is something of a grind"), blue and red oppose green and yellow. Players shoot in the alphabetical order of the colors. In a singles game, one player shoots both blue and red, the other green and yellow. The game is played on a soft felt mat that measures six feet by three feet. The mat in the basement rec room of Kahn's house in Vienna, Virginia, is white and spotless. "You'll see beer stains on the mats we play on when we go over for tournaments held in college gyms or pubs in England," Kahn says. "Some mats are dead, some are springy. Before you start playing you take some practice shots to know what the mat is like." Kahn's pristine mat is spread out neatly on a six-foot-by-three-foot foldaway conference table. When he watches television, he practices during the commercials. His tiddlywinks trophies are on a mantel above his fireplace.

Kahn is particularly proud of his dozen custom-designed "squidgers." These discs range from one inch to two inches in diameter and are custom-made from assorted materials—a rubber coaster, a spice-jar top, a button. "They serve different purposes, the way golf clubs do," Kahn explains. "In golf you usually blast out of a sand trap with a wedge and use a putter on the green. Certain squidgers are best for certain shots. If a wink is right next to the cup and you want to get it in, you use a flexible squidger."

Kahn became good at shooting very quickly. He excelled at the various shots that are used to free squopped winks, like the "bomb" (flicking your wink onto a pile of squopped winks, and scattering the pile), the "boon-dock" (a controlled blowout, which scatters enemy winks while keeping one's own winks nearby), and the delicate "piddle" shot, which frees one's own winks while keeping opponents' winks squopped. Some people who are unfamiliar with tournament winks have reacted to the game's vocabulary as Alice did after she was asked, in Lewis Carroll's *Through the Looking Glass,* to read "Jabberwocky": "It seems very pretty, she said when she had finished it, but it's rather hard to understand! (You see, she didn't like to confess, even to herself, that she couldn't make it out at all.)"

Kahn says he was hooked on winks from his first month at MIT. By the time he left the Boston area to take a job as an ocean engineer in Washington, he was known as a good solid player. "I wasn't at the top but I was near the top," he says. "I was about as good a partner as you could get in pairs. I was a top squopper. Strategy took me much longer to master, although it's strategy that draws me to the game. Some people say billiards comes close to winks, but it's two-dimensional and winks is three-dimensional. You can't stack billiard balls in a pile. Winks is often likened to chess. I play chess, but I think it's boring because it's just mental. Winks is mental and physical. Instead of picking up your piece and moving it, you have to shoot your piece. If you can't physically do the shot, it's as bad as picking the wrong shot and doing it correctly."

Winks is a tactical game. The most common way to win is not by shooting all the winks into the pot in the center of the table, although games may still be won that way. The more likely path to victory is to squop the enemy's winks to prevent them from scoring, and to take control of the game, which generally means controlling the area around the pot. Kahn sometimes refers to that area as "the war zone," when he isn't calling the whole game of winks "a war game which happens to be played on a three-foot-by-six-foot felt mat."

Each game of winks is worth 7 tournament points, with certain points awarded for potted winks and for winks that are free at the end of the game, and none for squopped winks. The tournament points from each game are added together. In world championship matches, the first player or players to accumulate more than $24\frac{1}{2}$ points wins. Matches are usually decided after six games have been played. "I'm the only person so far who has ever won a world singles championship in four games," Kahn says. "I seem to get more good luck than most players."

Larry Kahn's account of how he won the six major winks championships in the world, and the antecedents to his victory, gives an idea of his passion for high-level competition.

"In 1995 I finally achieved the Holy Grail of winks—holding all six major championships at the same time," he says. "These 'Big Six' are the NATwA pairs and singles, the ETwA pairs and singles, and the world pairs and singles. It's hard enough to hold more than three or four of these at once, mostly because it involves traveling to the other country to play in their championships while having won your own that year. Each year the two organizations, NATwA and ETwA, hold weekend-long national championships in pairs and singles that anyone can enter. Then the winners of those tournaments have a year to challenge the current world-title holders in head-to-head seven-game matches.

"I actually got close in 1985, maybe my best winks season ever. I started by winning the U.S. singles and pairs championships that year, and then in the fall eight of us set off on a brief tour of England. In the span of two weeks, I first won ETwA singles. Next, I won the world pairs title with my partner, Arye Gittelman, then the U.S. all-star team beat the Brits; and then I capped off the whole tour by winning the world singles title by a record margin. At that point I held five of the Big Six, with the only remaining title being the ETwA pairs the following spring. But I never went over for it. There were a number of reasons. I had just started going to England to play in their singles every year and hadn't realized it was about to become a habit with me instead of an occasional every-few-years event. Also, nobody had come close to winning all six before this, so it didn't seem to be overly important at the time. Plus, I was dominating the winks world and figured I'd be in a similar position—holding five out of the six—over the next few years. I didn't feel any urgency.

"Anyway, I didn't hold on to five out of six over the next few years and started regretting I had never taken a real shot at the sixth. In 1994 I got another chance. That was sort of a redemption year for me; I had done pretty badly during the previous two years, so at the beginning of 1994 I decided to get serious about practicing before the big events. I went to England in the spring and won their singles, then won our pairs and singles later in the year. I had neither of the world titles, though. That fall, one of my old partners, Dave Lockwood, and I decided to go over to the English pairs and try to teach some of the young upstarts—not really young, but about ten years behind us—a lesson. We won it, which made me the first person ever to win all four of the national titles in the same year. Sort of like the Grand Slam in golf.

"Since Dave and I would be at the English singles the following spring, I now had a chance to win both of the world titles and maybe hit the jackpot of all six if we could schedule both matches before the weekend match. Otherwise I'd have to also win the English singles to keep the streak alive. I was able to get the schedule arranged; I would try to regain the world singles title against Patrick Barrie on Thursday night, and then Dave and I would play Geoff Myers and Andy Purvis for the world pairs on Friday. Thursday went as planned. In a very close match that was tied after game six—only time that's ever happened—I won game seven to snag the world singles. The Friday match was tougher, and the games were so complicated that after five games we had to call it quits because it was so late. We decided to play the rest of it Saturday night, still giving me a chance to reach Big six history. Dave and I did hold our lead, so by Saturday dinner I had done it. Captured the Holy Grail, even if, as it turned out, I could only enjoy it for twenty-four hours. I finished second in the ETwA singles the next day. But at least I can say that I was the first, and so far the only, person to hold all the titles at once. I'm not sure if it's my greatest winks accomplishment, but it would definitely rank in the top three. Might be the most satisfying, though, since I worked extra hard that year and saw my effort pay off."

Kahn, who works for a high-tech consulting company, has always enjoyed extracurricular activities. He started playing bridge at the age of seven and played for an hour or so after dinner while at MIT. He had tossed a Frisbee around in high school and played the game at MIT. "Ultimate Frisbee was just starting in the early seventies and I played on MIT's ultimate team," he says. He continued to play when he moved to Washington and briefly held the distance record for throwing a Frisbee in a tournament in the nineteen-eighties. "I'm great with plastic discs," he says.

He also led an active social life. "Over a fifteen-year period, I must have met and dated close to a thousand women via the personal ads," he says. "Of course, most of these were just one-time dinner dates, but a few turned into long-term relationships. None permanent, though." In June 1994 he placed a personal ad in *Washingtonian* magazine. It read: "Enthusiastic, eclectic engineer, 40, athletic, irreverent, dependable, affectionate SWM seeks fit, witty nonsmoking SWF unswayed by typical Washington yuppiness. Happiness is marrying your best friend and sharing a spontaneous, *childfree,* lifelong romance. Failing that, free chocolate."

A SWF named Cathy Furlong who had never answered a personal ad was recovering from an operation. A friend gave her a copy of *Washingtonian* and suggested she answer some of the ads, pointing out that she had nothing better to do while recuperating. Furlong reluctantly consented. Her friend didn't think the ads she chose were any good, so she selected a few others for her. Larry Kahn's was among them.

The first time the two spoke on the phone, Furlong, a high school math teacher, asked Kahn: "If your house were burning down and you could take out only one thing, what would it be? What's your most valuable possession?" Without hesitating, he answered that he would take his squidgers. "They would be the hardest things to replace," he said recently. Furlong told him she would take a music box she had had since she was a little girl, one that reminded her of her childhood and of her parents.

The two met, bought a house together in 1995, and married in 1996. Over twenty winkers were among the hundred guests at their wedding. Furlong wore a custom-made hot-pink swing dress and Kahn a pair of white sneakers, turquoise shorts, and a shirt made from the same bolt of hot-pink cloth.

Perhaps because he hopes to play winks for the rest of his life, Kahn is worried about the future of the tournament game. "The game is in trouble here," he says. "England went through a time when they had fewer players than we did, but they've rebuilt. They got Cambridge going again. Their eight top players can now beat our top eight players. Our numbers have dwindled since the seventies and so far we haven't been able to get them back up. We've tried recruiting at schools in the Washington area. Winks didn't go over well at the University of Maryland because it's a jock school. We had no success recruiting at a regional meeting of Mensa or at the Billiards Café in Greenbelt, Maryland, where we play on the second and fourth Tuesday of the month. There are three other top-notch winkers in the Washington area—Dave, Rick, and a Brit who goes by the nickname of Sly. People seem to be more into computer games now. We'd like to get the Boston area going again. We're hoping that some of the students of my math-teacher friend at Ithaca High School, Severin Drix, go to Harvard and MIT and stick with the game. Boston is a city in which winks is likely to thrive.

"The game won't die off because we have a core of people who love it. The guys who moved from here to the West Coast would gladly play if they moved back east. We've played for thirty years and we still play. We enjoy winks and we enjoy each other's company. I'd like to see winks get bigger, so I could see if I'm as good as I think I am. I'd like to see if I could beat a thousand players rather than just the twenty or thirty I play in tournaments because they're the only ones able to qualify. It's cool to think that I've picked up this game and I've become the world champion and I've been able to keep up with the younger guys. It's cool to have won the most championships of anyone who has played the game.

"I can identify with Michael Jordan and Tiger Woods, because sometimes when I'm playing really well and really lucky it's like I'm in the zone. I don't mind admitting winks is sort of a silly game. Some of us play it to be good at something. I know that's one of the reasons that make me like it. It's nice being in the *Guinness Book of Records*. It's nice to be the best at something."

Thirty-five

Matt Dodyk:
Holing Out

There's a hush as Tiger Woods steps up to the tee, takes his famous looping swing, and sends the ball sky-high and far off to the right, a very un-Tigerish 148 yards into the adjacent fairway. The ball has barely come to a rest before golf's youngest legend pops up again, ready for the next swing, but this time Matt Dodyk is having none of it. With a shrug of the shoulders, Dodyk shuts down the computer in his off-campus house, hard by a railroad track in Lafayette, Indiana. "What can you do?" he says, as the screen fades to blank. "Tiger shanked it."

Even the great ones get humbled in cyber-golf.

A fourth-year computer science major at Purdue University when we talked, Dodyk has a collection of virtual golf games that includes at least half a dozen sanctioned by the Professional Golfers' Association of America—he's just been playing "Tiger Woods 2000 for Windows"—as well as several versions of "Links," the golf simulator series from Microsoft; "Golden Tee Golf," endorsed by longtime pro Peter Jacobsen; and a pocket-size portable Tiger Woods game "just for kicks."

Dodyk's not averse to a round of real golf, either, or to spending four hours on a Saturday or Sunday watching Tiger and the other touring pros go through their paces, or to rewatching the highlights of the day's action later in the evening or reading about his favorite pros on the Web or, in a pinch, in the newspapers. But the fact is, for a game that has come to occupy so much of his life in so many ways, golf was almost a nonstarter for him.

"I was nine or ten years old when I played the first time," says Dodyk, who grew up in Marion, Indiana, about two hours east of the Purdue main campus. "That was the last time for about seven years. It was so frustrating initially. I was playing basketball. Golf just didn't appeal to me at all, but after sophomore year in high school, a bunch of us got jobs as cart boys at the Shady Hills golf course in Marion. We got free golf, and that's how I got started. By then, I was able to hit [the ball] a long way, and that was all that mattered. Maybe it was because I'd played tennis by then or because my physical structure had changed. I'd come into my own."

Even with new muscles, there were the old ups and downs of the game to contend with—its maddening inconsistencies, for example, and the weird twisted fate that seems to bedevil even touring pros.

"One of the first times we went out and played—just us four cart boys— it was a par four, and all of us stepped up and had huge drives. We get up to the green. We're a bunch of hacks and still are, and we've finally gotten to a hole where we have a chance to do something. I'm standing on one side of the green; my buddy is on the other side. We're chipping. He skulls it straight across the green into my ankle, and I have to go into the pro shop. I can't finish the hole."

As Dodyk's interest in the game deepened, his golf multimedia net widened. Eventually, between cyber-golf and physical golf, between watching and playing, between the theory and the practice of the game, a kind of congruence began to emerge.

"I couldn't watch golf on TV before I started playing," Dodyk says. "I got to know the names of all the pros through the computer games. But once I started playing, then it was eat, sleep, and breathe golf. The computer games and the TV both make you want to play. You want to go out and make it look as easy as they do.

"I never had a lesson. Almost all my clubs are hand-me-downs. Everything I learned is from watching these guys and talking to my dad. It's an ongoing educational process."

Like many analysts of the game, amateur and professional, Dodyk credits Tiger Woods for the meteoric rise in golf's popularity in recent years, as both a viewing and a playing sport.

"The economy has something to do with it. People can afford to play more," he says. "But it's not that golf is getting any cheaper or that there are that many more courses. It's got to be Tiger. If it's not, what is it?"

Of Woods's influence on his own interest in golf, Dodyk has absolutely no doubt. He knew, he says, from the first time he saw Tiger play on television—when Woods was a Stanford University undergraduate competing in and eventually winning his third consecutive U.S. Amateur championship and Dodyk was a high school junior—that he was watching something and someone special.

"I'd never heard of him before, and I thought, Look at what he's doing and he's almost my age. Look at how much he has mastered the game—a game that can't be mastered. It was just Generation X: all that talent inside a Stanford Cardinal!"

The next spring, in 1997 just as Dodyk was finishing high school, Woods competed for the first time as a professional in the famed Masters Championship, played at the once-segregated Augusta National Golf Course in Georgia.

"I came home from school that Thursday and turned on USA to watch," Dodyk remembers. "He'd shot forty on the front nine, and I said, 'Oh, no, his first tournament, and Tiger's blown it.' Then he turned around and shot thirty on the back nine. He became more than a great golfer to me. He became someone who inspired me. He's doing so much off the course. He runs clinics for underprivileged kids, flies off and sees to his businesses, then he goes and wins a tournament on weekends."

By the time Woods took the Masters—by a record twelve strokes, the first African American and the youngest player ever to win the title—Dodyk also had had a personal connection with the golf phenomenon forced on him by his classmates. "In high school, I had really long hair, and I wore a bandanna. They called me 'Fluff.' It was a belittling term. Fluff was Tiger's caddy back then—he looked like this Grateful Dead follower. But after I made valedictorian, it became more a term of respect."

In an ideal week, Dodyk says, he might play eighteen holes first thing every morning, as soon as the course is open; spend an hour or two every day or two playing one of his "Tiger Woods for Windows" games (although he recently played a game called "Hotshots 2" for Playstation that he really liked) and another half hour or so each day paging through everything from *Golf Digest* to the growing host of Web 'zines devoted to the game. There are also the hometown pros to follow: the Golfing Gallaghers. Father Jim is a club pro in Marion. Sons Jim Junior and Jeff both play professionally, Jim on the main PGA tour and Jeff on the satellite buy.com tour. Sister Jackie Gallagher-Smith also plays, on the Ladies Professional Golf Association circuit.

Ideal weeks are mostly summer ones. The real life of a college senior trying to finish out his degree in style and find a good job on the other side of graduation doesn't afford as many chances for golf outings as Dodyk would like. Nor is north-central Indiana a golf paradise during the often bitter winter months. But when it comes to the nearly weekly tournaments that fill the PGA and international golf schedules, Dodyk is uncompromising.

"What distinguishes me from my friends is how much attention I pay to golf. If there's any kind of tournament that means anything, I'm all over it from Wednesday on."

In addition to whatever television channel is airing the tournament, Dodyk's number-one source of information, he says, is the Internet, especially PGATour.com: "I read that every day. I go there first and most often." After that comes the cable TV Golf Channel: "They get screwed out of showing the PGA tour—they've got to show foreign tournaments—but they do great analysis." Newspapers are "like Gate 3 or 4" when it comes to detail work on major tournaments, followed by the background information available in magazines like *Sports Illustrated* and *ESPN,* both of which Dodyk tends to read for free at his local Barnes & Noble. For a recap of the day's happenings, he also checks into ESPN's SportsCenter after play has ended: "That's the one my girlfriend really doesn't understand. Even though I've watched five hours of golf, I've got to see the highlights."

In addition to Tiger Woods and the Golfing Gallaghers, Dodyk says he's most likely to pay attention to Tommy Tolles and Fred Couples among the touring pros. "I've always liked Tommy Tolles. When he came on the tour as a young guy, I got a chance to see him in a tournament. He was just a nice guy. As for emulation, there's no one I'd rather emulate than Fred Couples. He has the smoothest swing in the game." Colin Montgomerie gets high marks, too, for being "so steady, so solid." Dodyk adds: "What I admire most about the pros is their tempo, the way every swing is the same. Part of it is hitting balls eight hours a day, but some people just have it and others don't."

Thanks to historical footage shown on the Golf Channel, Dodyk has had a chance to see some of the past greats of the game in action. "I love watching Ben Hogan and Sam Snead and Jack Nicklaus when he was young—how they come out of their shoes when they hit the ball and still stay in control."

There's also the game itself—the actual business of taking a slender, oddly shaped club in the hand; swinging at a small dimpled ball controlled by what appear to be irrational forces; and trying to propel it in the general direction of a hole no bigger than a fist. As devoted as he is to tracking the sport through television and into cyberspace, this is the part of golf Matt Dodyk seems to like the most. Not that he has quite mastered it: even in his own family, Dodyk ranks no better than third, behind his father and younger brother.

"My goal today would be to break ninety," Dodyk is saying as he settles in on the first tee at the Ravines, a public course some fifteen minutes due west of Lafayette. "My dad has been breaking eighty lately. That's his goal. My brother is more like break seventy."

Dodyk's first drive flies down the left side of the fairway, hung up at the end by a facing breeze but a good omen on a day when the winds promise to be tricky. By the third hole, though, the glow has started to come off the long game. "Golf's not enough of a challenge," he explains when his tee shot hooks wild to the left. "I like to come out and really see how hard I can make it on myself." A 250-yard drive dead down the center of the fairway on hole number five gets him back on track. Fortunately, too, neither the lost ball on the the third hole nor the other shots Dodyk sends sailing into unrecoverable locations during the round will work a hardship on him.

"My dad's job as an engineer involves lots of golf outings. He has pretty much an unlimited supply of balls that he's been given. That's why I can afford to keep playing the game."

Although he's no longer the high school golf-cart boy who took all his pleasure in the game from hitting long, Dodyk has the muscle—he's a rangy six-footer who likes to come out of his own shoes when he swings—to wallop the ball, and the driver remains his favorite and probably best weapon. He carries two with him, both of which sound as if they had been invented by a NASA subcontractor: a firm-flex Callaway Biggest Big Bertha 9 degree with a Pro Force 65 shaft and a Taylor Made TiBubble2 titanium model with a Burner Bubble graphite shaft and 7.5 degrees of loft. Of the two, he favors the Biggest Bertha "because it feels heavier at the head, where it needs to be, and gives me the confidence to grip and rip!"

The other favorite club in Dodyk's arsenal—one of the very few he has personally footed the bill for—is a Cleveland Tour Action Chrome 56 degree sand wedge with a steel shaft that he bought after it helped nail down his most successful day of golf.

"I had a thirty-nine–thirty-nine on the same day, but not on the same round. I chipped in from eighty yards, and I had another chip in, too. I was trying out the Cleveland wedge. After that, I decided I had to buy it. I really haven't had that round yet where I get to sit back and think about it—that hole in one, all the giant drives. It's all a process of working toward it."

By the back nine, though, driver and wedge have begun to pull together, and even the somewhat balky putter that he has been field testing for his grandmother (an Odyssey White Hot #4) has come around.

"This is where a smarter player like my dad or brother would take out an iron and hit it to the hundred-fifty [yard] mark," Dodyk says he steps up to the tee of the 277-yard fifteenth hole, "but, man, this is a drivable green!" Well, almost. Dodyk's drive stops about twenty yards short, on the right of the fairway. He caps the round off with an easy par four on the eighteenth, cutting the dogleg by driving left and leaving himself a short chip to the green. Maybe he broke ninety; more likely, he didn't. The scorecard has gone untended, and besides, the next round, not the last, is the one that matters.

"Another eighteen holes, and you'll be playing scratch golf," he says as the cart turns for the clubhouse. "That's what I tell myself after every round."

Dodyk eventually will take a job as a systems analyst with a division of the Guidant Corporation in the San Diego area—golf heaven, as it turns out, although he says that was not part of the decision-making process. "It will be an issue down the road, but for now, I figure that I'll be traveling so much, I'm just as likely to come home and play in Marion."

And that gets him back to what are truly his favorite moments in golf: not crushing a drive or snaking a putt fifty feet into the hole, but waking while it's still dark in the hometown where he first played the game and heading out to the course with some of the people who mean the most to him: his father, his brother if he's available, some family friends.

"There's nothing like the feeling of having a golf course to yourself. Nothing but you, your clubs, your close friends and family, the rising sun, and the course—no worries, no waiting, no carts running around everywhere. It's the combination of a good, friendly walk and the adrenaline-pumping thrill of competition all in one three-hour stint. And when you get out of bed at five in the morning, it's incredible how much you can get done. So many of my friends are just getting up at nine or ten or eleven. But it's nine, I've played golf, we come home and have breakfast, and I've got the whole day ahead of me!"

To, among other things, follow Tiger Woods on the TV or the computer screen. "Watching Tiger doesn't really help me," Dodyk says with a grin, "but I think it does."

PART 8

Passionate Pursuits

Thirty-six

John Sylvester Jr.:
The Things We Die For

The years 1968 to 1972 found John Sylvester Jr. living in Vietnam, part of that time in An Loc, due north of Saigon near the border with Cambodia. Sylvester had fought with the army in the tail end of the Korean war. At An Loc, he was serving with the State Department as the province senior adviser, heading a team of a dozen or so U.S. civilians and a hundred American army personnel that worked with a South Vietnamese colonel, the province chief.

It was, Sylvester says, a volatile place.

"An Loc was an ethnic minority area that had been carved out by the French for huge rubber plantations. The plantations had used many North Vietnamese workers. We were right on the border where some of the major North Vietnamese military units were camped. They would periodically come in. One of my successors as senior adviser got killed."

In April 1971, seeking to neutralize the menace on the border, American forces had crossed into Cambodia from the province and pushed ten miles into the interior. At the town of Snuol, the Eleventh Armored Cavalry Regiment fought a short, sharp battle that forced the North Vietnamese to withdraw. Afterward, Sylvester traveled to Snuol with the military commanders to have a look.

"There was debris of the battle lying around," he remembers. "I picked up some communist bullets. But I also found a scrap of ribbon lying there, and I picked that up. A year later, I went to Cambodia, into a medal shop, to see if the scrap of ribbon had come from a medal, and it had. I started avidly to collect ribbons. Later on, I got greedy and started collecting medals, and I became addicted."

Eventually, John Sylvester's collection would grow into perhaps the finest such assemblage of Indochinese medals in private hands in the United States—a thousand or more decorations, all of them dating from roughly 1870 to the present day and all from the broad region that so preoccupied his mind when he found that first scrap of ribbon.

"My own boundary for the collection is the medals of Vietnam, Cambodia, and Laos—the old French Indochina—plus foreign medals given for that region," Sylvester says.

Boundaries, though, are rarely impermeable, and collections tend to spawn more collections as surely as beer nuts demand more beer. And so it has been with John Sylvester. Everything fits the larger criterion: If an object can't show a connection to Indochina and some connection to the western presence in that part of Southeast Asia, it doesn't get in the door. Beyond that, space is pretty much the only limiting factor. Witness the kepis once worn by French troops sent to Indochina: About forty of the military caps, with their stiff visors and high circular crowns flattened at the top, form a ring below ceiling level in the upstairs office of Sylvester's spacious home along a golf course north of Durham, North Carolina.

"I started on the hats," Sylvester says. "They're all very interesting, but I ran out of room to keep the damn things. My wife used to disparagingly call this my hat-check room."

Sylvester ran out of room for the aigullettes, too—the ornamental cords, loops, and tags that sometimes adorn uniforms. "That came to a grinding halt," he says, as did his budding and complementary assemblage of Indochinese hat badges ("from the good old days, when armies dressed as they should, with helmets and plumes"). Even the brass flare guns had to be curtailed: six of them, magnificent pieces, are displayed low along one wall. Other collections died aborning: the French bayonets halted at a meager two. Sylvester's assemblage of Indochinese flags runs to a healthy ten, but even ten flags would barely seem to scratch the surface of possibility. If ten, why not twenty? If twenty, why not fifty?

Mayumi Sylvester, who died in 1998, had made her husband pledge that he would hold his objects to a single room, and thus far he has been both true to his word and tidy in his execution. No heaps crowd the floor. The desk drawers don't noticeably overflow. But if another wall were to magically appear within the confines of the present four, there seems no question that Sylvester would find a way to cover it with display cases, and in short order.

The heart of all this collecting, though, remains what it always has been: the core assemblage of medals and decorations that Sylvester began that day in Cambodia near the town of Snuol. And the heart of that, really, is a large part of his life's story.

John Sylvester Jr. was born in Newport, Rhode Island, and educated at Philips Academy, Andover, and Williams College, but, he says, "I've been involved with the Far East my whole life."

The Sylvesters were a navy family—hence the Newport address. Six generations of them, including John Sylvester's brother and his brother's two sons, have attended the U.S. Naval Academy. Generations, too, had served in the Pacific. Sylvester's grandfather, Harry E. Yarnell, had risen to full admiral and served as commander in chief of the Asiatic Fleet. Sylvester's father had served as his own father-in-law's flag lieutenant before becoming an admiral in his own right. From age six to age nine, John Sylvester had lived in the Far East while the family trailed his father around a succession of navy postings.

"We lived in Shanghai and Tsingtao in mainland China, and in Hong Kong and the Philippines. I remember some of the fighting at the outbreak of the war—the Japanese fighting German-trained Nationalists in Shanghai."

Weak eyes would keep Sylvester out of the Naval Academy and out of the family trade generally. He never rose above the rank of infantry sergeant during his army tenure, which included service in Korea during the last five months of the war. But nothing, it seems, was going to keep Sylvester from the Far East. After Korea, he had spent a year at the Georgetown University School of Foreign Service. From there, he signed up for the Foreign Service, where he would spend the next twenty-five years, most of that time in various State Department posts in Japan. Sylvester's wife had been a well-known Japanese actress when they married. "She gave up her career. She was earning more than I was." Together, they would raise a son.

Even after Sylvester left the Foreign Service, the Far East—and particularly Japan—wasn't far from his mind. The Sylvesters moved to Raleigh, North Carolina, in 1980. There, for fourteen years, he directed the Japan Center at North Carolina State University, charged both with helping the university strengthen its ties with Japan and with attracting businesses from the then booming Japanese economy to set up shop in the state.

In between duty in Japan as a young man and his university ties with Japan as an older one came Vietnam and all the bittersweet lessons of that war.

Before arriving at An Loc, Sylvester had been stationed in Vietnam's delta as deputy to "a very fine former Special Forces colonel." Once at An Loc, as part of the pacification program meant to bring stability to the provinces, he reported to "two very able bosses," he says: U.S. Foreign Service officer Charles Whitehouse and Army General Phil Davidson. Still, like most people who spent time on the ground in South Vietnam in those days, Sylvester came away with complicated feelings about the war, the country, and the American presence and performance there.

"I have very strong and somewhat conflicting views about the war," Sylvester goes on. "It was a just war, but not a wise war. South Vietnam was worth fighting for. It was a diverse, open, semidemocratic society that did not want to be conquered by the Stalinists and totalitarians in the North. I felt that if you had had a truly free election in Vietnam, the communists in the South would get between eight and ten percent of the vote. But you can prove anything you want about that war because everything was so diverse. Province by province, things were almost totally different. Pick your evidence, and you can make any case."

In a sense, the medals John Sylvester has gathered are his continuing tie to that time and place. The French, he says, are the primary collectors of such medals, along with German, Australian, New Zealand, and British enthusiasts. In pursuit of new acquisitions, Sylvester keeps up a lively global correspondence and sometimes swaps his own wares for other objects that help complete a subset of the collection. He also has returned to Vietnam four or five times, he says, "in part for my collection and partly just to see the place because I'm so interested."

American fascination with Indochinese memorabilia is high as well, on both the buying and the selling sides. Inevitably, the great bulk of those most interested—Sylvester estimates 80 percent—are former military, many of whom served in Vietnam.

"A couple of the major dealers are ex-army guys who have these militaria stores. They travel regularly to Vietnam. Then they have these gigantic flea markets. I was just at one at the civic center in Louisville, Kentucky. It's like a gun show: daggers, SS paraphernalia, uniforms, medals. You walk around with great fascination and find the little treasures. You see wives dragged along with that look of exquisite boredom that their husbands have when they take them shopping."

Some of the medals, too, are reminiscent of the most painful aspects of the Vietnam War—or the "American War" as it's known over there. In Sylvester's collection is a Vietcong medal he says was given "for killing Americans. They were freely given out to southerners and to northerners pretending to be southerners." There's also a nakedly symbolic American POW medal—a red, yellow, and green ribbon suspended above a huge and heavy bronze medallion that shows an eagle trapped in bamboo. "It was made as a neck award, to place over the head of a father or mother who had lost a son in Vietnam and who must have immediately been bent over by its weight."

But as much as John Sylvester's collection inevitably calls to mind the American military involvement in Southeast Asia, the medals also put that involvement in context with the century and a quarter of western intervention that had preceded the U.S. presence there and of which the American-led Vietnam War was, to an extent, only the prolonged denouement.

"Medals reflect man's vanity, his courage, and his merit," Sylvester says. "but they also reflect history."

"Vietnam is the cutting edge of the Sinitic culture," Sylvester says. "Laos and Cambodia are the cutting edge of Indic culture." It was these two cultures—the one spreading south from China, the other east out of India—that the French encountered when they went ashore in Vietnam in the eighteen-forties, ostensibly to protect Catholic missionaries, and began pushing into Cambodia and Laos, assuming the Vietnamese claim to both areas.

Sylvester's earliest pieces are singularly Vietnamese. The Khanh and its female equivalent the Boi were the traditional orders given out by the kingdom of Annam, which since the sixteen-hundreds had covered most of north and central Vietnam. Commonly hammered out of gold, and later in cast metal in a French version, Khanhs are in the shape of traditional Vietnamese gongs—roughly "the shape of a butterfly with its wings spread," Sylvester writes in one of the two monographs he has published to explain and illuminate his collection. High mandarins would wear the Khanhs around their necks, suspended from a silk cord that was red in normal times and green for mourning.

It wasn't long, though, before the French influence began to assert itself. The Order of the Dragon of Annam—a western-style award hung from a ribbon—was "the French Legion of Honor adapted for Vietnam. It could be issued by the president of France or the emperor at Hue with a different ribbon. It was a European inspiration of what an Oriental medal should be."

Sometimes, you can trace whole story lines in Sylvester's display cases. More than a hundred years of Cambodian history get told in the changing images of the rulers on the medals issued under their authority, just as the history of the Roman Empire gets told in the changing images impressed on its coins. (Medals are, in fact, coins adapted for the purpose of honoring and identifying the praiseworthy.)

Other times, the medals serve as a shorthand for individual biographies. One of Sylvester's display cases is devoted to groups of medals won by individuals and sewn together so that they could be mounted at one time on a single chest. One such group shows awards from French military campaigns in Italy, Casablanca, and Indochina—three "very different wars in three continents," dating from the last half of the nineteenth century.

The medals serve equally as a reminder that for more than a century and a half, Indochina has rarely been left alone by external powers. Sylvester has equivalents of the French Croix de Guerre from both South and North Vietnam, but, he says, "on the North side, you can see the cross disappear, replaced by the star and sickle." So stylized is Soviet art that the bust of Ho Chi Minh that appears on a number of Sylvester's medals is on first glance almost indistinguishable from a bust of Lenin.

Looked at in one light, Sylvester's collection is a miracle of balance, just as Vietnam itself is a miracle of balance today—between eastern influence and western yearning, between official communism and rampant capitalism.

"This little rinky thing is about the equivalent of the North Vietnamese Congressional Medal of Honor," Sylvester says, pointing to a particularly uninspiring lump of metal. "They have something called the Gold Star, which I don't have. You can get them, but they went to only a few people— Ho Chi Minh, Vo Nguyen Giap, Leonid Brezhnev—and they're very pricey. They don't come out easily. The Vietnamese will sell anything, but this has to be sold sub rosa."

Sylvester also has a display case devoted to all the nations that either fought in Vietnam during the American presence there or served on one of the seemingly innumerable international commissions that sought to bring peace to the region. Among his medals, too, is evidence of how often international ambitions have crashed against the shores of reality in Southeast Asia.

"This is a French campaign medal from Dien Bien Phu," Sylvester explains, referring to the famous and final 1954 defeat of the French army by North Vietnamese forces under the legendary General Giap. "Whoever won it had the back shaved off and replaced with: 'Bravery betrayed, a cause lost, etc.' He was so pissed off, he had it inscribed on the medal."

"Most of my medals," he says, "cost a few pennies to make, and a guy will run through machine-gun fire to get one of the damn things."

In an ideal world, with ideal access and ideal luck, John Sylvester would love to lay his hands on "an early French honor medal that was ascribed for Indochina. I'm only aware of one example of it, and I doubt I'll ever get it. But I've seen a photograph of it. I know it exists. It would be the Holy Grail."

In a less than ideal world, he'll settle for a medal from the governor general of Indochina that was struck for railway workers.

"It was the first version," he says, "from the early nineteen-thirties. It's not exceedingly rare, and it shouldn't be very expensive, but I've never seen it, and it's a little piece I'd like. It's a hole in my collection. It's just like stamps—you've got to fill that blank."

Thirty-seven

Sonia Young:
Color Me Purple

Sonia Young is widely known in Chattanooga as the Purple Lady, and no wonder. Her closets and drawers are filled with purple dresses, slacks, sweaters, blouses, skirts, lingerie, jumpsuits, shoes, handbags, scarves, and bathing suits. If she is invited to a black-and-white party she says she'll wear purple—or stay home. Her cashmere coat, raincoats, car coats, mink jackets, fur stole, and fur coats (two foxes, a mink, and a shearling) are in various shades of purple. She also has several purple feather boas. On her fingers she wears her diamond engagement and wedding rings, and four rings with purple stones.

The Purple Lady shares her symphony-in-purple house with her husband, Mel, and three Maltese dogs; the dogs are white but they wear purple collars, sleep on a custom-made purple canopy-covered bed, and eat from purple and lavender dog bowls.

The kitchen appliances are white, but the countertops are purple Formica, and the wallpaper is white with purple violets. The colander, dishes, glassware and plastic ware, trivets, bowls, trays, potholders, scrub brushes, sponges, trash cans, ice buckets, Palmolive dishwashing liquid, and Reynolds Wrap are purple, and the four sets of stainless steel have purple handles. The cookbooks contain recipes for Violets 'n' Vodka (vodka and grape juice) and pork in plum sauce.

For lunch Young may serve deli sandwiches with purple potato chips, called Blues. Purple M&M's and purple and white Good & Plentys are readily available. Neighbors provide homemade plum preserves. Mel Young and the Youngs' daughter Melanie, who has her own public relations firm in New York City, are always on the alert for purple presents for Sonia.

"Mel recently found me a purple wig at the mall," Sonia says. "And he got me a purple remote control device for the TV, and a new Sony purple CD player–radio–cassette player combination."

"If anything comes in purple, it comes to this house," Mel says.

The brass chandelier over the dining room table is festooned with purple ribbons, and when the Youngs entertain, the table is set with a purple tablerunner and purple place mats or cloths, napkins, candleholders, candles, and chargers. The dining room, living room, and den are furnished with purple carpets, purple and lavender sofas, purple chairs, and purple hassocks and footstools. The paintings on the walls are primarily purple, and the glass sculptures on the coffee tables are, too. "I've just bought a two-foot-high metal sculpture called *The Purple Lady* that was designed and made by a wonderful artist and old family friend who used me as his muse," the muse says. "I believe everyone should put a little or a lot of purple in his or her life."

The master bedroom is completely purple, and so is most of the master bath: "Carpet, spread and pillow shams, drapes, all bedding and towels, purple chaise longue, chairs, several purple throws, lots of purple bears and other stuffed animals, a Purple Passion Barbie doll, purple Princess Di Beanie Baby bear." Lavender soaps, lotions, potpourri, bath gels, and a tray of amethyst crystals are in the bathroom, which also has a purple shower.

At the center of the Youngs' one-story house is an atrium. In the atrium is an amethyst fountain and next to it a purple artificial Christmas tree—a gift from friends—which the Youngs keep up all year round. "We're Jewish but we're ecumenical," Young explains. The tree is decorated with hundreds of ornaments, most of them purple. She wraps birthday, get-well, wedding, and Christmas/Chanukah presents in purple wrapping paper tied with purple ribbons, and mails out purple greeting cards written in purple ink. She doesn't sign her cards and letters "Sincerely," but "With Lavender Love." The message played on the answering machine is: "This is the Purple Lady, Sonia Young. The rest of the world is keeping me busy right now but if you will leave your name, date, time of your call, and a brief message, I'll get back to you real soon. Now don't forget to wait until you hear the sound of the tone before you leave your message. Have a perfectly purple day. Lavender Love." The Youngs are listed in the telephone directory under Mel Young, Sonia Young, and "PURPLE, Lady."

Three cars are parked in the Youngs' driveway. Sonia drives a purple Sebring Chrysler convertible, Mel drives an amethyst Lexus. An old car, a purple Dodge Charger, is covered by a tarp. As luck would have it, Tennessee's state flower, which appears on its license plates, is the iris.

Sonia Young grows purple orchids indoors. The azaleas, pansies, petunias, impatiens, rhododendrons and most of the roses she plants outdoors are purple. The swimming pool has purple floats, the Japanese garden has a purple bridge, the outside furniture (tables, chairs, swing, and hammock) is purple. The landscape also includes a purple cow.

In the Youngs' basement, Mel has a wine cellar and a home office (he is writing his third book on the Civil War) and Sonia has a combination playroom and home office with purple calculators, mouse pads, rulers, file folders, clocks, radios, telephones, and caller-ID units; there are scissors with purple handles, a purple bubblegum machine, a grape Apple iMAC (her current computer), a purple scanner, and a purple typewriter (a relic). The sheet of music on the basement piano is "Deep Purple."

"When I was five years old, I took tap and ballet," Sonia Young reminisces. "I was an orchid in the dance recital. I thought I looked beautiful. My mother brought all her friends. I was a fat little girl with pigtails and I got lots of applause. It made me feel special. I'm convinced that the favorite color of ninety percent of girls under the age of twelve is purple. After the age of twelve, that changes. It didn't for me."

According to Young, there weren't many purple clothes made for high school girls in the nineteen-fifties; purple wasn't considered a color for the young. She was able to buy more purple clothes when she was in college, and she wore them more often.

Sonia Winer graduated from Tulane University in May 1956. She met Melvin A. Young, who was then in the army, the following month. They were married in February 1957—"the month with the purple stone, an amethyst," she points out.

"I wanted to get married in lavender but my mother said, 'Brides wear white, the color of purity and chastity, and no daughter of mine is going to go down that aisle in anything but white.' I carried white orchids with purple throats, found periwinkle-blue dresses for my bridesmaids, and wore an orchid pinned to my blue custom-made going-away suit."

During the first ten years of their marriage, Sonia Young worked part-time and got a master's degree in educational psychology. She has held a variety of paid jobs—as a teacher of speech- and hearing-impaired children and as a public-relations executive. For the past fifteen years she has taught courses in public speaking at the University of Tennessee at Chattanooga.

She has always been active in the community as a volunteer, and she discovered she had a talent for fund-raising. She has raised money for the Siskin Foundation (a rehabilitation center) and thirty-seven thousand dollars for a magnet school for the arts, and she led the campaign to raise six million dollars for building the Chattanooga Theatre Center. She wrote and produced a play—called *The Purple Princess*—for the opening of Children's Theatre, for which she also raised money. For her sixtieth birthday, in August 1994, she invited friends to a birthday party–benefit, even though it meant revealing her age to the entire community. The event, which raised sixty thousand dollars for Chattanooga Cares, was called "One of a Kind—The Arts Against AIDS."

The only time Sonia Young does not appear in her trademark color is when she acts in a play at the Theatre Center. "When I'm in a show, I can't wear any purple," she explains. "Directors tell me I can't be anyone else if I'm wearing purple and they're right." She played the lead in Alfred Uhry's *The Last Night of Ballyhoo* at the Chattanooga Theatre Center early in 2000. Her wardrobe was black, brown, and navy. She wore her mother's vintage nonpurple jewelry, which is usually kept in a safe-deposit box. She won the "Miss Annie"—the local Tony—for best actress for her performance as Beulah "Boo" Levy, the tyrannical mother. "Wearing colors other than purple on stage seemed appropriate," she says. "I was not me, I was Beulah Levy."

Sonia Young enjoys the recognition her passion for purple bestows on her. At her favorite restaurant, her dinner is served on a special purple plate. Other restaurants and clubs place bouquets of violets in front of her, or supply purple balloons or confetti. Mel often wears lavender jackets when they go out. Sonia first realized the positive value of wearing purple back when she taught children with learning disabilities. A pediatrician told children, "I'm sending you over to play games with this nice purple lady." The games were clinical tests and the children liked the purple lollipops she gave them. Deaf children signed "purple lady" as they passed her in hallways. She was pleased to find children seated in her convertible on days when she parked the car and left the top down.

"Earlier in my life I used the color as a positive attention-getter," she reflects. "With the kids at work I was the Purple Lady, but I was Sonia Young at home. I no longer go back and forth between the two. As I gradually furnished the house in purple, the color took over my house and my life. I put my nonpurple wedding gifts in storage. I never liked them anyway. Without being the Purple Lady I don't think I have an identity. More people know me as the Purple Lady than as Sonia Young."

Thirty-eight

Claudia Perry:
Love of the Game

It was books that first brought Claudia Perry to her love of baseball. Her father had been a diehard basketball fan, willing to take his young daughter to state high school hoops tournaments at the drop of a hat. He had even followed baseball occasionally, back in the days of the old Negro Leagues. But that was decades gone by. For him the national pastime was played in shorts and sneakers, with baskets suspended ten feet up at either end of a ninety-four-foot court.

"He'd tell me about seeing the Homestead Grays playing at Griffith Stadium," Perry recalls, "but at the start of every summer he'd cancel his subscription to *Sports Illustrated* and then renew it in the fall, just in time for the basketball season."

Worse, the hometown major league team of her childhood—the Washington Senators ("First in war, first in peace, last in the American League")—was mostly terrible, even when the great Ted Williams managed it in the franchise's final three years.

Still worse, in 1971, when Perry was still in elementary school and just beginning to seriously ramp up her interest in the sport, this second incarnation of the Senators (the first having become the Minnesota Twins ten years earlier) decamped for Texas, where they were renamed the Rangers but hardly reborn. Still under the guidance of the "Splendid Splinter" the team lost one hundred games during its inaugural year in the Lone Star State.

All of which hardly put a dent in Claudia Perry's enthusiasm.

"I'm not sure why, but I just loved the game. Probably when I was about nine or ten, I began really paying attention to it. I started reading every book on baseball that I could get my hands on. This was back in the days when they had kid and adult library cards—you could take out only so many books on a kid's card. I kept begging my mother to let me use hers. One of the first books I read was Bill Veeck's autobiography, *Veeck as in Wreck*."

The onetime owner of the St. Louis Browns and Cleveland Indians, Veeck is perhaps best remembered today for his ballpark-filling stunts, including sending midget Eddie Gaedel to the plate in 1951 when he owned the Browns, but during his Cleveland tenure in the late nineteen-forties, Veeck had signed the first African American to play in the American League, Larry Doby, and he followed that by bringing on board the legendary black pitcher Satchel Paige. (At least forty-two years old when he joined the Indians, Paige went six-one his first season, with a 2.48 earned run average.)

For the African American Perry, the combination of a race pioneer and an out-of-the-box baseball executive was irresistible. Reading Veeck's book, she says, was "a watershed moment. Veeck has a natural tie to kids' minds. He was a rebel."

Bill Veeck, though, was only the beginning. Another, deeper "watershed moment" came a year or so later, at a beauty salon where Perry and her mother had gone to have their hair done.

"It didn't take long to do my hair back then," says Perry, who now sports red dreadlocks. "I was sitting at the hairdresser's, waiting for my mother, when I came across an excerpt from Jim Bouton's *Ball Four* in an old magazine that was lying around."

Bouton's raunchy, insightful book—part a journal of his 1969 season, spent mostly pitching for the Houston Astros, and part a peek behind the curtain at the drinking and womanizing habits of such former Yankee teammates as Mickey Mantle—was guaranteed best-seller status when then-Commissioner Bowie Kuhn declared it "detrimental to baseball." Entranced, Perry moved from the excerpt to the book itself, and with that the hook was set and her passion had a specific if even more unlikely focus.

"Being just a kid then, I didn't know what all of *Ball Four* was about," she says, "but that began my love affair with the Houston Astros."

A decade and a half later, Perry was working as a cub reporter for the *Richmond* (Virginia) *Times–Dispatch* when she was assigned to cover the annual convention of the Society for American Baseball Research, a group of mostly amateur devotees of baseball minutiae and the people largely responsible for all those finely honed stats and details and comparisons that true fans of the game can't get enough of. And it was at SABR, which she joined soon after the convention, that Perry was to find a home for all her random and multifaceted fascination with the game.

Since 1987, Perry has served on SABR's committees on the Negro Leagues, on women in baseball, and on the business of baseball—as cochair of the latter two. Once a month, she travels from her home in Jersey City, New Jersey, near her job with the Newark *Star-Ledger,* to meetings of the Westchester County, New York, branch of SABR. Sometimes, too, she'll head out to the ballpark with SABR members. Two of them, both New York Mets fans, were with her in the summer of 2000 when she went to Shea Stadium to see the Mets take on her Astros. "It was a day that wasn't fit for man nor beast if he was wearing an Astros uniform," Perry recalls. "It was the ultimate humiliation." She would also throw her hat into the ring for the presidency of the organization.

As for the trivia and fine detail so beloved by the group's members, Claudia Perry already had shown she was no slouch at that.

Perry attended college at the Massachusetts Institute of Technology—a strange match, she says, in two ways. One, "I was a sports fan at a school where there were no teams. At MIT, the biggest thing was the chess team." And, two, "I knew I didn't want to be an engineer after my freshman year."

Eventually, she earned her degree in art and design. On the side, under the mentoring of the noted media critic Edwin Diamond, who lectured at MIT once a week, Perry found journalism. After graduation, she went to work for Boston's alternative *Real Paper* as a rock critic. When that paper folded two years later, she moved on to Jacksonville, Florida, and *The Florida Times-Union,* and then to Richmond and the *Times-Dispatch,* where she covered small-college sports for a living and the minor league Richmond Braves for recreation. Perry's next job—a six-year stint as a music critic for the *Houston Post*—finally got her to the majors and the team she had been admiring from afar for nearly two decades. Happily, the Astros, which had begun life in the sixties as an expansion team called the Houston Colt 45s, were firing from all chambers when Perry got there.

"My first year in Houston, 1989, there was a period in May and June when the Astros won some unseemly amount of games. They were playing with 'joy and verve and poetry,' as Annie Savoy says in *Bull Durham,* and I was there for that, including a twenty-two-inning game with the Dodgers when things got so bad the Dodgers had Fernando Valenzuela playing first base. I had to leave in the fourteenth to cover a band. I went home afterwards and saw the end on television. The Astros won and they went and won the next afternoon, too."

At seven hours and fourteen minutes, the Astros-Dodgers set-to of June 3, 1989, tied the major-league record for the longest game ever played. It was in Houston, too, where Perry came face-to-face with one of her true heroes in the game, Jose Cruz, who spent thirteen of his nineteen big-league seasons with the Astros, amassing a lifetime .284 average.

"Cruz was good, not great, but he showed up for work every day, and loved doing it. I met him at an Astros dinner after he'd retired. I was weak in the knees."

When the *Houston Post* folded in April 1995, Perry took a job with the *San Jose* (California) *Mercury–News,* where she got a chance to make her own competitive splash. As a baseball player, Perry says, "I was the perennial last person chosen." As a fantasy-league baseball player, she hasn't been so hot, either: "I've been working so much on the past of baseball that I tend to draft people who have already had their career years." The all-star *Jeopardy* team, though, was another matter.

"I'd passed the qualifying test once before when I lived in Houston, but nothing came of it. Then in May, I went back to L.A. for a rock critics' conference, and I played hooky one afternoon. I went out to the studio and took the test. I was one of maybe six out of sixty who passed it."

This time *Jeopardy* called back and asked her to be on the show.

"The first time was an absolute disaster. There were technical problems with the buzzer. I won a dollar and a fax machine—a *thermal-paper* fax machine. I had just gotten back home to San Jose when they called and said, 'We want you on again. You didn't get a fair chance.' So I went back in October 1996—they tape five shows in a day—and I won three straight games. By Friday, I had thirty-three thousand dollars."

Ten days later, Perry came back to continue her run.

"My fourth show I was, as the ballplayers say, in the Zone. I killed it. My two opponents didn't know what hit them. By 'Final Jeopardy,' they couldn't have caught me if they had doubled their money. I won twelve thousand dollars on that show."

Perry would lose in her fifth game, but her total winnings of $45,000 were enough to qualify her for the "Jeopardy Tournament of Champions," where she advanced to the semifinals. Although the show frequently uses sports categories, Perry says she never got one during her entire run.

"I did get music categories. One was priceless: 'Bands of the Eighties.' The nineteen-eighties were when I started working as a rock critic! I kept hoping for sports, but I got no sports categories. But one thing I noticed about *Jeopardy* is that the answers are sort of high relief. They want something the people at home can answer. Nine times out of ten if it's a baseball question, the answer is going to be Babe Ruth, not Heinie Manush or Bill Wambsganss. It's just not going to be. The people at home on the couch with the remote aren't going to know that."

For the record, Manush, an outfielder, batted .330 in seventeen seasons, mostly with Detroit and Washington. He was elected to the Hall of Fame in 1964. Known as "Wamby," Wambsganss won a spot in the record books—and in barroom trivia contests everywhere—with his unassisted triple play in game five of the 1920 World Series.

Perry can roll off her all-time Negro Leagues all-star team without breaking a sweat. "Satchel Paige would be on the mound, whatever team you put together." Behind the plate, no question, is Josh Gibson, the "black Babe Ruth," who might have hit as many as eight hundred home runs during his seventeen-year career, although it's always hard to tell with the Negro Leagues stars since maybe half or more of the 180 or so games they played each year were on barnstorming tours, where the statistics were casually kept and even more casually filed for posterity. At first is the great Walter Fenner "Buck" Leonard. Perry wants to think about her second baseman, but shortstop is a done deal: Willie Wells, who batted over .400 in exhibition games against white major leaguers and who was such a devilish fielder that fans in Mexico, where he played for four seasons in the early forties, knew him as "El Diablo." Beside him is the same third baseman who covered his wing on the Newark Eagles' "Million Dollar Infield" of the thirties: Ray Dandridge.

The list goes on through the outfield, as do the wonders of women in baseball, another subject about which Perry pretty much knows chapter and verse. There's Jackie Mitchell, for instance, who was taught to pitch by Dazzy Vance, brother of Dizzy. As a seventeen-year-old, Mitchell had been signed to a minor-league contract with the Chattanooga Lookouts of the Southern Association. On April 2, 1931, in an exhibition game with the New York Yankees, Mitchell struck out Babe Ruth and Lou Gehrig back to back. Not long afterward, she was banned from baseball on the grounds that it was too strenuous a life for the weaker sex. Even Mitchell, though, might be nothing next to shortstop Dottie Schroeder, the only woman to play all twelve seasons (1943–1954) of the All-American Girls Professional Baseball League that was the subject of the movie *A League of Their Own*.

"Chuck Dressen once said of her that she'd be worth fifty thousand dollars if she were a man," Perry says. Dressen, who spent sixteen years as a major-league manager, should know. Among the shortstops he managed was Dodger Hall of Famer Pee Wee Reese.

As much fun as all this data work is, though, Perry clearly prefers to take the long view: Statistics should serve history, not the other way around.

"It's the culture of the Negro Leagues that interests me. They were an example of the black economic community pre-integration. A lot of these teams were owned by local black people. Their downfall was that most of the owners didn't own the parks they played in, that valuable piece of real estate, but the teams and the players were a part of the community. People dressed up for the Sunday games. The players knew the black musicians of their time, and together they formed a black elite that people took pride in.

"I really wish black kids could be made aware of this element of their history. It's such a fascinating time. Yes, there was segregation all around, but that didn't stop these people. They wanted this, and they loved baseball, and they didn't let anything, even segregation, stop them."

As for the game itself, Perry says that what she most likes about baseball is that it creates its own sense of time.

"There is no clock. The game has to unfold at its own pace. There's no two-minute offense, no sitting on the ball. At some point the pitch is going to have to cross the plate, but all those spaces allow you to construct the narrative of the game. You go with friends, the game's going on, you're watching it, but all the time you're filling in the story. Just your being there fills in the story—that's why it doesn't work so well on television. If you miss that drive to the basket, that power jam, it's gone. The game has moved past it. But if you miss that great catch because you've gone for a beer, someone will describe it to you. 'You should have seen it!' You have time for that in baseball."

As the century was drawing to an end, Perry says, SABR sent out an e-mail to its members, asking them to pick an all-century team. Perry responded with her own idea. "I proposed in my e-mail that I was less interested in the statistical leaders of the twentieth century than in the people who have made you love the game."

Not surprisingly, Perry's own all-star team of those who have made her love the game runs heavily toward the hardnoses and off-beats and insurrectionists who first lured her to baseball. Jim Bouton is on the team, of course, along with Bill "Spaceman" Lee, the eccentric onetime Red Sox pitcher, and another former pitcher, "Bo" Belinsky, who spent his off hours with the Los Angeles Angels romancing actress Mamie Van Doren and a succession of Hollywood starlets. There also are two sluggers often portrayed in the press as moody, Dick Allen and Eddie Murray ("The fans liked both of them a lot better than the media did"); the Panamanian-born catcher Manny Sanguillen ("He had the greatest smile in the majors"); and a trio of former St. Louis Cardinals: Bob Gibson, Lou Brock, and Curt Flood. It was Flood who by refusing to accept a 1969 trade to the Philadelphia Phillies both ruined his own career and set in motion the legal machinery that eventually produced free agency for the players. "Like Jackie Robinson," Perry says, "he was a true race man."

Roberto Clemente is on her team, too: "He was a Latin player who didn't take any crap. He was a great player and an extraordinary human being. We won't see his kind again soon." She saw him play just once—during an exhibition game in the suddenly baseball-less Washington, D.C., before the start of the 1972 season—but once was enough, and all the chance she would get. Eight months later, Clemente died in a New Year's Eve plane crash, just as he was departing his native Puerto Rico with a load of relief supplies for earthquake victims in Nicaragua.

For good measure, Perry's team also includes the pint-size former manager of the Baltimore Orioles, Earl Weaver, as deft an umpire-baiter as ever stood on a dugout step. "I like him particularly for a quote he once gave Tom Boswell of *The Washington Post*," Perry says. "Boswell was talking with Weaver during spring training, just before a game. Finally, Boswell said, 'Well, I better go. You've got to get ready.' You know, all this stuff about getting your game face on. 'This ain't football,' Weaver told him. 'We do this every day.' That's how I try to look at my work as a journalist."

For every true fan of any team in any sport there comes a time when all the stars align for good or ill and everything you've ever cared about hangs in the balance. For Claudia Perry, that moment arrived on October 15, 1986, in game six of the National League Championship Series between the Astros and the Mets. The Mets led the series three games to two, but if the Astros could get through the sixth game, they had Mike Scott ready to pitch the seventh, and in two previous outings in the series, Scott had been all but unhittable, giving up a single run in eighteen innings and striking out nineteen. It wasn't to be. In what is often called one of the greatest baseball games ever played, the Mets scored three times in the top of the sixteenth inning and fended off a two-run Astros rally in the bottom of the inning to win the pennant. Perry, though, didn't get to see a moment of the closing drama.

"I was on assignment in Emory, Virginia, for the *Times–Dispatch,*" she recalls. "I had a meeting with the freaking basketball coach at Emory and Henry College. There wasn't even a hotel in Emory; I was staying in Abingdon, Virginia, and I had to leave my hotel where I was watching the freaking game. It was the Shenandoah Valley—all AM radio—and all I could get was high school football in the car. It was like I had violated the time-space continuum. I couldn't listen to the last innings.

"I'm convinced to this day that if I could have stayed in my hotel room and watched the rest of the game, we would have prevailed; Mike Scott would have won game seven; and the universe would have remained as it should. It's as if they stole my children and left them to die in the snow."

What would put the universe right again? Perry is asked over lunch at a Cuban eatery in Jersey City, just across the Hudson River from lower Manhattan. Not beating the Mets, she says. The Mets are small potatoes. She has her heart set on bigger things.

"I want the Astros to beat the Yankees in the World Series—beat 'em bad, like a drum."

She makes sure to say it loud enough so that the man wearing the Yankees cap at the next table over can't help but hear.

Thirty-nine

Daniel Chapin: Route Man

When Daniel Chapin left his home in a Baltimore suburb to drive with his parents to Boston College in September 2000 he didn't have to consult a map. Chapin, eighteen, who was beginning his freshman year at B.C., is a map whiz. He knew, simply knew, four or five different ways of traveling from Baltimore to Boston. The one he chose was I-95, Delaware Memorial Bridge, New Jersey Turnpike, short attempted use of I-287 to bypass New York Metro area congestion (it was rush hour on the Friday before Labor Day weekend), exited off I-287 after coming to a total stop (a truck had overturned five miles ahead), U.S. 1 north to Garden State Parkway, Garden State Parkway north to I-87, across Hudson on Tappan Zee Bridge, I-684 north to I-84, I-84 across central and northern Connecticut to Massachusetts Turnpike (I-90), eastward toward Boston.

"It seems that I have always known the interstate highway system," Chapin says. "I cannot remember when I didn't. We always had maps lying around the house. Maybe I just absorbed roads from maps. I think it had a lot to do with my interest in geography. If you can understand the special qualities of geography—which path rivers and mountain ranges follow, where cities and political boundaries are—then it's easier to grasp all of the lines of the interstate system. I have, in fact, memorized the U.S. interstate system and can tell a person how to get from any major city to any other. This odd ability was always a crowd pleaser at high school."

Chapin's first interstate love, he says, was I-95, mostly because it carried his family the better part of the way from Baltimore to Holden Beach, North Carolina, near Wilmington, for an annual summer vacation. He was only age eight or so when he first made a list of all the exits between Washington, D.C., and a little south of Smithfield, North Carolina, where they left the interstate system in favor of U.S. and state routes. By age ten, he was ready to make dramatic improvements in his inventory system.

"I decided beforehand to make a list of all the exits on I-95 in Virginia and North Carolina, as well as those on the newly opened stretch of Interstate 40 between Benson and Wilmington. In a frenzy, as I was before every trip to Holden Beach, I got out my ruler, paper, and pencil and created a list that spread out over two or three pages. I made boxes for 1) the road name; 2) the route number; 3) the exit number; 4) the mile number; 5) the cities, towns, and villages the road went to; and 6) any relevant special information that caught my eye. The list took me a while to make, because the ruler lines would not make perfect boxes."

Box number one got filled by the intersection of I-495, the Capital Beltway; I-395, which continues northeast toward the District of Columbia; and I-95, heading south to Florida. By the time the Chapin family hit North Carolina, three hours later, Daniel wasn't missing anything.

"One exit in North Carolina was for Flower Road. The only reason Flower Road had an exit was because on the side of I-95 sat several gas stations, a Burger King, a Pancake House. I know every exit in the South has a Pancake House, yet I have heard from people that some exits have two, one on each side of the interstate, and some cheap motels. Otherwise, Flower Road led to massive fields of tobacco and corn and to some dusty-looking houses. Several years ago, North Carolina appropriately changed the name of the road to Truck Stop Road. They changed the sign on I-95, and when we passed by at seventy miles per hour the next year, I immediately noticed the difference.

"Traveling on all interstates in fun. The roads themselves are full of energy. Cars move fast. It is exciting to go seventy miles an hour down a highway with many other cars around you. There are big trucks that whiz by. They don't seem dangerous when you're too young to drive. Transportation is motion. It's how people and things get from point A to point B that I'm interested in. When I see other cars on the road, I wonder where the people are going, and what route they will use."

In addition to traveling and cataloging the interstates, Chapin has also read heavily in the somewhat limited literature of superhighways. Robert Caro's *The Power Broker*, about the life of New York's master public works builder Robert Moses, is one of his "all-time favorite books." "Caro says

Moses was devastating to the city." Chapin says, "but his legacy in public works is enormous." Another favorite is Tom Lewis's *Divided Highways*.

"One amazing part of that book is a section about Interstate 40's construction in California. The plans called for the road to cross a mountain in the middle of the Mojave Desert. The engineers were baffled about how to get the highway across it. A tunnel was impossible and the mountain was steep, so a simple up-and-over approach was not going to work, either. This being the early sixties, some engineers decided that the best way to get I-40 across the mountain was to detonate something like twenty-three atomic bombs on the mountain, creating a large pass. This proposal was actually considered for a while! The federal government under Eisenhower and Kennedy and Atomic Energy [Commission] officials looked favorably upon using atomic science for peaceful and productive purposes. Fortunately, after studies revealed that most of Arizona, including Flagstaff and Phoenix, all downwind from the site in California, would have been contaminated by radiation for many years, the plan was called off. They eventually got I-40 across the mountain by normal means.

"In high school classes, when I was bored, instead of drawing circles, I drew highways. My desk at home is a repository of old drawings. As a summer project a few years ago, I drew a complete city with expressways, streets, and open spaces. It is spread out, taking up all the available floor space in one room in the basement."

Just as Chapin's knowledge of highways set him apart from the run of the mill in high school, so it's given him a minor celebrity status on his college dorm hall. "One guy from Los Angeles asked me what the PCH was. I answered the Pacific Coast Highway, California Route 1. He was surprised, especially since I told him I had never traveled west of the Mississippi River. In fact, I haven't even seen the Mississippi River. The farthest west I have been is Sea World of Ohio, southeast of Cleveland, and Savannah, Georgia. They are actually nearly on the same longitude.

"I guess knowing maps is sort of a hobby, but I would rather call it a fascination or a passion. I really do enjoy highways. I suppose having maps in your head is useless because you can always turn to a map for what you want to know. I don't think you can find many jobs just by knowing maps—not even with AAA—but it makes trips a lot better. You're not just seeing scenery go by you. It's knowing where you are.

"It's very helpful to know where you're going ahead of time, something that rarely happens in life."

Forty

Don Betty:
Crossover Artist

For Don Betty, part of the thrill of catenary suspension bridges—the Brooklyn Bridge, Delaware Memorial Bridge, and Golden Gate Bridge are notable American examples—lies in their exquisite, hidden logic and in the raw bravery that achieving the logic demands. The word "catenary" comes from the arc created by the two main cables as they sag between the towers. The bridge towers themselves generally sit on top of caissons that rest on the bedrock beneath whatever chasm the bridge is seeking to span. And it's in these parts—towers, caissons, and catenary cable—that the greatest construction danger lies.

Up top, men are working in sometimes treacherous weather conditions, laying the small cables back and forth atop the towers, from shore to shore, literally thousands of times before the smaller strands get spun and compressed into the huge, seemingly single cables that support the vertical cables from which the roadway is suspended. Down below, at the bottom of the river if that's what is being crossed, things are likely to be worse. Muck has to be taken out and forms made dry so concrete can be poured, and the deeper you must go to find something solid to rest the caissons on, the more perilous the job gets. Before it became associated with deep-sea diving, the medical condition known as "the bends" was called "caisson disease." Men by the score died of it trying to set the towers of the Brooklyn Bridge on the bedrock far beneath New York's East River.

"It's a very dangerous world," Betty says. "Fourteen people died in the construction of the Golden Gate Bridge alone. In 1936, in the height of the Depression, people were queued up, hoping someone would be killed so they could get their job."

All this life-threatening construction is only the window dressing of cate-nary bridges. The towers and the sag of the cables give the bridges their dis-tinctive geometry. Constructing tower, caisson, and cable creates the drama, but it's what you can't see that keeps you safe. Between towers and shores, the main cables—now known as side spans—descend at roughly forty-five-degree angles to their anchorages, and it's these often invisible junctions of cable, concrete, rock, and steel that do the real work of a catenary suspen-sion bridge. Let an earthquake jolt the bridge, and you're likely to have a serious road-repair job on your hands. Pour a bad caisson, and you'll get a cockeyed tower. But let a side span pop loose, and you'll begin spilling cars and people into eternity as surely as a snapped washline spills clothes to the ground.

"You think the car is held up by the roadway," Betty says, "but it's held up by what's embedded in the anchorages."

Don Betty took his degree in mechanical engineering from Bucknell Uni-versity, in Lewisburg, Pennsylvania, in 1951 and went on to become vice president and director of engineering for Armstrong World Industries—the people who make flooring and other house products. He has an engineer's love of numbers, and that also is part of the thrill of catenary suspension bridges: they are quantifiable.

"All catenary suspension bridges are measured by the distance between their towers," Betty says, and he can pretty much rattle off all the distances anyone might need to know, and any other bridge statistics, too. San Fran-cisco's Golden Gate Bridge, a favorite example, is 4,200 feet between its towers. The bridge's main cables are composed of 27,572 wires, each the thickness of a stick of lead in a mechanical pencil, that "have been com-pressed into a circle with an outside diameter of 35.6 inches." When the Golden Gate was completed in 1937, there was nothing to match it in the world, nothing even close. By the close of the twentieth century, the Golden Gate had become the seventh longest catenary suspension bridge in the world, and its rank was falling fast.

At 4,260 feet—"It was intentionally built sixty feet longer than the Golden Gate"—the Verrazano Narrows Bridge between Staten Island and Brooklyn stole the world's-longest title when it was opened in 1964, but that fame proved fleeting, too. By 1981, a 4,626-foot bridge had opened across the Humber River in England. The longest catenary span as of cen-tury's end was the Akashi Kaikyo Bridge in Japan, at 6,532 feet. "It's an amazing structure," Betty says, "more than one and a half times longer than the Golden Gate Bridge. The tower is nine hundred thirty-two feet out of the water."

By comparison, the Brooklyn Bridge is nothing—"fifteen hundred ninety-five feet and six inches between towers"—and very nearly every-thing: "The eighth wonder of the world to people like myself. It was completed in 1883. They did everything by steam, manually."

From there Don Betty is off to the Roeblings, John Augustus and Washington Augustus, father and son and the great engineers of the Brooklyn Bridge. The father had been injured in an accident while trying to establish the exact location of the bridge and died of tetanus before construction ever began. Son Washington took over, but he soon became so debilitated from a case of the bends contracted in an inspection of the caissons that he had to monitor construction from his Brooklyn apartment through a spyglass. And from the Roeblings it's back to numbers, dates, and tower definitions. (Betty can recite the specifications for the towers of the fifty longest cate-nary bridges in the world.) And always, always, there's the steel to consider as well because that's another part of the attraction of catenary suspension bridges: what they are made of. Don Betty has steel in his blood.

Betty was born in 1928 in the Dundalk section of Baltimore, not far from what was then the huge Bethlehem Steel plant at Sparrows Point. Every one of his male relatives had been employed at the plant at one time or another, and Betty himself had worked there in the summers. "I like anything huge and man-made, and steel is one of man's greatest inventions."

Betty had been intrigued by suspension bridges as early as 1971, he says—particularly the picturesque one that crosses the Capilano Canyon, 230 feet above the river of the same name in North Vancouver, British Columbia. But it was the Golden Gate Bridge, which he first saw two years later, that seemed to bring it all together for him: the history, the elements, the logic, the danger, the numbers, and the steel.

"Having researched the background of how it came to be, I appreciate the visionary exploits of Joseph Strauss," Betty says of the man who was the driving force behind the construction of the Golden Gate Bridge. "It's a pri-vately financed bridge. In the middle of the Depression, Strauss convinced people to mortgage their homes and take out loans because the bridge would be in the best civic interest of the area. I love the sheer beauty of the bridge, the aesthetics, the color, the towers, the setting, and the way it was all built by Bethlehem Steel. All the steel used for the bridge was fabricated at Sparrows Point, or at Steelton [in Pennsylvania, near Harrisburg] or Bethlehem, and taken west by rail or through the Panama Canal."

No wonder Don Betty fell in love with the Golden Gate. For Betty, though, the final and greatest part of the thrill of catenary suspension bridges is both simpler than their history and engineering and his own blood ties to them, and deeply anchored in all three: Betty loves to walk the bridges.

"I don't know of anyone else in the world who has this hobby."

The entry in the 1996 edition of the *Guinness Book of Records* reads simply:

Suspension bridge walking Donald H. Betty of Lancaster, PA, has walked over 46 suspension bridges, including the 13 longest in the world.

Betty was first included in the *Guinness* rankings in 1994, after he had been nominated for the honor by his son, Clifford. The nomination, he says, "energized" him, and how. That year—1994—he walked 17 bridges. He slowed down some in 1995, completing only 11. Then the lid came off. In 1996, Betty walked 19 bridges; he cleared another 23 in 1997 and 20 more in 1998. In 1999, he did 17 of them scattered all around the world: the Paseo Bridge in Kansas City, Kansas; bridges in Portsmouth, Dresden, and Columbus, Ohio; the Hennepin Avenue Bridge in Minneapolis; five in Germany, all across the Rhine; four more in China; and three in Japan. And all this despite knee-replacement surgery in 1991 that led to a near-fatal blood clot.

By the end of 1999, Don Betty had walked 128 catenary suspension bridges, including the 30 longest in the United States and the 26 longest in the world. He had walked bridges in Turkey (the Faith Sultan Mehmet and the Second Bosphorus, with spans of 3,576 and 3,524 feet respectively, the eleventh- and twelfth-longest in the world); in Finland, Norway, Sweden, and Denmark, including the Storebaelt, at 5,328 the second-longest in the world; throughout China and Japan (12 in the latter alone, including the remarkable triple-loop catenary suspension bridge that steps across the Kurushima Straits between Onomichi on Honshu Island and Imabari, on Shikoku), and pretty much everywhere else there was a bridge upon which foot could be set, including all across the United States.

The "upon which foot could be set" part of the equation is important because with notable exceptions—the Brooklyn Bridge and the Golden Gate Bridge with its gorgeous eight-foot-wide walkways on either side—catenary suspension bridges tend to suspend cars, not pedestrians.

"My challenge," Betty says, "has been to get permission to walk these bridges." Sometimes that has meant going through the back door.

Betty entered marathons to cross the Oakland Bay Bridge and Verrazano Narrows Bridge—the latter in the handicapped division, thanks to his replacement knee, which never regained full flexibility. New York City's Bronx–Whitestone suspension bridge, which connects the northern end of Queens with the south side of the Bronx, stymied Betty until he read about a New York state senator and fellow Bucknell University alumnus who was in charge of the committee that oversaw state highways.

"I wrote him and heard back, and a few days later I was at the Bronx–Whitestone. This crusty fellow's waiting for me. 'I don't know who the hell you are, buddy,' he says, 'but you get over that bridge fast and get your ass back to Pennsylvania.'"

Betty's longest-standing frustration had been the Delaware Memorial Bridge, which connects the Delaware and New Jersey turnpikes across the Delaware River. "I wrote to Senator [Joseph] Biden, a lot of officials in both states. The bridge is only sixty miles away from where I live. I would always get these letters back that said, sorry, we can't let you, insurance, et cetera."

Then one day, he and his wife, Joan, stopped for a visit in Millville, New Jersey, where they had once lived, and fell into conversation with Frank the Barber, who cuts the hair of someone who knows someone who knows the head of the bridge authority, and not long thereafter, Betty was being escorted across the Delaware Memorial by the bridge authority head himself. In honor of the event, Betty has worn a distinctive red Delaware Memorial cap and jacket for nearly all his subsequent bridge walks.

Abroad, the problems of bridge crossing are complicated by custom, the practical difficulties of flying thousands of miles to make a walk of a few thousand feet across a span that might open to foot traffic once in its whole existence, and the fine points of language. To the untrained eye, catenary suspension bridges are not all that different from cable-stay bridges, in which the weight of the roadway is borne by cables descending at an angle from a tower. To Betty, such distinctions are critical.

Betty crossed the Angostura Bridge near Ciudad Bolívar, in Venezuela, in the middle of a coup. To confirm that a catenary bridge crossed the Rio Coatzacoalcos, below Veracruz on the Caribbean coast of Mexico, he wrote the Mexican embassy, called consulates, found a hotel near the bridge, and talked with the manager there. "'Sí, señor, sí,'" he says he was told; there is such a bridge.

"So I hop on a plane, fly to Houston and from there to Mexico City and on to Veracruz. We're driving from the airport to the Rio Coatzacoalcos, and I see this lovely cable-stay bridge, and I say, 'Oh, my God.'"

In 1997, Betty flew 51,000 miles round-trip for a chance to walk the Tsing Ma Bridge in Hong Kong—then the world's fifth-longest bridge—because "it was the opening, and if you weren't there for the opening, with the Chinese Communist takeover, you weren't going to get to do it." The next year, he crossed what had just become the world's longest catenary span, the Akashi Kaikyo Bridge, which links Kobe, Japan, with Awaji Island over the Akashi Strait.

In 1999, Betty was setting out to walk the Xiling Bridge over the Yangtze River—"2,953 feet, 3.5 miles upstream from the Yangtze Dam, across the Xiling Gorge"—when an armed Chinese guard turned him back. "I didn't have permission. We drove past the guard onto the bridge, and I knew I'd be rejected. I did not walk across that bridge, but I still count it."

Betty tallies the bridges he crosses in two ways: by keeping a running list on his computer, and by placing dots beside the bridges he has walked on a U.S. Department of Transportation list of catenary bridges worldwide that was compiled in August 1999. He keeps track as well by samplings of the debris he finds on the bridges—rivets, washers, beverage can tabs, fan belts; all meticulously labeled and filed—and by the slides that document his crossings. Betty's "trademark" is a vertical shot of the towers, taken by lying down in the middle of the roadway.

"People say to me, 'What are you thinking about when you're walking between the towers?' And I say, 'The next bridge.' This one's done. I've put the dot beside it."

The "next bridge" is, in fact, an increasing problem. As he talked, Betty had letters out to departments of transportation in Texas, Oklahoma, and Arkansas, all trying to confirm the existence of catenary bridges that may well have been torn down and replaced. Otherwise, the holder on top of his desk where he normally has his airplane and rail tickets lined up for the next adventure was bare.

There's talk of a 16,404-foot span that will link Gibraltar and Morocco. China has at least five bridges either completed or scheduled that will be longer than the Golden Gate. A nearly 11,000-foot span is on the drawing board to tie Italy and Sicily across the Strait of Messina; if it's finished in his lifetime, Betty says, he'll be pushed over it in a wheelchair if necessary. But the bottom line is that he's not getting any younger, walking isn't getting any easier, and for whatever reasons, he settled upon a hobby that offers a shrinking number of opportunities. Even the *Guinness Book of Records* has turned a cold eye on suspension bridge walking: it dropped the category in 1999 as part of a general reorganization.

Occasionally, though, the gods that guard passionate pursuits smile on us all.

"Joan and I went to Iceland in 1998," Betty says, "because it looked like a place where there could be no suspension bridges. I asked the tour guide, and there were two of them there. So we took the bus to them, and I walked over them. It just nonplussed Joan. Every once in a while, a blind pig finds an acorn."

And there's always the hope that the gods have one last smile left in them. "My ultimate aim," Don Betty says, "would be to have a heart attack on a suspension bridge and die there."

Acknowledgments

This book has been a multiple collaboration: between two authors, between the authors and their subjects, and between the authors and all those who helped point us in the right direction. We are grateful, first and foremost, to the people who appear in these pages. Thanks for all the time and for answering so many questions, and apologies for the ones that were so ill informed. Thanks most of all for letting us into your lives and sharing your passions and pursuits with us. Our own lives have been enriched accordingly.

In one sense, the research for this book came easily. We asked friends and family for suggestions, and they—and their friends—deluged us with great possibilities that ultimately led to the people profiled here. Judy and Gil White put us in touch with their niece Hilary White, who led us to back-country skier Lisa Ball. Al Strickler nominated his former colleague, the bridge walker Don Betty. From George Burke came his neighbor and fellow doctor Tom Blake. Peggy Dickson of the talking birds was suggested by Anne and Lee Ravenel; marathon swimmer Jim Dreyer, by Mary Ellen and Brewster Willcox. Ted Furey, who has done so much to preserve the work of Patrick Charles Keely, came to us via Mag and Sherwood Willard. Gambler Kim Eisler is an old friend.

Steve Everett, the downhill skater, was a gift from his daughter, Kim. We met Kim Everett as a result of buying some books illustrated by Edward Gorey from her on eBay. We would never have started bidding on eBay if Patsy Sims hadn't suggested that we include her University of Pittsburgh colleague, Harry Kloman, in this book. Andreas Brown not only owns our favorite bookstore (where we've been buying signed Edward Goreys for thirty years before the existence of eBay) but is a formidable postcard collector and historian. Andreas Brown proposed Leonard Lauder.

A history teacher at the Gilman School in Baltimore, Jerry Thornbery, introduced us to his student, Daniel Chapin, the map whiz, and to Bob Strupp. Thornbery spends his summers in Wisconsin and plays Sheepshead. Kathie Swift, of the Iowa State Fair, also blessed the book twice, by providing Robin Tarbell-Thomas, whose cookies win more ribbons than anyone else's at the fair, and Jerry Traufler, the self-taught carver of *The Last Supper*.

We have the Internet to thank for two of our chapters. Ann and Sam Ritter maintain a handsome site devoted to kiting. When we plugged "golf" and "fanatic" into the hotbot.com search engine, it took us straight to the home page of Matt Dodyk at Purdue University. Mike Gaines, the late-in-life stock car racer, is an old friend of Dana and Scott Lacy. James Pettus delivered a document to the Capitol Hill office of Janet Blum and began talking about his love of bonsai; Janet called us directly. Leannah Harding nominated her fellow Bruce Springsteen fan, Marietta Phillips, while Bambi Nicklen suggested her onetime fifth grade classmate Henry Sakaida, who specializes in reuniting former World War II combatants.

Bill Mead, a terrific baseball historian, led us to the Society for American Baseball Research, and SABR led us to Claudia Perry. From the prolific author Paul Dickson came the prolific word-sleuth Barry Popik. Restaurant critic Tom Head put us in touch with Simone Rathlé, who led us to her sister-in-law, New Orleans food-lover Alexandra Stafford. The McDonald's marathon eater Peter Holden came to us from Jane Podesta, as did marble collector Cathy Runyan. Colleen Carroll gets credit for globetrotter Gig Gwin and whale-watcher Patricia Corrigan. We have Tom Barnes to thank for John Sylvester Jr. and his collection of Indochinese military decorations. Among Marilyn Dickey's many suggestions was one that pointed us along the track that eventually arrived at Steve Spreckelmeier and his steam engine. When we described this book to Jeff Smith, he said, "You've got to include Walter Pforzheimer." Jeff was right.

Our old and cherished friends Barbara and Soc Glasrud answered a letter requesting prospective subjects by saying "We do have someone for you": Jim Murphy, the canoeist whose friends ask him if he goes paddling in the Canadian arctic because Fargo isn't cold enough for him in July. Another friend of very many years, Elizabeth Rich, gave us David Hanschen's e-mail address (it has "pre" and "cancel" in it). Sally Leach, of Austin, has had a couple of treasures purchased by Cathy Henderson at garage sales. Pamela Walker works with Larry Kahn, and knew he played tiddlywinks—in world-class fashion—during his off-hours. Paula and Ed Goldfader go back a long way with David Kerben and told us about his wife, Claire Miller, and her ardent pursuit of genealogy.

We thank Lindy Neely of Chattanooga for telling us about Sonia Young, that city's Purple Lady. We found Judy Konnerth and her arks in an agreeable Tinkers-to-Evers-to-Chance sequence: Ellen Pollack, of Nashville, to Juli and Ralph Mosley, of Nashville, to Dan Hixon, of Nashville, who had met the Konnerths, of Mundelein, Illinois, at gatherings of the Antique Toy Collectors' Club. Another complex exchange put us in touch with Nan Ides, who knew Donna Heron, who knew wool-spinner Rose Kramer. Jennifer Johnson proposed Doug Fishbone, the banana sculptor. Providence put us on Roger Swicegood's mailing list fifteen years ago.

We also want to thank our literary agents, Robert Lescher of Lescher & Lescher, Ltd. and Rafe Sagalyn of the Sagalyn Literary Agency. Alice Mayhew at Simon & Schuster has been everything an editor should be, and her associate, Anja Schmidt, has been indispensable. No expression of gratitude would be complete without thanking our best editors and most valuable advisers: Neil Sheehan and Candy Means.

Susan Sheehan
Washington, D.C.

Howard Means
Bethesda, Maryland

About the Authors

SUSAN SHEEHAN is the author of seven books, including the Pulitzer Prize–winning *Is There No Place on Earth for Me?* She has been a staff writer for *The New Yorker* since 1961, and has written for *The New York Times* and *Architectural Digest,* where she is a contributing writer. She lives in Washington, D.C.

HOWARD MEANS is the author of three books, including *Money & Power: The History of Business,* and coauthor of two others. Until recently a senior editor at *Washingtonian* magazine, he lives in Bethesda, Maryland.

MAY 2005